A CHANCE
TO WIN

A CHANCE TO WIN

Boyhood, Baseball, and the

Struggle for Redemption

in the Inner City

JONATHAN SCHUPPE

Henry Holt and Company
New York

Henry Holt and Company, LLC
Publishers since 1866
175 Fifth Avenue
New York, New York 10010
www.henryholt.com

Henry Holt® and ® are registered trademarks of Henry Holt and Company, LLC.

Distributed in Canada by Raincoast Book Distribution Limited

Library of Congress Cataloging-in-Publication Data

Schuppe, Jonathan.
A chance to win : boyhood, baseball, and the struggle for redemption in the inner city /
Jonathan Schuppe.—1st ed.
    p. cm.
ISBN 978-0-8050-9287-5
1. Drug addicts—Rehabilitation—New Jersey—Newark.   2. Drug dealers—New Jersey—
Newark.   I. Title.
HV5840.U6.N49 2012
363.45092—dc23
[B]   2012034298

Henry Holt books are available for special promotions and premiums.
For details contact: Director, Special Markets.

First Edition 2013

Designed by Meryl Sussman Levavi

Printed in the United States of America

1   3   5   7   9   10   8   6   4   2

To Amy

I do not understand what I do. For what I want to do I do not do, but what I hate I do.

—Romans 7:15

In the little world in which children have their existence, whosoever brings them up, there is nothing so finely perceived and so finely felt, as injustice. It may be only small injustice that the child can be exposed to; but the child is small, and its world is small . . .

—Charles Dickens, *Great Expectations*

A CHANCE TO WIN

Rodney sat.

Every day, he parked himself at the far end of the slate-gray platform outside his apartment building, midnight-blue Yankees cap pulled low over his eyes, arms folded across his chest, tensed jaws masked by a thick, black beard. He glared out at Elizabeth Avenue, numb to the block's clatter and thrum. Young men with hard stares swigged beer outside a bodega, radio growling angry rap. Young mothers tugged kids past the front-door security glass. A procession of medical transport vans and livery cabs idled in the curved driveway, then rattled away. New Jersey Transit buses moaned up the hill along Weequahic Park. Still, Rodney sat, despondent and alone.

Every so often, something broke the spell. A boy stopped and waited for Rodney's massive hand to land on his skinny, outstretched palm. Someone in a passing car sang out, "Rock!" A corner boy raised his clenched fist, a street salute. Former customers, weathered beyond their years, ambled up for a quick hello. All had some place to be, something that kept them moving. But not Rodney. He just sat there in the thin shade of two bare pear trees and wondered how he was going to live the rest of his life like this.

Even before his injury, Rodney had been guarded and brooding; that veil had now hardened into a shell. He spoke in gruff, clipped sentences and never made eye contact. He did not talk to you if there was someone else around. If you were alone, and he trusted you, he might let down his guard, a little. But there were not many people he trusted anymore.

Under most circumstances, I would not have even considered approaching him, let alone engage him in a conversation. But on a late-winter afternoon in 2005, Rodney was waiting for me.

I was a reporter for Newark's daily newspaper, the *Star-Ledger*, researching an article about the physical and emotional toll of living in one of America's most violent cities. He was a former high school pitching ace and corner-level drug dealer who had lost the use of his legs. Our meeting was arranged by an anticrime activist I'd met at the scene of a homicide. After the activist introduced us, Rodney motioned for me to follow him inside—he couldn't be caught talking to me on the street. We waited at a bank of three balky elevators. No one in the building remembered when all of the cars worked at the same time, and it took several minutes to make it to the sixth floor, where Rodney led me into his dim one-bedroom apartment. There, beside a big-screen television flashing muted SportsCenter highlights, he told me his story.

Rodney had no scrapbook or pictures to illustrate his life; almost all of his personal possessions had been lost or stolen years ago. Instead, his home was cluttered with seemingly random odds and ends: a helmet from an adult-league football team, a ceramic bust of an African woman, a two-foot-tall stuffed replica of Foghorn Leghorn, bottles of Windex and aerosol air freshener, a portable stereo, a Tiki Barber bobblehead doll, scattered papers and DVDs. Nothing of much meaning.

When we finished, I thanked him and went on reporting my article, which ran a few weeks later, accompanied by a photo of him outside his building, looking the same as when I'd first encountered him. The piece got mixed reviews among his friends; many were proud of him for speaking openly about his ordeal, but Rodney had also broken a cardinal rule among drug dealers: stay out of the public eye. Old partners warned him about the blunder, and some began keeping their distance out of fear that the article would draw attention from police. But Rodney didn't care about that anymore. Nothing good had come of his allegiance to the streets. Just lost hope, failed potential, prison, paraplegia. He had fallen about as low as a man could go.

I didn't expect to speak to Rodney again, but for some reason he held on to my business card, and sometimes he called, with no seeming purpose other than to chat. I couldn't understand this. I wondered if he expected something more of me. Maybe he needed help. But he asked for nothing. Years later, when we'd become close, I'd ask him why he, a dealer, continued to pursue a relationship with me, a reporter. He told me he saw something vaguely beneficial in knowing me and wanted to hold on to whatever shred of positivity that existed in his life. He wanted to make amends, and perhaps he needed someone to help him believe it was possible.

Every once in a while, I found myself driving past Rodney's building and saw him posted on the platform—same stare, same despair. Sometimes I hopped out to say hi, and we'd go talk. Upstairs, there were things Rodney felt more comfortable sharing with me than his closest confidants—his depression, his regrets, his desire to somehow make up for all the damage he'd done, not only to himself, but to his neighborhood. He was still traumatized from his injury, which was more than a decade old, and no less permanent. He'd lost his manhood, his control over his bladder and bowels, his self-worth. He'd converted to Islam, aiming to find some new strength or wisdom, and there were times when he believed he'd made a connection with God. But those moments were fleeting glimmers of light. He was weak. He could not resist the quick money of drugs. He knew it was wrong, but it was easier than looking for a job, and even if he tried, he could not imagine anyone wanting to hire a disabled ex-con.

Casting through memories, Rodney kept returning to the moment when his life began to break: the summer he turned fourteen, his first year out of Little League, just before he started high school. It was the last time he remembered being truly happy. When he looked around Elizabeth Avenue now, he saw hundreds of children just like him, growing up just as he had—poor, fatherless, coasting through an inept school system, fascinated with the streets, confronted with the decisions that, fairly or not, would define their adult lives. He knew what they needed: someone to steer them from the path that had been so easy for him to take, the one that now ended at the front curb of the building where he grew up, parked in his wheelchair, watching the world go by. He just needed a way to reach them.

He found his answer in June 2007, when public works crews showed up in the park across the street. For as long as anyone could remember, the spot had been a patch of stubbly grass and pebbly dirt that served as a makeshift baseball diamond. No one played there anymore, but the head of the struggling local Little League had persuaded officials to build something that could spark a new interest in the game. Through the summer, the crews cleared and flattened the land and carved out a new field with bleachers, dugouts, lights, a scoreboard, and a carpet of artificial turf. Children hopped the fence and were smitten. The surface was spongy under their feet, like nothing they'd ever felt. They tested it out, swinging imaginary bats, running the baselines. Some of them knew how to play, or at least thought they knew, based on what they'd seen on TV or their Wii video game systems. Soon they were battling each other in raucous pickup games, using old bats and balls salvaged from someone's uncle's closet. Rodney saw this and knew what he had to do.

Baseball was the only thing—besides dealing drugs—that he knew well. He'd once been among the city's most promising schoolboy pitchers, with a fastball clocked in the low nineties, good enough for a chance at a pro career. He'd blown it, but the game remained dear to him; it was a symbol of childhood, of an unspoiled life.

He called me up and said he had news: "I'm going to coach baseball." How, he wasn't sure. He'd never coached anything before and knew of no other wheelchair-bound men who had. He had no plan or strategy, and no guide, other than his heart.

Baseball seemed an unlikely way to reach inner-city boys and girls. In Newark, and across urban America, the sport had been eclipsed in popularity by football and basketball. There were many reasons why city kids didn't play—expensive equipment, decrepit facilities, poor marketing, the disproportionately small number of baseball scholarships available for big-time college programs. But there was another disturbing trend that didn't get as much attention. Baseball had always been a game that children learned from their fathers, and in too many cases—six out of ten, according to Newark's census figures—fathers weren't around.

For decades, Newark had been a national emblem of urban dysfunction, the butt of jokes on late-night talk shows. The prevailing narrative was of long-faded glory and municipal despair. Some of it was true, but not all of it, nowhere near. You could pick out parts of Newark and fit them into the caricatured vision of the American ghetto—countless already had—but anyone who bothered to look past this superficial portrait found a place that was vibrant and resilient, capable of terrible brutality, but also of extraordinary acts of compassion. Its future was being paved by the devout, the reformed, the strivers and strugglers—people finding promise in the shallowest of footholds. Their victories were small and their progress modest, but they were proud to say they were from Newark. They called it Brick City and wore homemade T-shirts that boasted, WE HIT HARD. Working there as a crime reporter, I came to think of Newark as a prizefighter, the battered former champion in a comeback match who refuses to go down. Not winning, but not losing, either. And with the start of each new round came a renewed sense of possibility, even as the fighter charged into another storm of blows.

Newark's longtime mayor had spent much of his twenty-year tenure trying to recast Newark's image as a "renaissance city," but had just left office under a pall of corruption. In his place was Cory Booker, a young, charismatic graduate of Yale Law School. Booker had grown up in the suburbs, but his supporters looked past that and saw him as what they badly needed: a new way of doing things. Booker seized the role, promising to help Newark reclaim its place among the country's most desirable, productive cities. He proclaimed that Newark—with a murder rate twice that of the Bronx, a third of its residents living in poverty, and a 40 percent high school graduation rate—was "a front line of what I believe is a fight for the American dream."

If that was true, if Booker was right, if Newark truly did represent what was possible in America's neglected postindustrial cities, then I wondered where that left Rodney. For much of his childhood, and for most of his adult life, Rodney had contributed to the blight and dysfunction. He'd been the problem. Now he wanted to turn things around and, in some small way, be part of the city's resurgence. If Newark was a front line, then Rodney was one of its soldiers. Newark's success depended at least as much on people like him as on Booker. Their journeys, I came to realize, were intertwined.

On an early evening in April 2008, I met Rodney at his apartment, where he was getting ready for the debut of his team, the Elizabeth Avenue Eagles. I came because he'd asked me, and I wanted to show him support. But I also kept a notebook in my back pocket, just in case.

I sat across from Rodney as he slipped a black hooded sweatshirt over his thick shoulders and twisted a San Francisco Giants cap onto his shaved, size 8 head. He yanked the brim down to the bridge of his nose. He looked to his lap, where a blank scoring book balanced on his knees, and took a heavy breath. The sweet odor of Cool Water incense lingered faintly in the air. A smoke alarm, running out of power, bleated above him. He pressed the joystick of his newly donated electric scooter and spun from his living room, down the front hall, and out the door.

He rolled outside, and I followed. Across Elizabeth Avenue, pin oaks glowed green and yellow in the lowering sun. Birds twittered inside them. The scrim of low-floating clouds that had hung over the neighborhood that morning had faded. A milky wisp swirled into the otherwise radiant blue sky. Rodney huffed into his fists and motored up the hill along the sidewalk that hugged the park. He passed three pink magnolias in full blossom, and he was struck by a giddy sense of anticipation he hadn't felt since he was a boy, when the winter weather broke and the day felt fresh and full of potential.

Over near the bleachers, kids were playing pickup, using stumps and branches as bases and the trunk of an old oak as a backstop. Many were wearing the same clothes they'd gone to school in: polos and rugby shirts, blue jeans, cargo pants, shorts, sneakers. Seeing Rodney, they surrounded him and battered him with questions.

"Coach Rock, who we playin' today?"

"Can I pitch?"

"We gettin' uniforms?"

A few minutes before six p.m., the league president arrived bearing a Rite-Aid bag of cheap white T-shirts—interim jerseys, blank in front, red numbers on the backs. "Oh bay-bay!" a boy shouted. They grabbed at the shirts and bickered over numbers. One of them, who went by the nickname Pooh, muscled through the tangle and pulled off his shirt, revealing boxer shorts that had ridden up past the waistband of his black sweatpants. He slipped number 10 over his doughy frame. "Let's go!" he cried.

The umpire announced that it was time to play ball. Rodney wheeled to the dugout, scratched in the lineup, grunted the assignments. Everyone put their hands together. Someone counted to three and they barked in unison, "Eagles!" Then the home team took the field.

The pitcher, a boy in cornrows, glossy basketball shorts, and unlaced high-tops, wound up and, on the first pitch of the season, drilled the leadoff batter in the left arm. On the next pitch the runner stole second base; on the next, he took third. Then the pitcher delivered a fastball down the middle, and the number-two hitter dribbled a grounder through the left side of the infield. The runner scored. A teasing cheer erupted from the visitors' dugout.

The Eagles fell silent. Rodney sat in the third-base coach's box, eyes locked on the field, saying nothing. A gulp of dread moved down him. He was afraid of what would come next. He considered calling time-out and summoning everyone back to the dugout, telling them that he'd been thinking about it and maybe this hadn't been such a good idea after all, that they should all go home and find something else to do. Then he snapped back to reality. This moment was months in the making—years, really. He'd come too far. He could make this work. He had to.

* * *

For the next few months, I tagged along with Rodney and his new charges. I sat in the dugout, lounged in the bleachers, hung out in their homes. As the season progressed, it sometimes felt to Rodney that Little League was more difficult than the drug business. His players were unpredictable, excitable, brash, disorderly; they fought over every error, and someone was always threatening to quit. He had to cool their tempers and soothe their tears. He had to consult with complaining parents, negotiate with opposing coaches, scramble for missing equipment. Before games, Rodney often found himself stuck with half a team. As the clock struck six, a pack of them would emerge from Elizabeth Avenue, shirts untucked, caps askew, greeting him, as if nothing was amiss: "What's up, Coach?" In the dugout, they chomped on candy, made fun of each other's mothers, sparred, wrestled, farted, flirted with girls through the chain link. Once, between innings, three helmeted Eagles took turns banging each other on the head with bats, chuckling through a game of on-deck Whac-A-Mole while the opposing pitcher warmed up. "See, it's all about comedy," an adult chastised. "That's why y'all be losing." One night, after dozing off in front of the television in his apartment, Rodney awoke to a rerun of *The Bad News Bears*. He watched for a few minutes and thought, *That's us.* But maybe that wasn't such a bad thing. At the end of the film, the Bears didn't win, but they left with their pride intact. He'd settle for something like that.

About half of the Eagles were what Rodney called "street"—they came from the lower end of Elizabeth Avenue, in the high-rise apartment buildings that faced the park, and freely roamed the neighborhood. The others lived a little farther up the hill, in buildings that were marginally better, or in stand-alone houses elsewhere in the South Ward, where they were more sheltered and less likely to be seen walking around without supervision. These distinctions were invisible to a stranger like me, though. To my outsider's eyes, they swaggered and scowled and talked tough in ways that made them seem precocious beyond their years. But emotionally, they were clearly still little kids. When they got a hit or scored a run, they acted as if they'd won the Little League World Series, swarming each other, dancing in the dugout, taunting the opposing team. When they screwed up, it was if those victories had never happened. The cruel world—or at least the umpire—had, once again, turned against them.

I got hooked by their story. I'd grown up in a small, uniformly white suburb that was six miles, and a universe, from Newark. In my cloistered boyhood existence, Newark had been a lawless frontier, a place to avoid, or ignore. My only visits were in a baseball uniform, arriving by school bus with my varsity teammates, pummeling the unskilled, poorly equipped kids of the West and South Wards, then fleeing back down Interstate 78 without bothering to look out the window. Back then, Newark meant nothing to me; it was absent from my history books, so I had no appreciation for what the city had once been—an engine of American industry, one of the country's busiest commercial centers, a hub of the civil rights movement. I didn't learn any of that until I became a reporter there.

At the end of June 2008, I wrote an article that documented the Elizabeth Avenue Eagles' inaugural season, including an improbable run through the play-offs. When I finished, I couldn't walk away. I'd grown attached to them and to what they represented. Their lives spoke volumes about what it was like to survive in one of America's most neglected, star-crossed cities. I'd only scratched the surface of a deeper story: of children growing up in an unforgiving world; of parents struggling to show them the way; of a man trying to do the best he could, not only for himself but for the kids. To tell that story, I needed to follow Rodney and the children as they went on with their lives, far beyond the bounds of a newspaper article. That is how this book came to be.

Eventually I settled on four people to follow: Rodney; two players, DeWan and Derek; and a father named Thaiquan.

DeWan was an earnest boy, the son of a single schoolteacher mother. He had budding dreadlocks and an easy, gap-toothed smile and had never played baseball before. At school, DeWan was chastised for not living up to his potential. At home, he ached for a man's attention. But at the ballpark, he found a place where he could shine. Even when he struck out, which was often, he ran back to the dugout, head high.

Derek, by contrast, was a brooding veteran. He was one of only two Eagles with any baseball experience, which automatically made him a key element in Coach Rock's constantly shifting lineup; he used Derek at nearly every position—outfield, shortstop, pitcher. Derek moved homes almost as often as he changed positions; he was raised by a network of extended family, shifted from place to place depending on who was least busy or less ill. Sometimes that person was his father, but it never was his mother.

Thaiquan Scott was a cleaned-up ex-con, a father trying to do for his kids what his own father didn't do for him, and one of those things was baseball. Before every game, Thaiquan's minivan arrived at the field and disgorged his five children, his wife, an array of nephews and nieces. He loved them so fiercely and he worried about them so intensely that it gave him panic attacks. But he was determined to prove that the family curse of prison and poverty ended with him.

The lives of DeWan, Derek, and Thaiquan only rarely intersected off the baseball diamond, and I went where they led me. They welcomed me into their homes. They shared their deepest hopes and fears. I went to birthday parties, football and basketball games, jazz concerts, church events, court hearings. I stuck around for more than three years and came to consider them my friends.

Through it all, Rodney remained the heart of the story, and I devote a good portion of this book detailing his adolescent trespasses, his evolution as a thug, and the chain of events that transformed him from predator to victim. The more time we spent together, and the more I got to know him, the more I rooted for his redemption. All good journalists aim to maintain an impassive distance from the people they write about, but I couldn't help but take a personal interest in Rodney's life, in the decisions he made. The attention that resulted from my article about his first season as a coach brought him new options and better resources. But he didn't always take advantage of them. Watching this was often frustrating. I gave him counsel when he asked, but the choices, of course, were ultimately his to make. Every day he had to persuade himself to keep going, even if he wasn't sure how. Every day was a battle against his dark side, which he feared he'd never escape. After observing his struggle for some time, I realized that for someone like Rodney, in a place like Newark, the path to success wasn't always obvious or clear; it was studded with complications and disappointments, constantly testing his resolve.

I saw this same struggle everywhere in Newark. Every time something good happened, when it seemed the city was gaining a little momentum, something else set it back. The people had to choose: waver and quit, or step back into the fight. Sometimes winning meant simply holding your ground. Not losing. There was a certain dignity in that. And dignity mattered.

Everyone documented in these pages agreed without hesitation to allow me to write about them. They believed their stories needed to be told, not only to dispel popular myths about their city but, more important, to provide an accurate portrayal of the myriad economic, social, and psychological forces they wrestle with every day. Many of the adults have made terrible mistakes; they've hurt the ones they loved, committed crimes against friends and strangers, poisoned themselves with drugs and drink. Their bad decisions haunt them and often overshadow the good they try to do. But they do not stop trying, if not to save themselves, then to make things better for their children. Among the most common phrases I heard from them was the need to "break the cycle," to help the next generation avoid repeating their mistakes, to give their kids opportunities they never had: to make better things possible.

Even though this book covers a period of several years, there is no tidy ending. Life doesn't work that way, especially for the children, who, as I write this, still have high school ahead of them and are navigating the perilous road to adulthood. For them, this is the beginning.

CHAPTER 1

If you drive south from New York City on the New Jersey Turnpike, Newark appears rather suddenly, about five miles out, as the highway curls across the Hackensack River, climbs a hundred feet above the Meadowlands, and cuts through a formation of volcanic rock called Snake Hill. Atop the cragged peak, the road bends westward, and you find yourself looking out over a vast mottled carpet of factories, warehouses, landfills, highways, and railroad lines. Plumes of steam dissolve into the air over oily mudflats and windblown beds of wheat-colored reeds. Up ahead, the three-mile-long black-steel skeleton of the Pulaski Skyway stretches over the Hackensack and Passaic Rivers, and to the right, at the southwestern horizon, along an S-shaped curve in the Passaic, stands the downtown skyline, a striking combination of art deco, Beaux-Arts, and modernist skyscrapers built in the city's golden age, when Newark was the most industrialized city in America, producing just about anything Americans used, from curling irons and soap to sheet metal and celluloid. Catch the view late in the afternoon, with the sun hanging low over the Watchung Mountains and reflecting off the sandstone and glass, and you understand what it must have been like for twentieth-century travelers arriving in Newark for the first time, immigrants fresh from Eastern Europe and Latin America, and African-Americans from the Jim Crow South, stopping short of New York to stake themselves in a rough-and-tumble city with still so much to prove.

On the road toward Newark you pass piles of automobile carcasses, oil tanks, fields of empty Lego-like shipping containers stacked seven stories high, trucking bay after trucking bay. Soon the turnpike carries you under the rumble of airplanes descending into Newark Airport. A half-dozen apartment towers, each more than twenty stories tall, rise above a tangle of jug handles and overpasses. The towers stand on Elizabeth Avenue, a major municipal artery that begins at the edge of downtown, runs into the South Ward, and keels westward along the slope of Weequahic Park and traces the southern boundary of the neighborhood that shares the park's name. The brick-and-steel towers are clustered around that sharp turn at the park's corner, at the periphery of an industrial zone littered with scrap-metal yards, recycling plants, auto-glass works, and methadone clinics.

The towers were the result of an ambitious and ill-timed development blitz aimed at preventing Weequahic's middle- and upper-income residents from fleeing to the suburbs in the 1960s. Billed as luxury high-rises, the buildings were supposed to bring modern living to a city desperate for revitalization. They boasted saunas, pools, recreation rooms, maid and porter services, marble lobbies, and easy bus access to downtown Newark and Manhattan. The key feature was an unencumbered vista of the 311-acre park, which featured a lake and golf course and was designed by the same landscape architectural firm that created Central Park.

It didn't work. The upwardly mobile Jewish families who had migrated to the neighborhood decades earlier continued to retreat westward, a trend that hastened after several days of rioting in July 1967. They were replaced by striving working-class blacks from Central Ward slums, some of whom could afford the rent in the new towers or in the squat 1930s-era art deco buildings between them. But there weren't enough middle-income tenants to keep the buildings filled, and the developers were forced to rethink their business plans. That included the backers of Zion Towers, a twenty-eight-story building conceived as a residence for elderly Jews. When the project was finally finished in the early 1970s, the sponsoring temple, B'nai Zion, and its partners applied for government subsidies and opened the apartments to a wider array of residents.

At the time, Clara Mason was a single mother of five children, facing eviction from a house down the street that had just been sold. A scrawny woman with angular features, a jutting lower lip, and light brown skin, Clara grew up in Norfolk, Virginia, and quit school at seventeen to marry a navy-yard worker thirteen years her elder. Many members of her family disapproved of the marriage, including an uncle who'd moved to Newark seeking work. He sent for Clara, offering her the chance to finish school and start over. She agreed, but her husband, James, followed her, finding work as a truck driver. She moved in with him and ditched her plans. They began having children, but James was a carouser and an abusive alcoholic. They separated, but he would still stop by from time to time. "It was like he would come around long enough to get a baby," Clara told me, a scratch of bitterness in her drawl. "You know. One of them things." James never stuck around long enough to play much of a role in his children's lives, and he died in the early 1970s. Clara found work in an airplane-parts factory, then in a doctor's office, supporting her three daughters and two sons on her own.

Desperate for a new place to live, Clara went to her pastor, who worked as a chaplain at a local hospital alongside a rabbi from B'nai Zion. Despite Zion Towers' struggles, the building still boasted luxury amenities: mail chutes on each floor, juice and milk machines in the lobby, a recreation center, a playground. When Clara was accepted for a three-bedroom apartment on the tenth floor, at $167 a month, "I thought I was living in paradise," she said. "I thought I was rich."

The Masons were among the first black families to live in Zion Towers, and they weren't exactly welcomed. Soon after they moved in, Clara stepped into an elevator and started riding it down with an older white woman who sneered, "I'm going back up and calling Rabbi Klein, because he told me when I moved in there wasn't going to be any blacks coming in here."

"You got something against blacks?" Clara asked.

"Yes," the woman said. "They have too many babies."

The rabbi often stopped by to inspect Clara's apartment—more often than he did her neighbors'. After looking around, he'd say, "Miss

Mason, I am so proud. You have all these kids and your apartment is spotless." She thanked him, but she wanted to say, *What do you think, that all black people are dirty?* After that, Clara was afraid to let her kids play in the hallways for fear that she would get kicked out. But years later, she would recall the inspections fondly; they reminded her of a time when people cared enough to keep the neighborhood clean.

Clara made a decent living, but she developed excruciating ulcers that doctors blamed on stress. An ill-advised surgery removed parts of her stomach, but she remained in chronic pain and was unable to eat much. She was forced to quit her job and go on disability, but her government checks barely covered rent and groceries. Clara's three oldest children moved out of the house, leaving only Rodney and Darlene.

Rodney, the baby, was a quiet, pensive boy. He kept to himself and did not give his mother much grief. If he did something wrong, all she had to do was flash him a stern look and he would burst into tears. He grew up tall, slender, and bowlegged, prone to long bouts of silence and a habit of biting his nails. He was obsessively hygienic; he refused to wear anything stained and took long showers that often made his sister late for school.

When Rodney was six, Clara showed him a photograph and pointed to a man she said was his father. He was thin, light skinned, with a mustache, and was laughing. Rodney wanted to ask Clara why that man was so happy, but before he got a chance, she took the photograph back and put it away. Rodney never saw it again, and his father remained a fuzzy snapshot of a memory. He was rarely spoken of at home; Clara only acknowledged her husband when someone else brought him up, and then she quickly changed the subject. If Rodney asked her about him, she would reach for a cigarette, light it, and shoot him a look that said, *Boy, why are you bugging me with this?*

But his curiosity grew. The other boys at Peshine Avenue School talked about their fathers all the time, and when he went to their houses to play, the men were always around. Rodney wanted what they had. "What was my father like?" he asked his oldest sister, Pam. "Did he look like me?" She replied brusquely. "Rodney, he was your father. Him and Mommy used to get into it, but he was a good father, and he died." For years, that was about all anyone would tell him: that James was a drunk, that he beat his mother, and that he passed away when they were young. He learned to live with the unanswered questions but told himself he'd ask his mother about it again someday, when he was older.

Rodney spent most of his childhood outside, playing sports. Each building, and block, had its own baseball, football, and basketball teams and challenged each other to games in a section of the park they called "the battlefield." Rodney became one of the neighborhood's biggest and best athletes, and Clara signed him up for the South Ward Little League. He loved the regimen—the daily practices, the repetitive drills, the cookouts and parades, the adult men who seemed to care so much about helping him do well. He wore his first uniform—white polyester pants, candy-striped stirrup socks, tight powder-gray T-shirt with BRAVES in burgundy across the chest—to school on the day before his first game in spring 1976. He became a star pitcher and fantasized about making it big and coming back to visit the neighborhood, kids chasing after him like he was Muhammad Ali. With his success on the field came an aura of cool that attracted the affections of girls and the envy of boys. Many of the younger kids started calling him Brown Hornet— after the superhero in the Fat Albert cartoon series—because of his long face and stiff voice.

At home, Clara had increasing difficulty keeping the kids fed. They ate whatever was in the cupboard, which was sometimes just a can of beans, or cereal, or syrup sandwiches. Their neighbors saw what was happening and tried to help. One woman across the hall would go food shopping for them; others invited them over for dinner. Rodney didn't like having to depend on others. He felt a growing desire to change things. Lying in bed with his stomach growling, Rodney would tell himself, *I can't go another night like this.*

In the summer of 1981, when Rodney turned fourteen and was preparing to enter his freshman year at Malcolm X. Shabazz High School, he approached a man who sold joints in his building. Rodney asked if he could help out, and the man agreed, apparently figuring that he would make more money in the long run with an apprentice. He gave Rodney 100 joints, which Rodney sold for a dollar apiece, and took home $30 or $40. Soon, Rodney was selling 250 joints a day and pocketing $100. The money opened up his life, giving him not just the cash to join other kids at the pinball machines and hot dog joints, but also to buy groceries. He didn't tell Clara where the money came from, and Clara chose not to ask.

Rodney was not only a weed peddler. He and his friends regularly took the bus to Plainfield, where they shoplifted jeans and shirts from Bamberger's. He also began shaking down a neighborhood kid who worked at McDonald's, demanding a cut of the boy's paycheck and threatening to beat him up if he did not comply.

Rodney began to admire the neighborhood "old heads," career criminals who worked the corners and sometimes shared their expertise with the younger boys. "Like any kid who grows up without a father figure, I was looking for that manly type," Rodney told me. One of them let him sell some cocaine on consignment. After a few weeks of modest but steady sales, the old head gave Rodney a career-changing piece of advice: cut out the middle man and go into business for yourself. "Go *uptown*." Rodney didn't know where uptown was, so the old head offered to show him. They drove over the George Washington Bridge into New York, stopping at the intersection of Broadway and West 163rd Street, in Washington Heights. It was the center of a sprawling open-air drug market run by Dominican drug gangs who worked with Colombians to supply the entire Eastern Seaboard with heroin and cocaine—traditional powder, and a new form known as crack.

Rodney and his guide were inundated by calls from dealers and touts: "Yo, *Papi*, over here!" "Ay, *Papi*, what you need?" Rodney bought five grams of powder cocaine for $100. Then he went to a pharmacy and picked up dozens of glass vials and a container of Inositol, a type of sugar that was commonly used as a cutting agent. Back in Newark, Rodney sold the entire package in a few hours, without leaving his building, and cleared about $250. That night, he found a ride back to New York, bought ten more grams of coke, and sold half of it before bed. He finished the rest the following morning and returned to

Washington Heights again. "From that," Rodney told me, "I was on my way."

Even as he was getting pulled into the drug business, baseball remained Rodney's singular passion. He was turning into a powerful pitcher and had ambitions of making the Shabazz High School varsity baseball team, whose coach had recruited him in Little League. Rodney had all the tools to become a star: fluid motion, long stride, and good command of his pitches, which included a fastball with movement. He also possessed a certain quality that the coach didn't think could be taught: a poise that allowed him to battle through the most difficult situations. Rodney tried not to let his money-making pursuits affect his prospects on the ball field, but soon that became impossible.

During Rodney's freshman year, a boy got shot at Shabazz in an argument over a pair of sneakers. Before then, only the roughest street criminals carried guns. But a new era was dawning across Newark and the rest of urban America, fueled by crack. By dealing crack, young men found an easy way to buy things that otherwise would have been impossible to obtain. Their goal was to be "the freshest" on the block, the one with the biggest "dookie rope" gold necklace, the flyest sheepskin coat, the latest British Walker shoes, the sharpest fade haircut. Smoking a concentrated form of cocaine was more addictive than snorting it, and the customers, formerly respectable people whom the young men might have looked up to, people with nine-to-five jobs and tight families, got hooked and became, in street jargon, "fiends" who did whatever they needed to do to buy their next hit. At the same time, the crack trade gave rise to a secondary industry of "stick-up boys" who specialized in robbing dealers at gunpoint. Soon teenagers were arming themselves for protection and gunning after those who ripped them off. Authorities were caught flat-footed; the Newark Police Department's narcotics unit was tiny then, with maybe a half-dozen detectives working days and another half-dozen at night. Between 1984 and 1989, Newark's crime rate jumped by 41 percent, exceeding those of New York, Baltimore, and Philadelphia.

Elizabeth Avenue became an open-air drug market. That development coincided with an economic downturn in which many of the low-rise apartment buildings were lost to the city in tax foreclosures, then appropriated by squatters and dealers. The high-rises continued to operate, but with vacancy rates that forced owners to seek more federal subsidies. With the new money came requirements to keep rents affordable for low-income residents, which in turn triggered a turn-over of the tenant rolls: poorer people moved in, and the remaining middle-class residents fled. Many of those who left blamed the rental subsidies for the neighborhood's rapid decline. "People came in who didn't value the community as much as we did," one told me. "And the drugs. Some of the kids we knew as babies blended in with the new tenants and unleashed hell in that neighborhood. It became just like the projects."

Security in the towers was minimal; they employed guards, but many either were addicted to drugs or let the dealers come and go as they pleased, occasionally even holding their guns for them. Halls and lobbies and stairwells were open to virtually anyone who wanted to cop or sell. At Zion Towers, Clara noticed an influx of children who ran unsupervised through the building, destroying property at random. They poured hot water and garbage into the mail slots, smashed the vending machines. One day, Rodney ran into the building's man-ager after crackheads made off with the TV and videocassette player from the recreation room. The manager stood in the lobby, shaking his head, saying, "I wouldn't let my dog live in here."

Some apartments in Zion Towers became crack dens, where tenants rented out space in exchange for drugs. Rodney often went there to cut and package his cocaine because he could not do it at home; he was still, after all, only a teenager.

Rodney and Clara rarely spoke of his drug dealing. She knew where he got the money that filled the Pathmark bags he left in her kitchen, and the new sneakers and clothes he wore. But she felt powerless to make him stop. At least once, she walked in on him cutting and bag-ging his coke. "Get that shit out of here," she hollered. As he got up to go, she told him, "Boy, I'm praying for you. Keep that up, and you're going to go to jail."

The only family member with whom Rodney spoke candidly was

his sister Darlene. She understood his motivations and that underlying his cool posturing was the desire to provide for himself and his family. They knew it wasn't right to feed drugs to their fragile community. Rodney told Darlene, "This is not what I want to do, but I'm tired of struggling. I'm tired of not having."

"Me, too," she said.

In the spring of Rodney's sophomore year, the Malcolm X. Shabazz Bulldogs, after a string of losing seasons, were poised to compete for the city championship, led by a senior outfielder who was being scouted by major league clubs. Rodney's fastball was clocked in the low nineties, and he became a key part of the starting rotation. Even the fiends who were losing their families and earthly possessions respected his commitment to baseball. "Yeah, Rock," they greeted him when he returned home from practice. "Keep doin' what you doin'. You gonna make it." Rodney went 5-1 that year, and the Bulldogs ended up with a 15-9 record, placing second in the city league but getting knocked out of the state tournament in the first round.

After the season, Rodney returned to dealing full-time, paying crackheads $50 worth of rock to drive their car on supply runs to New York. He took the business seriously, like a real job. He usually started his daily shift by walking down the hill toward Meeker Avenue, where, along the way, one customer after another would approach him. The street seemed out of *Night of the Living Dead*, with drug-addled zombies outnumbering the clearheaded working people. He met his friends at the corner of Elizabeth and Meeker, where there was a constant flow of customers along a block-long strip of storefronts. This was the early days of hip-hop, and passing cars pulsed with the raps of Run-DMC, Biz Markie, Rakim, KRS-One, Big Daddy Kane. Amid the noise, Rodney would hang out and buy food while haggling with clients, a front in case the cops came. To keep his finances manageable, and his risk relatively low, Rodney never kept more than 125 grams of product at any one time. He made a good living this way; after "taking shorts" from those who couldn't pay full price, he would typically end the day with about $900 in his pocket. Then he would step away from the street, going upstairs to his mother's apartment for a nap. Later, he joined friends in the park to drink and smoke pot.

Rodney and his friends were curious about what kept their customers coming back for more, and they began experimenting by crumbling a bit of crack into their joints, concoctions they called "woolys." Rodney told himself it wasn't as bad as smoking crack straight out of a pipe; he had yet to learn the meaning of what Michelle Pfeiffer's character warned in one of his favorite movies, *Scarface*: Don't get high on your own supply.

The woolys kept him up night after night, dealing and partying all over the South Ward. He'd remain away from home for days on end, crashing in crack houses, breaking dawn in the projects. After one weekend-long bender, Rodney found himself on the streets at seven a.m. on a Sunday, strung out and exhausted. Instead of walking home, he trekked a mile to his mother's church, where services were under way. Clara, thinking he was there to repent, saw him and cried, "Praise the Lord." Rodney knelt to pray, telling himself, *I gotta change. I gotta change.* From then on, Rodney told me, he never did any hard drugs, just the occasional joint. He also stopped dealing, but he changed his mind when money got tight again. It required little effort to slip back into the routine.

By his junior year, Rodney had abandoned any pretenses about wanting to finish school or play professional ball. Every now and then, he would brag to his friends that he could strike out Mets slugger Darryl Strawberry, and they would dismiss him, saying, "If you keep hanging out in the streets, you'll never strike anyone out." Rodney rejoined the baseball team that spring but rarely showed up for practice. He started one early-season game against rival Weequahic High School but, winded from weed and cigarettes, he was pulled from the game in the second inning. He threw a tantrum in the dugout, and his coach threatened to kick him off the team. Rodney apologized and said he wanted to keep playing, but that didn't last.

Clara pleaded with Rodney to graduate, so during his senior year he doubled up on classes and told his coach he wanted to return to the team. While waiting for a physical examination, Rodney got pulled into someone else's argument with the school nurse, which led to an argument with the vice principal, which led to Rodney threatening to beat him up. Rodney was expelled. He tried to find another school that would let him finish the year, to no avail. He enrolled in summer school but blew off his exams. He applied for a GED course but dropped it after buying a forged diploma on the street. Every now and then, when he tired of dealing, or if there was too much pressure from police, Rodney would use that diploma to get a job—at McDonald's, cleaning planes at the airport, hauling furniture for a moving crew— convincing himself that he could keep a foot in both worlds. He managed to keep his adult criminal record clean until he was nineteen, when he was arrested with a small packet of cocaine as he drove back from New York. The following year he was caught with coke in Newark. In both cases, he was sentenced to probation.

In 1988, three years after he was thrown out of school, Rodney's mother talked him into enrolling at Essex County College, where she and his sister Barbara were already taking classes. He signed up for a program in which he would earn his GED and an associate degree, putting him on track to attend Rutgers-Newark, where he hoped to play baseball. Rodney received a $2,500 student loan for books and supplies, which he promptly cashed and took to Washington Heights. He continued dealing as he attended school. That lasted about a year, until September 26, 1989, when he was pulled over in a cab that was driving him home from Penn Station. Rodney saw the lights through the rear window and started stuffing his stash under the seats. The officers ordered him out of the car, slammed him against the trunk, and started searching him. Rodney wrestled free and took off running. He made it a few blocks before officers tackled him and fished two bulging bags of coke from his pants. He was twenty-two.

Rodney sat in the county jail for months, unable to make bail, while his mother enlisted friends at Essex County College to help him. Prosecutors offered him a deal that would put him behind bars for a year, but Rodney refused and his mother's allies could not persuade prosecutors to go easy on him. On the eve of his trial, during which he would likely be convicted, Rodney told prosecutors he'd reconsidered, but their first offer was off the table; this time, they were not nearly as generous. A judge sentenced Rodney to five years behind bars, with a minimum of eighteen months before he could be considered eligible for parole.

He ended up at a work camp for nonviolent offenders in the farmlands of western New Jersey. Because he stayed out of trouble, he was accepted into an "intensive-supervision program" that allowed him to return home early. The rules were strict: he had to find a job, submit to drug testing three times a week, attend group meetings, keep a curfew. His mother persuaded the Zion Towers management company to hire him as a maintenance man.

Around that time, Rodney started getting stopped in the street by strangers who said they knew him. Their conversations were always the same: they asked how his mother was doing, remarked how tall he'd gotten, and told stories about playing with him when they were kids. "You probably don't remember me," they said, "but when you was a baby, your mother used to bring you around and you'd be playing with my brothers and sisters, and I used to be babysitting you." Rodney was baffled by these encounters, but didn't let on. He just nodded and said *Okay, uh-huh, see you around.* But as he continued running into these same people, Rodney started asking them questions, and they were happy to talk. They said his mother had spent a lot of time with their father when they were young. In fact, their father, they said, was *his* father—and his youngest sister, Darlene's, too.

Clara had always claimed that her husband, James, was the father of all her children. She still refused to talk about him, though, and Rodney never asked. He remembered how nervous the subject made her. She didn't handle stress well—she still suffered the aftereffects of stomach ulcers, was prone to depression, and practically chain-smoked—and Rodney didn't want to make things worse. But this new information made him wonder. He told his sister Darlene about it, and she said the purported siblings had approached her, too. She'd asked Clara about it, and Clara had insisted it wasn't true. But the more Darlene spoke to these people, the more she believed their story.

Rodney felt conflicted. He wanted to know the truth, but he didn't want his mother to think he doubted her. He confided to a family friend, who confronted Clara. Clara wouldn't answer, and the next time Rodney saw her, she looked wounded. "Why did you have to mention that?" she said. She began to cry. Rodney apologized and promised himself he'd never bring it up again. *If she ever wants to tell me, she'll tell me*, he thought.

Rodney went on to earn his GED and got back into shape playing on adult-league baseball and football teams. One day, he came across a newspaper article about the New York Mets holding open tryouts. He sent an application and was rewarded with an invitation. His parole officer granted him a one-day leave, and Clara joined Rodney for the bus trip. He arrived at a minor league park in Albany, New York, with about five hundred other hopefuls. At twenty-five, this was his last shot.

When his number came up, Rodney took the mound and threw about fifteen pitches, including five fastballs that clocked in the high eighties, far short of the speeds he'd hit as a teenager, but impressive. A scout asked how old he was. When Rodney told him, he looked disappointed. "I wish you'd come out here when you were a little younger," he said. Rodney tried to take it as a compliment and left to get back home before nightfall. A few weeks later, he got a letter saying four prospects at the camp had been offered a chance at a pro contract, and he wasn't one of them. They invited him to another tryout, but Rodney didn't go. At his graduation from the intensive supervision program, the judge congratulated him and urged him to stay straight. Instead, Rodney went right back to dealing drugs.

CHAPTER 2

Rodney never considered himself a thug, just another guy out to make money the quickest and easiest way he knew how. While many of his friends aspired to run their own corner operations, he stuck to his 125-gram-at-a-time limit and never rose above a street-level dealer. He was satisfied earning enough money to pay his bills, stock his mother's cupboards, and keep himself looking fresh. But years in the streets had taken a toll. He'd been arrested and robbed, ambushed and pistol-whipped, and had narrowly escaped more drive-by shootings than he could count. He carried a gun regularly now, and though he'd never shot anyone, he'd used it to pistol-whip a man who'd robbed him. He beat his girlfriend Prudence so badly once that she ended up in the hospital, and he might have been sent back to prison if she hadn't decided against pursuing charges against him. Despite what he thought, Rodney was indeed a thug.

By now, many of the old heads Rodney emulated were either dead or locked up, as were many of the guys he came up with. One got sliced in the throat during a bar fight and bled to death on the floor. Another was killed by younger guys in a battle over turf. A third was shot by police. A fourth was gunned down by a pair of dealers he'd robbed. Deadly violence was part of the daily landscape, and Rodney dealt with it the only way he knew how: by not thinking about it. He did not—could not—let himself get scared. He treated death like an abstract event that had more to do with fate than self-inflicted risk. He told himself things like, *If it happens, it happens, and if it don't, it don't,* and, *When my time comes, then it's meant to be.* Rationalizing it in any other way would have made it psychologically impossible for him to return to the streets every night.

In Rodney's world, guys generally only got shot when they robbed or shortchanged a dealer or trespassed on someone else's operation. But there was a new generation of criminals who lived by a different code and were far more willing than Rodney's contemporaries to kill. The new boys would shoot you over an insult. Some had started claiming allegiance to Los Angeles–style street gangs like the Bloods and Crips. Eventually he couldn't ignore the fact that the streets had become more dangerous. He told himself he needed to cool it.

In late 1994, Rodney heard that the owners of a property up the street were looking for maintenance men. Such projects were popping up all over Elizabeth Avenue, as the city tried to reclaim the buildings that had been commandeered by squatters and dealers. Rodney introduced himself to Seymour Alpert, the patriarch of the company that just won a renovation contract. The old man hired Rodney on the spot and after a few months made him superintendent of a blond-brick low-rise apartment building at the corner of Elizabeth and Custer Avenues.

Rodney knew the place well. For many years it had been a *New Jack City*–style drug den that operated around the clock, taking in more than $15,000 a day and patrolled by lookouts on the roof and sidewalks. After the police shut it down and put the ringleader in prison, the city sold the building to Alpert. He asked Rodney to live there, alone, rent-free, on the third floor, to keep out the addicts who made a habit of ripping out metal fixtures and selling them to scrap yards. Rodney accepted, and at the age of twenty-seven he moved out of his mother's apartment for the first time. He continued, though, to spend his nights and weekends in the streets. When Seymour saw him on the corner, he warned him to stop. "I like you, Rodney, but please, you don't need to be around them kids."

Rodney was also still seeing Prudence, despite the fact that she'd moved in with another man. Prudence told Rodney she really only loved him, and was with the other guy because she and her young daughter needed a place to live. She wanted Rodney to leave Elizabeth Avenue and start a new life with her, and Rodney told her he'd try to make that happen.

But the other man, who was known as Hawk, was very jealous. He suspected Prudence of sneaking off to see Rodney. Hawk and Prudence got into a fight, and he beat her up and told her that he'd kill her if she left him. Prudence ran to Rodney and told him what happened. Rodney didn't take the threat seriously. They kept seeing each other.

One Monday in October 1995, Rodney returned home from work and found his apartment ransacked. His dishes had been pulled from the kitchen cabinets, his clothes from his dresser drawers. The mattress was pulled from the bed, and the 9mm pistol he kept hidden there was gone. Rodney found a handwritten note that said, "You bitch ass nigger, I got her now, suck my dick."

Rodney went berserk. He and a friend jumped in a car and found Hawk standing on his porch on Willoughby Street, his white Cadillac out front. They parked and turned the headlights off. "I'm gonna kill that motherfucker," Rodney said, reaching for a gun resting on his friend's lap. His friend yanked it away and told Rodney to relax, but Rodney was already out the door, jogging up the block toward Hawk. "What's up now?" Rodney called.

Hawk took off running. Rodney and his friend lost him. They ran back to their car and saw Prudence sitting in Hawk's Cadillac. Rodney couldn't understand why she was there. He told her to come with him, and she refused; it could get Rodney killed. She felt that she was trying to protect him. But that made Rodney angrier. He wondered if she'd set him up. He smacked her. His friend pulled him away, and they drove off.

Rodney tried to figure out what to do next. Hawk was probably going to report to the police what had just happened. So Rodney decided to try to head him off by telling the cops that Hawk had broken into his apartment. He stopped at a pay phone and called 911. The dispatcher told him to meet a patrol car outside his building, and Rodney jogged home. On his way, he saw a cruiser parked on Custer. "Y'all here for me?" he asked the officers. They told him they were on another assignment, so he should go home and wait.

A minute or two later, the officers came up behind Rodney and ordered him against their car. Someone had reported being threatened with a gun by a man who fit Rodney's description. They patted him down, and when they found nothing, they left. Rodney sat on a wall outside his apartment building and caught his breath.

It was just after dusk, and the stoop, bathed in the yellowy halo of a nearby streetlight, had fallen quiet. Rodney rested his head between his hands. He told himself that he needed to go inside, somewhere safer, and figure out what to do. But he lingered a few more moments, and then a few more, until, suddenly, it was too late.

When he looked up, the car was already bearing down on him in a shriek of skidding tires. It was a red Honda Civic CRX with a man in a dark hood leaning out of the passenger's side window, reaching across the roof. Rodney knew it was Hawk. He stood to run and heard three sharp cracks as he ducked for cover beside a parked van. He pressed himself against the cool metal door. The Honda braked and idled. Hawk had missed and now was probably getting out of the car. Rodney could think of only one thing to do: run.

Just as he cleared the van, the gun blasted one more time. Rodney felt a burn in his lower back. His legs went rubbery and weak, and he slammed onto the sidewalk, a heap of sprawling limbs. "Ahhhh!" he moaned. "Shit!" Then he heard Hawk say, "I got your ass." The car sped away.

Quiet returned, as if the gunshots had sucked the air out of the street. Time seemed to slow. Rodney tried to turn himself over and realized that the lower half of his body had gone numb. He waited for the deadening to swallow the rest of his body. He closed his eyes.

Rodney heard footsteps and shouting, and soon people were crowded over him, trying to roll him on his back. One of them, a friend, was weeping. Rodney thought about his mother. He didn't want her to see him like this, blood soaking his clothes and puddling beside him in what could be his final moments. He could hear sirens getting closer. He tried to calm himself but could not. It would have made sense to him if he had been shot by a rival dealer or stickup man, but not this. As the medics pulled up and started loading him into an ambulance, he thought that this would be a lousy way to die.

The drive to the hospital seemed to take forever. But, in reality, everything was happening very quickly, and Rodney, given what had happened, was fortunate. He was headed to University Hospital, which handled more than three thousand trauma cases a year, about a quarter of which were shooting victims. They were so good at keeping people alive that patients often walked away wondering how they'd survived. Homicide detectives said their jobs would be much busier, and the murder rate much higher, if it wasn't for University.

When the ambulance pulled into the trauma bay, a response team in blue scrubs and white coats rolled Rodney inside. A nurse checked his pulse, blood pressure, and breathing. A doctor probed his mouth and throat. A second doctor was searching for the wound. Someone slipped an IV into his arm. Another person cut off his clothes. It was chaos, but controlled chaos, not unlike a NASCAR pit crew, or a scene from *ER*.

Outside, it seemed that all of Elizabeth Avenue had showed up to see what had happened to Rodney. Soon a tall doctor came outside and said, "He wants to see his sister. Which one of you is Darlene?" She stepped from the crowd.

Rodney lay awake and alert in a mess of tubes and wires. He grabbed Darlene's hand and held tightly. "Don't let them put me to sleep," he pleaded. "And don't let them give me no type of drugs."

"Do you know who did this?" Darlene asked.

"Yeah."

"You sure?"

"I'm positive."

"Who?"

"Hawk."

The doctors wheeled Rodney upstairs to the intensive care unit, and Darlene walked back outside, to Rodney's friends. "Hawk did it," she told them. But they already knew. They were heading out to find him.

Clara arrived. She and Darlene waited a long time before another doctor emerged. "He's holding his own, he's in good condition," he said. "That's the good news. The bad news is he got hit in the spine and it shattered and it doesn't look like he's going to walk again." Darlene burst into tears. Clara's shoulders slumped; she walked away and lit a cigarette. A nurse handed her a bag containing everything that Rodney had on him when he was shot: black leather jacket, two T-shirts, blue jeans, tan Timberland boots, Fossil watch with a black leather band, black Pagenet beeper, a set of keys, a nail clipper, and $22.82.

When the doctors allowed another visit, Darlene went up alone. Clara couldn't bear to see, and Rodney didn't want her to.

"I ain't fighting this no more. It hurts," Rodney said.

"You can't leave me here," Darlene said.

Rodney grabbed her hand. "You don't understand. It hurts."

"I don't care if it hurts. It's not going to hurt forever."

Then Rodney's grip loosened. His pain medication was kicking in, but Darlene panicked. "Don't do this to me!" she shouted at him. Rodney shook his head and closed his eyes.

The next few days were a blur of painkillers, medical tests, teary visits from family and friends, and a brief interview by detectives. Rodney could not feel or move his legs or go to the bathroom, but because of the sedatives he could not quite understand what was going on.

A doctor came in to check him and, without looking Rodney in the eyes, said, in some foreign accent, "No walk," and left.

"What the fuck was that?" Rodney asked. The nurses seemed embarrassed by the doctor's lack of tact. They told him not to worry, that someone would come by to explain what was going on.

The next day, doctors brought in a pile of MRIs, X-rays, and a model of a spinal cord and laid it out for him. The bullet had slammed into his spine, then ricocheted up, splintering bone before lodging into the spinal cord just below his belly button. It appeared to be a 9mm slug. Rodney wondered if Hawk had shot him with his own gun. But detectives had not found the weapon, or Hawk, so it was impossible to know.

The impact crushed the bundle of nerves in the rigatoni-size cord, instantly shutting off communication between the brain and everything below the point of impact. The brain could not tell Rodney's legs to move, and Rodney's legs could not tell the brain what they were feeling. Everything from his lower abdomen down had immediately gone dead, like a switch had been flipped. Only for Rodney, the switch could not be flipped back on. The damage could not be undone. His injury was, in medical jargon, "complete," putting the chance of recovery at less than 1 percent, with room for those highly rare exceptions that doctors could only call miracles.

Rodney refused to believe that he wouldn't walk again. In all the years that he had played sports and ran the streets, he had barely even twisted his ankle. He fell into a deep depression that frightened his mother and worried the doctors. He couldn't sleep, wouldn't eat or bathe, told nurses he wished he was dead. He had flashbacks of the shooting but would not talk about them. Rodney refused doctors' attempts to give him antidepressants, saying he "would handle the situation myself."

One day, Rodney's right leg twitched, and he excitedly reported it to his doctors. They checked him and said they saw no evidence that he had regained control of his lower body. It must have been a muscle spasm, they said. Soon, they told him, he would be released to a rehabilitation hospital, the same place where the actor who played Superman was recovering from a horse-riding accident. By then, Clara had filled out Rodney's application for Medicaid, which would cover his care. He'd be in good hands there. Miracles sometimes happened, the doctors said, but they cautioned Rodney not to expect one.

CHAPTER 3

Rodney arrived at the Kessler Institute for Rehabilitation in suburban West Orange feeling like he was a newborn baby—unable to take a bath, dress himself, move around, or go to the bathroom on his own. On his first day, he lay on his side while a male nurse inserted suppositories in his rectum to help clear his bowels. When lunch was announced, Rodney rolled to the cafeteria, saw all the people in wheelchairs, and did a U-turn back to his bed. His hair started falling out in clumps. A social worker visited Rodney in his room, where a large window framed a few craggy pine trees and the staff parking lot. She drew the curtains around his bed, sat beside him, and told him that it could take a long time to see anything but despair, but he would need to focus on learning to live with his injury and returning home.

"What are you going to do when you get out?" she asked.

Rodney had no idea. "I'm going to be all right," he stammered. He repeated it, as if that alone would make it true. He began to sob. "I'm going to be all right . . . I'm going to be all right . . ."

He looked up and saw that the social worker was weeping with him.

Rodney had never thought much about people in wheelchairs before. Most of them were old and feeble and probably going to die soon. But he began to see things differently. Kessler was one of the world's premier rehabilitative hospitals. Many of the other patients were shooting victims like him, young, poor, and black, but there were also white suburban kids injured in car accidents, middle-aged men disfigured in construction mishaps, dyed-haired ladies recovering from tennis injuries. At Kessler, doctors and nurses told him that he was part of a new community and that after he learned how to get around in a wheelchair, catheterize himself, and empty his bowels, he could live a fulfilling, independent life.

In the Kessler gymnasium, therapists wrapped his legs in splints and bandages and taught him how to walk between parallel bars. The goal was to improve strength and prevent bone loss, but Rodney saw it as a step toward walking again. He threw himself into the exercises. Focusing on them dampened his anxiety. Doctors were impressed by his progress and began preparing him for a December discharge. A staff member handed him a brochure that guided new patients through the process of obtaining their own wheelchairs. But Rodney refused to look at it. He felt like they were asking him to choose his casket. "Y'all got me picking out chairs like I'm going to be in one for the rest of my life," he told them.

Returning home was considered the most difficult stage of rehabilitation. During inpatient care, which staffers called "the Kessler bubble," nearly every minute was planned, and Rodney was surrounded by people going through the same thing. He saw doctors several times a day, had access to round-the-clock nursing care, worked out three hours a day, and took part in organized recreational activities. At home all he had was his mother and a visiting nurse. Hours stretched by in which there was nothing to do but sit. Rodney and Clara orbited around each other, the air heavy with regret. He caught her looking at him and saw the sadness in her dark, sunken eyes. She babied him, and he resisted. She tried to get him to tell her how he was feeling; Rodney avoided conversation. "I'm all right, Ma," he always said. He watched a lot of SportsCenter and played PlayStation with a neighbor, but when the apartment got claustrophobic and he tired of his mother's pity, he retreated to the platform at the edge of the Zion Towers driveway.

Rodney had spent untold days—years, maybe, if he added them up—outside the front entrance, people coming to him at all hours for fixes or for help fronting a package. Now he was just a passive observer, left to think about his wasted life. He wondered if things would have been different if he'd had a father at home. Every boy needed a man to look up to, and all Rodney had when he was young were the old heads. He wanted to know more about his father, but he still couldn't confront his mother. The time never seemed right. She was sad enough already.

Whenever someone asked how long he was going to be in the chair, he said he didn't know. Seymour Alpert, the developer who'd hired Rodney to look after the building where he was shot, happened by and told him there was a job waiting for him as soon as he was able to walk. Rodney asked if he had something in an office, and Seymour promised to check. He began to walk away, then turned and said, "I told you, Rodney. I told you . . ."

Rodney ran through his memory of the shooting, over and over and over again. He still couldn't believe it happened over a girl. He worried that Hawk—who remained on the run—still wanted to kill him. He wondered if there was a reason to go on living.

Sometimes Rodney's old drug-dealing buddies would pull into the driveway and holler for him to come for a ride. He always refused. He did not want people seeing him like this and did not want trouble. What if his friends had stuff in the car with them? What if they got pulled over? They'd all probably jump out and run, and he would catch a charge.

Rodney dreamed about the shooting almost every night, though the details often changed. Sometimes, the flashback played out as it had in real life. Other times, the dream was more abstract; he was being fired at but wasn't sure where he was, who was shooting, or why. Always, though, the fear and panic remained vivid, even after he opened his eyes, heart fluttering. Caught in the foggy transition between sleep and wakefulness, he was not immediately sure whether the dream had been real. Sometimes he woke up thinking his legs had fallen asleep. He would slip his hand under the covers and rub his emaciated thighs, pinch them, and feel nothing. He would try to move them. Then he would remember.

A wave of pins and needles occasionally washed over his legs. When it first happened, Rodney believed that his nerves were trying to come alive again. His doctors at Kessler called it "neurogenic pain," a mysterious reaction by the spinal cord that was unpredictable, and difficult to treat. Most important, it did not mean he was getting his legs back. They told him he would get used to it, and eventually he did. He learned not to believe everything his brain told him, and as those dreams continued, he knew to wait for the confusion to pass and to force himself out of bed, into his wheelchair, and back to reality.

The only time Rodney ventured beyond the curb of his building that winter was three days a week, at around noon, when a medical transport van took him to Kessler for outpatient physical therapy. He was assigned to an attractive, upbeat twenty-one-year-old intern named Denise, who nearly froze in fear when she saw him for the first time. She was five feet, eight inches tall, weighed about 115 pounds, and had grown up in a largely white middle-class town. She had hardly any experience with black people, let alone an angry six-foot, three-inch ex-con with a bullet in his spine. She helped him strap on a pair of custom-made leg braces and rise to his feet. She handed him a walker, got behind him, and held his hips, praying that he would not topple on her. But Rodney did not waver, and soon she had him staggering down the hallways on forearm crutches, a rare feat for someone with an injury like his. Every visit, Denise came up with new challenges for him, and he met them all. At one point, she had Rodney stand unassisted in his braces while she tossed a ten-pound medicine ball at him. Rodney caught it and kept his balance, something many of her colleagues had never seen. She had him climb and descend steps in his wheelchair, using only the railing for support. She had him get out of the chair, sit on a bottom step, and pull himself and his empty wheelchair up the stairs. Rodney never missed a session, never came late, never left early, and never lollygagged. The point was to teach Rodney to maneuver through the most difficult circumstances, but he was thinking just one thing: he was going to walk. That became his motivation, no matter what anyone said about the permanence of his injury. He wanted to use the braces at home, but Denise and the doctors would not allow it, saying it was too dangerous. Rodney ignored them. Using a borrowed walker, he did slow, staggered-step loops around his mother's living room, sometimes with friends spotting him. He played and replayed his favorite album of the moment, Tupac Shakur's *Me Against the World*, taking the troubled rapper's words, written in prison and barked over silky R & B samples, as if they had been written for him. *Keep your head up, and handle it.*

That spring, a lawyer from the Essex County Prosecutor's Office met Rodney to talk about the case against Hawk who, after four months on the run, had turned himself in. The prosecutor, Harry Moskowitz, was sympathetic to what Rodney had been through. He was interested in Rodney's personal story—not the drug dealing, but his once-promising baseball career and his failed pro tryout. Moskowitz said the state had a pretty good case against Hawk for attempted murder, but the charge would be difficult to prove at trial. One option was to see if Hawk would plead guilty to aggravated assault, which carried a much lighter prison sentence. But the thought of Hawk somehow getting off on a lesser charge angered Rodney, and he urged Moskowitz not to let it happen. Moskowitz went to his supervisor and they decided to back Rodney. Hawk's public defender said he was willing to plead guilty if the government recommended a sentence slightly short of the legal maximum. Moskowitz went ahead and cut the deal, and in June Hawk pleaded guilty, telling the judge he had shot Rodney "because we had a fight over a girl."

Later that month, the New Jersey Victims of Crime Compensation Board sent Rodney the first installment of a $25,000 payment that was supposed to make up for his lost wages. The first envelope contained two checks totaling $13,000, which covered the months since the shooting. From then on, he would receive checks of $5,900 once a year until the $25,000 ran out. Rodney had no bank account, so he took the envelope to a check-cashing place down the block and left with a massive wad of bills.

The money bolstered Rodney. He stocked his mother's kitchen and took a cab downtown, where he bought new clothes. He filled out an application for a rent-subsidized apartment of his own in Zion Towers.

Word quickly spread of Rodney's new fortune. Friends approached him for help flipping a package. Relatives needed something "to get me back on my feet." Neighbors asked help making ends meet. Rodney refused none of them. He hoped that if the situation was reversed, they'd do the same for him. Some already had, and he owed them. Others were the kind of people to whom he simply could not say no. That was how things worked in the underground economy, where every day was a fight: when you had something you spent it, if not on yourself, then to build goodwill. Cash had a way of slipping through your fingers like water. Rodney, who'd burned through untold riches over the last decade, understood better than most: you took shorts, you spread the wealth, you got robbed, and then you went out and made it back.

In mid-summer, when his compensation package had nearly run out, he took his last few hundred dollars and paid a cabbie to drive him to Washington Heights, where his old Dominican suppliers sold him four ounces of high-grade marijuana at a discount. Within a couple of weeks, Rodney had upgraded to coke and heroin. Eventually he got his friends to go to New York for him, and later some Dominicans agreed to deliver the drugs in person. He bought a .25-caliber handgun for $300 on the street. The incongruity of spending his compensation money on a firearm did not occur to him. Guns came with the business, and Rodney did not want to be caught unprepared.

On the first day of August, just after 9 a.m., a small group of Rodney's friends and family slid into the wooden benches of Judge Serena Perretti's courtroom on the twelfth floor of the county courthouse. Hawk stood with his lawyer, sleepy-eyed in a green jail jumper and a goatee. Rodney sat with Moskowitz, the prosecutor. Behind him, his friends insulted Hawk under their breath. Next to them sat Rodney's sister Darlene. Rodney looked over at Hawk and thought he saw him smirk.

Perretti asked if Hawk had anything to say.

"Yes," Hawk said, standing. "I'm sorry for crippling and shooting Mr. Mason."

Moskowitz urged the judge not to show leniency on Hawk, calling Rodney "a victim in every sense of the word." Perretti sentenced Hawk to a longer prison term than what the lawyers had agreed upon: sixteen years, six of them before he could become eligible for parole. An officer led Hawk from the courtroom, and Rodney heard the prisoner tell his mother, "Ma, I'll be home."

Moskowitz asked Rodney if he was satisfied.

"Whatever," Rodney answered. Nothing could make up for what Hawk had done.

A few weeks later, Denise, Rodney's physical therapist, announced that he had "maxed out" his potential and there was nothing more she could do for him; his outpatient therapy would end. An apartment on the sixth floor of Zion Towers became available, and Rodney moved in. Because he was, by the books, dependent on disability checks, he had to pay only $175, or 30 percent of his income. He used his Victims of Crime Compensation checks and his drug profits to furnish the place with a new bed, sofa set, kitchenware, and a TV. Rodney began dealing out of his place, and soon apartment 6K developed a reputation. His old friends came up to his apartment to smoke pot and play Madden NFL on his new PlayStation, betting $50 or $100 a game. Most seemed happy to have him back in their circle. But not all of them. One said, "They be locking guys up in wheelchairs. And that ain't a pretty sight, Rodney. You *do not* want to go down there in that wheelchair."

Outside, a younger generation of Zion Towers boys who had looked up to Rodney were now selling drugs. He sat on the platform with them deep into the night, urging them to go home and do their homework. But Rodney was no longer the Brown Hornet, the tall and imposing big-brother type. Now he was a casualty, symbol of broken hopes, a living mistake. He was what they prayed *not* to be. He wished there was a way he could change that, to teach them something worthwhile.

CHAPTER 4

When I arrived in Newark as a crime reporter in 2004, the city was in the midst of a staggering surge in gunfire. The number of shootings was headed toward levels not seen since the end of the crack era more than a decade earlier, when *Money* magazine dubbed Newark "America's most dangerous city." Authorities struggled to explain it. Modern police strategies, including computerized statistical analyses and a crack-down on quality-of-life crimes, combined with stricter prison sentences for drug offenses, had put thousands of young men behind bars and pressed the overall crime rate down to historic lows. But now, several new trends were converging to cause the uptick in gun violence. More young people were growing up with the notion that it was okay to use firearms to solve petty disputes. A large number of them were joining street gangs, which made such disputes more prevalent. The street narcotics trade still flourished. And each year a steady flood of ex-cons, the targets of those tougher drug-sentencing laws, were returning from prison and trying to reclaim turf seized by the new guys, who were holding them off with superior firepower. Variations on this scenario, along with straight-up gang battles, dominated my reporting. It was tempting, especially among public officials, to describe these attacks as having occurred in a sort of underworld vacuum, with no greater harm done. After a string of gang-related executions at the end of 2004, officials tried to calm a jittery public by saying that law-abiding residents were at "minimal risk" of getting shot. But that simplistic explanation overlooked the fact that long after the gunfire stopped, shootings continued to reverberate through communities.

While covering the aftermath of a gun fight one evening, I started talking to an antiviolence activist named Thomas Ellis, an unassuming nondenominational minister in his midforties who'd found his calling after getting robbed and shot outside a gas station. Instead of shouting slogans and holding sidewalk vigils with the other protesters, Ellis took it a step further, tracking down victims and their families, praying with them, and trying to help them cope with their trauma. Every year, he held a Thanksgiving dinner for people who had lost loved ones to guns. Ellis told me that there were thousands of survivors scattered throughout the city, physically and psychologically damaged, living in fear of running into attackers who had not been caught. It was easy to see how, over years, chronic gun violence could wear at a community, unraveling its social fabric and destroying people's faith in each other. "We need to educate the public about this, because people don't understand what's happening," Ellis said.

I asked him for help telling that story, and a few days later he called and said he'd found someone I should meet. I picked him up, and we drove to Zion Towers.

At first, Rodney seemed an intimidating figure: massive hands, dark stare, and a build, from the waist up, like an outside linebacker's. Once we started talking, my impressions changed. He was meek and insecure. He apologized for the mess in his apartment. He didn't look me in the eyes. Although it had been nearly a decade since the attack, he still seemed traumatized. Hawk was now on parole after serving seven years in prison, and Rodney worried that he might still want to kill him. He entertained thoughts of revenge but felt powerless. Instead, he spent most of his time thinking about what it would have been like if he'd done things differently. "There would be some closure if I woke every day and was able to stand up," Rodney told me. "But waking up every day and getting into a wheelchair, there will never be closure for me."

At Kessler, doctors and nurses had told Rodney that many patients with spinal cord injuries saw their disabilities as a way to find more meaning in their lives. Some became closer with their families, while others got involved with charities, religious organizations, and other community groups. The ultimate example was Christopher Reeve, who, after leaving Kessler, had become a world-renowned advocate for spinal cord patients. But there were countless other people who were not famous or rich but had touched the world in special ways. Their change came about slowly. For those like Rodney, men from the inner city who used to depend on their physical prowess to survive in the streets, the choice was stark: adapt or withdraw. But Rodney still struggled with overpowering questions about who he was, what he wanted to be, what people thought of him. He knew he had some goodness in him. He just needed to decide he was ready to embrace it, and let it guide him. Each night, after his friends and drug customers left, Rodney went to bed with his television on, trying to drown out the turbulence in his head. But when he awoke, that uncertainty was still there.

Rodney had first explored this ambivalence about a year after he'd come home from Kessler. It was sparked by a chance meeting with an old childhood friend, Ron Christian. Ron was driving by Zion Towers one day and noticed Rodney sitting on the platform, moping alone in the cold. The sight startled Ron because he remembered Rodney as a strapping "ghetto superstar" who always had people hanging around him. Ron had escaped the neighborhood, gone to college, and become a sergeant for the New Jersey Department of Corrections, but had blown everything on a coke and dope habit and was convicted of stealing from Northern State Prison, where he worked. The last time Ron and Rodney had seen each other was long before the shooting, outside a Bergen Street restaurant. Rodney saw Ron picking through the garbage and bought him a meal. Ron vowed to repay Rodney someday.

Ron was now out of prison, preaching at a nearby church and telling his story to schoolkids and youth groups. He asked Rodney to join him. "We need to talk to these young people," Ron said. "We need to make sure they don't do what we did. *You* need this, Rock. You're going to tell your story, I'm going to tell my story, and we're going to make a difference."

The thought of speaking in public made Rodney's stomach twist. But he couldn't say no to Ron. They landed their first gig in front of an audience of rowdy eighth graders at Peshine Avenue School. It was Rodney's first time on a stage, and at first he spoke haltingly, leaving long silences that the children filled by shifting in their seats and chattering. Then Rodney raised his voice and said, "I remember when I was just like you. I didn't think it could happen to me. And it happened in a second. Do you think it's fun being in a wheelchair? I have to take this tube and stick it in my penis when I want to go to the bathroom." The kids fell silent, and Rodney finished his story. "You could hear a pin drop," Ron told me. "I *know* that lives were changed and touched from that moment."

They spoke at more schools, churches, and youth jails, and Rodney began to feel for the first time like he was doing something meaningful. But the engagements happened only once or twice a week and lasted only a couple of hours. The rest of the time he was out on the platform or in his apartment with his friends in a haze of pot smoke, customers coming and going. He tried not to think about how fraudulent he was.

Before long, Ron became a licensed minister. He hobnobbed with politicians and took humanitarian trips to West Africa. He would leave town for weeks or months at a time, but when he returned he would always try to arrange gigs with Rodney. Rodney felt that Ron was leaving him behind, and instead of trying to keep up, Rodney started blowing his friend off.

"I have something to do," he'd tell Ron.

"What are you doing?" Ron would reply. "You're in your chair, you have no job. What's more important?"

Ron was dismayed. They were both at potential turning points in their lives, but Rodney could not see it. "He was still captured in his environment," Ron told me later. "I wanted to yell: 'Do you know who you are? You have so much to contribute!' But he just didn't get that."

* * *

Several months later, Rodney was back on the platform when one of his neighbors asked if he was okay. She must have known from the look on his face that he wasn't. "I was wondering," the woman said. "Would you like to go to *jumu'ah* with me?" Rodney knew a little about Islam from some of his friends who had converted; *jumu'ah* was communal Friday afternoon prayers. As with Ron, Rodney could not think of a reason to say no.

She drove him to Lincoln Park and stopped at a brownstone mansion, where four men picked him up and carried him up a narrow flight of steps to the second-floor landing. They showed him how to do *salat*, the ritualized series of prayers and postures that ended with a recitation of the Koran's opening chapter, *Al-Fatihah*.

In the name of Allah, Most Gracious, Most Merciful.
Praise be to Allah, the Cherisher and Sustainer of the worlds;
Most Gracious, Most Merciful;
Master of the Day of Judgment.
Thee do we worship, and Thine aid we seek.
Show us the straight way,
The way of those whom Thou has bestowed Thy Grace, those whose
    (portion) is not wrath, and who go not astray.

Then they sat and listened. Services were already under way, one floor above them in the packed main worship hall. Rodney could hear the imam piped through speakers. The slow rhythm of the foreign words, the placid responses from the worshippers, relaxed Rodney, and soon he was lost in the drone of their voices. The imam gave a sermon about respecting yourself, respecting others, doing good deeds. Rodney felt instantly at peace. *This is where I need to be*, he thought.

He returned the following Friday, and the one after that. Many of the worshippers were guys like him, from the street, and welcomed him like a brother. He followed them when the imam moved services to a space in a Bergen Street boxing gym, rolling every week past the spot where he had gotten shot. Rodney told the imam about his public speaking and that he wanted to find a way to help young people avoid the streets. The imam pointed out that Islam required its followers to perform acts of charity, and helping kids could be a path to righteousness. *"That's* your charity, Rodney," the imam said. "Find a way to make it happen."

There was one big problem, though. Rodney was still dealing. His crime-victim payouts had long since expired, and he could not contemplate living on just $600 in monthly disability checks. He hadn't done hard drugs since that bender in his teens, but the lifestyle was all he knew; it was the only place he felt he belonged. He prayed for the strength to stop. He often returned to the words of *Al-Fatihah*. One line rang out at him: *Show us the straight way.* That's what he had to find. But he didn't know where to begin.

Rodney was alone on his sofa one afternoon when there was a loud knock at the door.

"Who?" he shouted.

"Newark police."

Rodney hoisted himself into his chair and found his stash, a small bag of coke, and stuffed it into his sock. He opened the door, and a half-dozen officers flooded the apartment. The sergeant pulled a badge from under his shirt and said, "We're getting a lot of complaints that you're selling narcotics out of here."

"I ain't doing that shit."

"Well, we gotta do our jobs and check it out."

"Go ahead."

During the search, one of the officers began admiring some old trophies Rodney kept on his television case. "You used to play ball?"

"Yeah."

"You ought to leave that shit alone and mentor some kids instead," the cop said.

They left without finding anything, but Rodney knew he hadn't fooled the police. He'd just gotten lucky.

When my 2005 story about shooting survivors, featuring Rodney, appeared, his friends told him he'd fucked up and brought too much attention to himself. The traffic in his apartment thinned, and his old partners didn't stop by or call as often as they used to. But others—neighbors, relatives, friends who weren't criminals, strangers on the street—said they were impressed that he'd shared his burden so openly. One was Jeff Billingsley, a former classmate from Shabazz High School who'd dealt drugs and survived several shootings himself. He was now running a recording studio and working with Operation CeaseFire, a program that enlisted ex-offenders and social service agencies in a public health-style campaign against gun violence. He saw Rodney passing by the studio one day and called out to him. "Come and chill with us," Jeff said.

Rodney did, and returned to the studio just about every day, talking to whoever happened by the studio, mostly members of Newark's growing antiviolence movement. He joined Jeff at CeaseFire events and told his story to small audiences, similar to what he had done with Ron. Jeff encouraged Rodney to branch out on his own. Rodney decided to try to start a mentoring program in Zion Towers. Jeff helped him apply for a city-administered grant, and Rodney was surprised when he won $4,500, along with an invitation to city hall to receive his check. The day he heard, he called me up, and I noticed that his voice had softened. It sounded like he was smiling.

When the president of the Zion Towers tenants association heard about Rodney's plans, she protested. She knew what Rodney did for a living and apparently convinced the management company, which withdrew support. Rodney went back to the nonprofit foundation that was administering the grant and explained what had happened; he was told not to give back the money, just do what he could with it. Rodney bought kids back-to-school supplies, arranged a trip to the city's new minor league baseball park, hosted a pizza party and a Halloween party, and bought a computer. But when the money was gone, Rodney felt empty.

CHAPTER 5

A little after noon on July 1, 2006, Cory Booker climbed the stage of the New Jersey Performing Arts Center, a 250,000-square-foot glass-and-brick centerpiece of Newark's prolonged downtown resurgence, to introduce himself as the city's first new mayor in two decades. If there was ever a sign that a new day was dawning in Newark, Booker was it. In Newark, authenticity, especially among blacks, was perhaps the single most important factor in determining a politician's viability. That meant paying your dues, not only by working within the local Democratic machine, but also by proving your street cred. Then along came Booker, a light-skinned, blue-eyed, thirty-seven-year-old African-American who was raised in the suburbs and moved to Newark after graduating from Yale Law School. A former Rhodes scholar and Stanford University tight end, Booker didn't eat meat, claimed to have never had a sip of alcohol, counted Hollywood stars and New York investment bankers among his supporters, and had served one term as a reformist city councilman, during which *Time* magazine had put him on a cover with the headline, "The Savior of Newark?" In 2002, Booker had taken on Mayor Sharpe James, the very model of an inner-city political boss: charismatic, ruthless, adored, feared, and the survivor of a number of corruption scandals. James destroyed Booker that year in a vicious campaign that exploited the city's insularity and resistance to change; he called Booker gay, Jewish, Republican, even white ("You have to learn to be African American," James taunted. "And we don't have time to teach you."). But Booker did not retreat. Unabashedly earnest and a natural self-promoter, he knew James's days were numbered, and he cast himself as a symbol of Newark's rebirth: post-racial, unburdened by liberal urban political orthodoxy, a champion of school choice, and a darling of conservative think tanks. He amassed a huge campaign war chest, and the next time around, the seventy-year-old James decided not to run for a sixth term. The mayor offered no protégé to take his place, allowing Booker to coast into office.

Booker's choice of the performing arts center—one of James's pet projects—as the site of his inauguration ceremony was another break from tradition and injected a bit of glamour into the event. Dressed in a dark blue suit, his head shaved so smooth that it reflected the stage lights, Booker gave an intense speech that lasted nearly an hour, describing a city teetering at a historic precipice, primed for a turnaround but staggering under the weight of violence, poverty, and government negligence. He was a gifted extempore speaker, and got so worked up that spittle often flew from his mouth as he waxed poetically on matters gritty and grand, from street tales of uncertain provenance to Greek philosophy. His favorite quote was from Gandhi: "Be the change you want to see in the world." He was so eager, so seemingly pure in his ambition, that it struck cynics as corny or fake. But even the most hard-bitten Newarkers in the audience that day couldn't help but applaud when Booker outlined his top two priorities: cutting violent crime and expanding recreational opportunities for children. Thrusting an index finger in the air, almost shouting at the crowd of two thousand, he implored, "Stand with me, Newark, because I tell you right now, I can *smell* the future. The future is *now*."

As the event wore on, and the temperature and humidity rose, I was in the streets on an assignment to gather a snapshot of the city as it fell into Booker's hands. By numbers alone, the challenge appeared daunting. After two decades of James's so-called renaissance, a quarter of all residents—and half of families with children—lived in poverty. The municipal government remained the city's largest employer. And at midyear, Newark was on pace to record the most murders since 1990. Booker had campaigned on the phrase, "A renaissance for the rest of us," and today I was out for a view from the ground.

First I stopped at the bleak, grassless Seth Boyden public housing complex on the farthest edge of the South Ward, where drug dealers, addicts, and mentally unstable transients often lurked in the sulfur-lit courtyards. The heat wave had temporarily driven them elsewhere, and I found some children playing under a canopy of drying bedsheets while their parents gathered in the shade of a few sickly trees. The adults told me they didn't listen to politicians' promises anymore, even those coming from Booker. "Our little children gotta stay in the house twenty-four-seven," one mother said. "The situation is terrible."

I made my way to a city-owned vacant lot on Broad Street, where Booker had once held a campaign press conference to protest James's selling of public land to politically connected housing developers. When I arrived, three young boys were swinging from a tree on a two-by-four secured to a thick branch by a cord of twine. "I hope they make a baseball field or a playground," one of the boys said. His mother nodded. "We don't need no more houses," she told me. "We need something for the kids."

Back on the street, I happened upon a Pop Warner football team running drills on an asphalt playground. One of the coaches explained that their home field was in a park a couple of blocks away, but it had been left to molder, and despite the city's pledge to renovate the gridiron, they had no other place to practice. "We want to see a field get built so we can say to our children, 'You have your own place to play,'" he said. "They deserve more." He encouraged me to take a look for myself. I cruised around the corner, to Jesse Lee Allen Park, where weeds grew knee high and glass crunched under my shoes. The bleachers had been taken over by squatters. Basketball hoops hung off kilter. Empty chip bags rolled in the wind like tumbleweeds. Not one child. I thought of something Clement Price, the city's preeminent historian, once told me: "When Newark stopped looking after its kids, that's what hastened its decline."

* * *

Newark always had more pressing things to worry about than parks and recreation and it showed. Its Little League diamonds were arguably among the country's worst, and near the bottom of that heap was the Jackie Robinson South Ward Little League's home at the St. Peter's Recreation Center on Lyons Avenue. It flooded in light rain and grew lumps that sent ground balls caroming into infielders' faces. Before each game, coaches cleared away crack vials, beer bottles, and other trash and poured ammonia into the dugouts to wash away the urine.

The situation was nauseating, particularly in light of the league's daring creation, in 1967, months before the riots, by five determined fathers who'd grown disillusioned with the dwindling after-school options for their sons. They obtained the ball field in a donation from the St. Peter's Orphanage and got a construction crew to bulldoze it. They enlisted volunteers to walk the property, shoulder to shoulder, military-style, clearing debris. They carved out the infield and base-lines by hand, often working late into the night, illuminated by car headlights. They built bleachers and a concession stand, which was looted. The city donated money for fences and a backstop, which were destroyed by vandals. But they remained undeterred. That spring, scores of boys representing a dozen teams paraded to the new field in full uniform behind a South Ward Little League banner, accompanied by the brassy honks of the Weequahic High School marching band.

The league grew to include more than three hundred boys and girls and expanded into a fall bowling league, a Women's Auxiliary, and joint ventures with other community groups. It flourished during the grim 1970s and endured the free-fall 1980s. But in the mid-1990s, the league faltered. Some of it had to do with abrupt leadership changes and general disorganization. But there was a broader set of circumstances decimating youth baseball, not only in the South Ward but in cities across the country, where decades of chronic poverty had disintegrated families, leaving fewer adult males around to coach. Colleges focused their scholarship money on the more lucrative sports, basketball and football. Baseball, meanwhile, became a specialized sport that catered to the wealthier suburbs. Eventually, black kids stopped recognizing faces like theirs in the major leagues. Baseball became uncool, a white man's game.

In 1995, the South Ward Little League went dark. It may have remained that way, if not for a mother named Kelley Spear. Kelley grew up in the Weequahic neighborhood and returned after college to raise a family. She was an avid baseball fan and wanted her young sons to play the game. When she couldn't find something nearby, she founded her own T-ball league. Eventually it was merged into the South Ward Little League just before it started to sputter. When the league shut down, Kelley took it over, resurrected it, renamed it the Jackie Robinson South Ward Little League, and began spreading the word.

At that time, Kelley worked for Communities in Schools of Newark, a nonprofit social-service organization that partnered with Newark Public Schools to help students focus by taking care of whatever they needed outside the classroom. She was assigned to Peshine Avenue School and was deeply troubled by what she saw: five-year-olds walking to school alone, sixth graders acting as caretakers for their younger siblings, dozens of students showing up every day hungry, sleepy, and in dirty clothes. Most of these kids were from the Elizabeth Avenue high-rises, including Zion Towers. She thought they would make ideal recruits for her league, but she got few responses; parents were either uninterested or worked hours that prevented them from taking their kids to games. Letting them walk to the St. Peter's field, about a mile away, was out of the question; the side streets were considered too dangerous. But Kelley had an idea. Just a few blocks from Peshine, on the edge of Weequahic Park, was a dilapidated old ball field with a warped chain-link backstop and deep grooves worn into the rock-hard baselines. Kelley appealed to Joseph DiVincenzo, a former Newark high school football star who had recently been elected Essex County executive. After lobbying him for months, he finally agreed to meet her at the park, where she described her vision.

"Kelley," DiVincenzo said, "if I build the field, will you get the kids to come to it?"

She said she would.

* * *

Cory Booker started the summer of 2006 with a call for all hands on deck. He sent more cops into the streets and ordered social-services agencies to fan across the city's poorest neighborhoods looking for young people to enroll in recreation activities and job training programs. But the post-inauguration honeymoon didn't last into fall, and his first year became an unrelenting lesson in governmental dysfunction. Shifting political alliances made it nearly impossible for Booker to implement reforms. He discovered that his predecessor, James, had hidden a massive budget deficit, forcing him to hike property taxes and lay off city workers. When suspicious credit card bills in James's name showed up at city hall, Booker called federal prosecutors, who, it turned out, were already investigating lavish trips James had made at taxpayers' expense. A spate of murders at the end of 2006 left Newark with its highest number of killings in sixteen years. Booker turned to experts outside the city for management help but was accused of favoring white outsiders over local blacks. His critics—including supporters of James, who would soon be arrested on corruption charges—began picketing city hall. The city teachers' union bought billboards around town that screamed HELP WANTED: STOP THE KILLINGS IN NEWARK NOW. One piece of good news came from the U.S. Census, which revealed that Newark's population had risen faster in the past seven years than any other city in the Northeast, thanks in large part to urban pioneers drawn to Newark's cheap housing. But many of those new residents soon found themselves drowning in debt, the result of a nationwide proliferation of subprime mortgages.

Booker tried to maintain a bullish front. "We've reached a turning point," he declared as his first year came to a close. At times he seemed to be trying to single-handedly will Newark to a better place. He kept an exhausting schedule that often ended with his riding the streets with his security detail, looking for drug dealers. He traveled the country to talk about his experiences in Newark, hoping to drum up financial support. But he peppered many of his speeches with stories about crack houses and drug addicts and gunshot victims, which backfired at home, at one point forcing him to apologize for reinforcing negative stereotypes about the city. By the summer of 2007, even some of his supporters began to wonder if he was more hype than substance. At a fund-raiser, Booker leaned wearily at the podium, a rare public display of weakness. "I'm worn," Booker confessed to two of my colleagues at the *Star-Ledger*. "Everything is hard." But it would soon get much worse.

A little before midnight on August 4, 2007, four young Newarkers, two men and two women, either in college or headed there—the embodiment, in many ways, of Newark's potential—gathered in a West Ward school yard to hang out and listen to music. They were approached by a half-dozen young males, and, sensing danger, the friends started to leave. The crew surrounded them; one of them pulled a gun. Three of the victims were lined up at a brick wall and shot in the back of the head, execution-style. The fourth was sexually assaulted, slashed with a dull machete, shot behind the ear, and left for dead. It was as senseless as a killing could be. The victims were good kids who had made all the right choices and, until that night, avoided the hazards of coming of age in Newark. There was no logical way to answer the question on everyone's minds: *Why?*

The murders broke the city's heart and propelled it into a period of dark, penetrating self-examination that deepened as police began to round up the killers, some of whom were as young as fifteen and claimed allegiance to a notoriously depraved street gang called MS-13. Booker had repeatedly told Newarkers to judge him by his ability to reduce violent crime, and statistics showed he was starting to deliver. But to many, the killings showed that he hadn't done enough. Whatever progress was being made in Newark, none of it mattered when stacked up against the image of kids executing kids.

For much of the week, Booker struggled to find his footing. In press conferences, he asked Newarkers to "unite around their common challenges," but his pleas were largely overlooked until Saturday, when he took the podium at the funerals for all three murder victims. He started out repentant in the morning and grew more commanding throughout the day. "How dare I or any other Newarker crumble to the ground?" he said at one service, as mourners began to stand and call back in approval. "How dare we give in to fear? How dare people turn on their brothers and attack them, blame them?" Later, he called on the city to go to battle for a new future. "I tell you, Newark, this tragedy will not define us," he boomed. "*We* will define us. Our children buried today are not the exception to the rule, they *are* the rule. Long live Newark!"

Slowly, something turned. The city began to rally behind the mayor. A crush of volunteers flooded the city's Big Brothers Big Sisters program. Other antiviolence and children's programs found more people offering to help. A newly formed Newark Community Foundation pledged to raise the $3.2 million needed to install a camera-driven gunshot detection system, a key element of Booker's antiviolence platform.

That summer, a temporary orange plastic fence went up at the Weequahic Park ball field, and work crews began tearing it apart. Rodney noticed the construction, but it was not until later, when the scoreboard and outfield fence and dugouts were erected and fifteen-foot rolls of green artificial turf lay waiting to be spread across the land, that he realized what was going on. The sight sparked memories of his own Little League days. Kids today grew up even faster than he had. Maybe he could help them hold on to their childhoods a little longer. Maybe he could play a part in that new "spirit of unity" that people had been talking about since the school yard murders.

He showed up at the Jackie Robinson South Ward Little League's monthly meeting and introduced himself to the committee. Kelley, the president, wondered if Rodney was up to the challenge. Every year, new coaches quit after realizing how difficult and time-consuming it was. And they weren't in wheelchairs.

"Are you sure you can do this?" she asked.

Rodney looked up. He fixed his eyes on hers. "I can do it."

The resolve in his face convinced her. She gave him an equipment bag and a rule book and told him to pick a name for his team. The league used old Negro League nicknames, and she showed him a list of those that were available. He chose the Newark Eagles.

When Rodney told his mother about his plans, she cautioned him against it. She'd been working as a substitute teacher in the South

Ward and was appalled by the children's lack of discipline and respect for authority.

"Those kids is off the hook," Clara warned her son. "You ain't going to be able to do it."

"Mom," Rodney said, "I think something's wrong with me because I like doing stuff with bad kids."

His sister Darlene could not understand how her stoic, withdrawn younger brother was going to pull it off.

"To coach he has to talk and communicate with people," she told Clara. "How's that going to work?"

"I don't know," Clara said.

That fall, county officials held a ribbon-cutting ceremony at the new field. Rodney came to watch. Fallen leaves coated the new playing surface, and the trees beyond the outfield wall had turned the color of rust. Rodney sat near the home dugout in a black leather jacket and his Yankees cap. The South Ward councilman Oscar James II, who had been instrumental in helping Rodney obtain the 2007 city grant, walked over to say hello. "This man," James announced to everyone, "is going to get the children in these buildings to come out and play on this field." DiVincenzo, the county executive, asked Rodney to join them. Rodney squeezed between Kelley and the councilman, who wrapped an arm around his shoulder as the camera clicked.

After the ceremony, kids began meandering onto the field. Rodney told them about his team. He printed up flyers and posted them in the lobbies of the high-rises. He overheard people scoff at him, saying that no one gave a shit about baseball anymore. Rodney worried whether they were right. But he asked around and was told that there were 240 children listed on leases in Zion Towers alone, with another 278 in Carmel Towers down the block. That was a lot of kids with nothing to do. Surely he could find nine.

CHAPTER 6

Rodney woke just before dawn and for a while lay still, trying to coax himself back to sleep. When the first slants of sunlight began to break over the trees of Weequahic Park and through his window, he gave up, pulled himself to his wheelchair, and rolled into his living room. He flicked on the radio, toggling between hip-hop and R & B stations before he found a song he liked. Then he slalomed through a narrow hallway and into a tiny bathroom littered with medication bottles and unopened urine collection kits. He twisted the tub's hot water knob, poured a handful of Epsom salts into the deepening pool, and watched the granules swirl and dissolve. He dropped himself in, pulled his knees close to his chest, and let the mineralized water soak his aching body.

Don't panic.

For weeks, Rodney had been combing the neighborhood for recruits, but now it was late March, a couple of weeks before the start of the 2008 Little League season, and he had only a handful of completed registration forms. Baseball just didn't seem to be on many people's minds. Some kids had actually told Rodney that they *hated* baseball, recoiling as if it were some kind of social disease. He couldn't understand it. This was the national pastime, the game *everyone* played when he was growing up. What happened to all the boys who'd been scrambling on the soft, new artificial turf last fall? Where were all the kids he'd counted on the tenant lists? In the sluggish span of winter, his outlook on coaching had evolved from *How hard could this be?* to *What the fuck am I doing?* He needed a half-dozen more kids, at least, just to field a team. Desperate, he'd told Kelley, the league president, that he might need help filling out his roster and wouldn't mind if she sent some strays his way. Then, to hedge his bets, he'd called me for help. He didn't want to spend money on an ad, but he thought maybe I could slip something in the local news section. I told him it wouldn't be a problem and wrote a brief article that appeared in the paper in late March:

Little League in South Ward Seeks New Team in Newark

The Jackie Robinson Little League in Newark's South Ward is looking for kids living along the Elizabeth Avenue corridor to form a new team that will play on a new field.

The team, to be coached by Rodney Mason, will host games on a renovated diamond in Weequahic Park.

For years, the Jackie Robinson Little League has had trouble recruiting players from the Elizabeth Avenue area because most games were played in far-off sections of the South Ward, league officials said. That will change with the new county-owned field.

Mason, executive director of the Elizabeth Avenue Youth Recreation Program, is holding registration sessions for prospective players. The next session will be held Saturday from 10 a.m. to 1 p.m. at the new baseball field at Elizabeth and Mapes avenues.

Today was the day. If kids didn't show up this morning, then they never would. Rodney settled back into the effervescent water. His mind drifted back to a well-worn memory of pitching for the Shabazz Bulldogs. He was a sophomore, 190 pounds, all legs and arms, looking down from the rutted clay pitcher's mound of Untermann Field. Sun seared his face. Sweat stung his eyes. His right hand squeezed the dusty cowhide of a five-ounce Rawlings Official League baseball. The batter from Central High School shifted his feet in the dirt. Rodney toed the pitcher's rubber, stepped back with his left leg, tucked his throwing hand into his glove. Pivoting off his back foot, he shifted his momentum forward, pulling his hands to his chest and drawing his left knee toward his shoulder. He was now balanced on his right leg, his chin tucked into his chest, eyes narrowed like a sniper's. For a fraction of a second, he paused at the top of his windup, cocked and ready to release. Rodney knew little of the physics behind his delivery, just that it could be his ticket to pro ball.

He uncoiled his body and pushed off the rubber with his right foot. He reached back and drove his left leg forward in a loping stride that dropped him off the edge of the mound. His arm followed and sent the ball home in a red-stitched blur in less than half a second. It slammed into the catcher's mitt with a high-velocity collision of leather on leather that sounded like a pickax on ice. The pop of a called strike. The sweetest sound he'd ever known. What he'd give to hear it again.

Rodney hoisted himself out of the tub and dried off. He slipped on a condom, fitted it to a urine collection bag, and strapped the contraption to his right leg. He ironed his jeans and white T-shirt and switched to a battery-powered scooter that the family of an elderly neighbor had given him after the old man died. Then he rode a lurching elevator to the lobby and rolled out into the gray chill. The neighborhood was just starting to come alive, people stepping onto their stoops, assessing the weather, waving to neighbors, retreating inside. The field was empty. So was the parking lot. Rodney pulled up to the dugout, jammed his hands into the pockets of his Yankees windbreaker, and waited. *Please, God*, he prayed. *Help me make this happen.*

Sometimes, when he was not working and his children were at school, Thaiquan Scott stopped by the Jackie Robinson South Ward Little League's old field at the St. Peter's Recreation Center to catch a game. The diamond was lousy with lumps and the quality of play was terrible, but he occasionally noticed a gifted athlete who, if he found the right coach and stuck with it, could probably go on to play in high school or college. Thaiquan wondered why more black kids weren't interested in baseball.

Thaiquan stood a shade under six feet, with an athletic build and a midsection that was starting to soften. He worked an overnight shift at the Beth Israel Medical Center emergency room, returning home each morning as his wife and children were getting up. He'd been on this schedule for the better part of a decade and carried himself like a man in need of a nice, long, deep sleep. He moved languidly and spoke in a sandy drawl that combined a Newarker's cropped vowels and a Southerner's unhurried tempo. His cheeks were often taut with worry, and his drowsy eyes gave him a solemn, menaced appearance. He wore a short row of braces inside his bottom front teeth, and a thin tuft of hair darkened his chin. He had the names of three of his children inked on his skin: one on his right arm, another on his left biceps, the other on his right hand. He never got around to adding his two stepdaughters, and that bothered him because he loved all his kids with equal ferocity. He dressed in loose-fitting blue jeans, white T-shirts, work boots, and a black do-rag over his head, the intentionally generic look embraced by a generation of inner-city boys who sought protection in numbers. Thaiquan looked as if he could still blend in with the guys on the corner, and he still could relate with them on a certain level. But Thaiquan had turned his back on that life seven years ago.

He and his family lived on the second floor of a narrow three-family house with cream-colored vinyl siding on Peshine Avenue, about a mile north of Weequahic Park. Their block was not what you'd call kid-friendly, though there were many children. Dope fiends and drunks puttered around in the abandoned lot across the street. Brash young drug dealers played noisy games of dice on the stoops of homes, the tenants too frightened or too complacent to complain. A few days after the Scotts moved in, a thirty-nine-year-old woman was killed in a drive-by around the corner. A little while after that, as Thaiquan lay in bed listening to the distant pounding of a Friday night football drum line at Shabazz High School, he heard gunshots, went outside to investigate, and found a teenaged boy bleeding to death on the corner. When the block's dealers began shooting craps at the foot of their house, Thaiquan retrieved a gun he kept hidden in the house and gestured for one of them to come talk. "You will *not* be dealing drugs outside 203 Peshine," Thaiquan told him, the weapon heavy in his waistband. "Kids *play* right here. I'm not a snitch, but this is where me and my family live at. This is a drug-free zone." The young man said, "Cool," walked away, and never came back. Later, when Thaiquan told me this story, and I expressed astonishment that he'd kept a firearm in a house full of kids, he shrugged. "This is where we live, brah," he said. "I had it for the protection of my family. Everyone should have one for the days and times that we live in."

Thaiquan and his wife, Shamira, wanted to leave Peshine Avenue, but their house was one of the only places they could find that was cheap and large enough for the seven of them. So they made the best of it by keeping the kids busy and trying to expose them to the world outside the city. Every July, they piled into their coughing minivan for a trip to see family in Atlanta. He told his kids stories about friends who'd blown opportunities at college. He also talked openly about how he'd lost his way as a young man and gone to prison, but had pulled himself from the brink in time to become a father. Now, any threat against his kids—biological or not—he took as a personal affront. If they were in the car and came across some dealers or junkies, he would point them out and say, "I don't care how old I get, if I see you on the corner looking like these motherfuckers, I'm going to KILL YOU!" They'd laugh nervously, and he'd crack a smile, but everyone understood how serious he was.

Thaiquan saw baseball, and sports in general, as a bulwark against the streets; the more his kids played, the less chance that something bad would happen to them. He also believed that baseball ran in his family. His father had been an amateur ballplayer—a damn good one, he'd heard. But drinking got in the way, and the old man left home without ever passing the game on to Thaiquan. That didn't keep Thaiquan from trying; as a young boy, he'd wander the block with a bat and ball, trying to start a game of pickup. The other kids made fun. "That's some white-boy shit," they'd say. "Corny." Now he wanted to give his two oldest children—Nasir, his biological son, and Kaneisha, his stepdaughter—that chance he never got. He pledged that as soon as they reached playing age, he'd sign them up for Little League.

That day came just after the first thaw of 2008, when his wife noticed the newly renovated field on Elizabeth Avenue, along with a sign announcing registration for the coming season. "It's time," Thaiquan told Nasir and Kaneisha. He drove them to Modell's and bought them gloves, sweatpants, turf shoes, and baseballs. Then he took them into the street with a beat-up twenty-nine-inch, thirty-two-ounce aluminum softball bat that Nasir had found somewhere and began hitting them grounders. Too many rolled into traffic, so they moved to the rocky vacant lot across the street. The ping of the bat and the shrieks of their voices drew other kids on the block, none of whom had played baseball before. Soon they were splitting up for pickup games, using construction debris—bricks, flattened cardboard boxes, two-by-fours—as bases. Soon the children no longer needed Thaiquan to motivate them. They went door-to-door calling out for each other, gathering in the vacant lot for noisy games that adhered only to the most basic rules: three strikes to an out, three outs to a side, and when you hit the ball, run like hell.

In late March, Thaiquan got word that Nasir and Kaneisha had been assigned to a team. They went to meet the coach and were surprised to see that he was in a wheelchair. Thaiquan introduced himself and felt like he understood Rodney immediately. "He's from the struggle," Thaiquan told me later, a phrase he often used to describe men, like himself, who had come of age in the streets. "But that don't mean that he's not about the kids. He's a product of his environment, so he knows how the kids are and how they grow up. I could tell right away that he was doing it from his heart."

It began with a trickle: a child here, another there, and soon there was a crowd. Among the first arrivals was Derek Fykes, who arrived with his grandmother Irene. He was ten but had the face of a tired man: eyes narrowed, brow rumpled, lips slack. He had just been removed from his father's apartment by the state child welfare agency. This wasn't the first time he'd been abruptly pulled from one home and placed in another. Probably wouldn't be the last, either. Irene worried about the lasting damage of such an unsettled childhood. But baseball was one of the few things that helped Derek regain his footing. It was the one sport he was good at, and the ball field was the rare place where he could forget the sting of feeling unwanted. The game calmed him, and that was important, because Derek had a propensity for sudden, violent outbursts that frightened his family. When Irene had first volunteered to take him home with her, she'd looked around for a ball team and found Rodney's newspaper announcement. She sighed and told herself, *God is good*.

Derek was an anomaly in that he'd played Little League before. Just one other boy, a heavy trash-talker named William (who went by "Pooh"), had any experience. The others were young and scrawny and clueless; most didn't have gloves, and some didn't know if they threw right-handed or left-handed. DeWan Johnson, a magnetic ten-year-old with a gap-toothed grin and nubby dreadlocks that poked from his head like spring shoots, was one of the most promising recruits. No one had taught him how to swing a bat or throw a ball or encouraged him to play baseball at all, for that matter. What little he knew about the game came from watching kids in the park and the Yankees on TV. But he had a unique ability to mimic the postures and movements of other good athletes, and immediately stood out among the rabble of rookies that day. He had an untethered rocket of an arm and bravely planted himself in front of hard-hit grounders. Rodney assigned him to third base.

DeWan was eager to learn. At home, he clacked around his apartment in his new turf shoes and practiced his throwing motion and batting stance in front of a mirror. His mother did not protest, even when he broke a light or stepped on her foot, because she was happy to see him so excited about something new. She also wanted him to find a man he could look up to. His father lived elsewhere, and his stepfather was in prison for drugs, but maybe Rodney—this new version of Rodney—could help fill some of the void.

The kids were arriving in packs now. A pickup game began. Rodney suddenly looked overwhelmed. A couple of fathers offered to hit grounders, keep the books, whatever they could do to assist. Another man showed up and said he, too, wanted to coach; his father had been a founder of the original South Ward Little League, and he wanted to be of service to the organization that had helped mold him into a young man four decades ago.

By that afternoon, Rodney figured that he'd talked to about a hundred people. When Kelley, the league president, stopped by to see how things were going, she found dozens of kids calling themselves Eagles. They threw like shot-putters, swung bats like axes, ran shrieking through the infield with little clue what they were doing. It was hard not to chuckle, watching them swirl around Rodney as he tried to figure out what to do next. His sister Darlene showed up and was startled by the sight.

"Where did you get these kids?" she said, aghast. "They *cannot* play baseball."

Rodney didn't care. The hardest part, in his mind, was over; he now had something to work with, something that he could shape into a team. It would not be pretty. But it would happen. Finally. He couldn't wait to get started.

"That's all right," Rodney told his sister. "I'm-a teach them."

CHAPTER 7

This had to be the worst team Derek had ever played on. It was hard for him to imagine anything in their future but defeat. Most of his teammates hadn't spent any time on a baseball diamond. They cowered under pop-ups and pounced on grounders like they were fumbled footballs. They gripped the bat cross-handed and stood on top of home plate, begging to be beaned. They didn't know the difference between a ball and a strike, so they swung at everything—balls over their heads, balls at their feet, sometimes even balls that *hit* them. Those who didn't swing at everything swung at nothing at all, too frightened to lift the bat from their shoulders. During warm-up sprints, the Eagles lined up under Coach Rock's instructions, then zigzagged off on their own trajectories, whooping and throwing their gloves at one another. Curses, including "nigger," were forbidden, the punishment a lap around the field, but banned words slipped from their lips as thoughtlessly as breath itself, and it was impossible for Coach Rock to keep up. The team's green canvas equipment duffel contained just three flimsy rubber bases, a pair of scuffed batting helmets, battered catcher's gear, three aluminum girls' softball bats, and a chipped wooden children's bat. They didn't even have proper uniforms. Some kids had sweatpants. Others wore last season's football pants. One boy wore the trousers from his tae kwon do outfit. But most showed up in their street clothes— baggy jeans or knee-length basketball shorts with untied high-tops. Whenever someone called "Who are we?" and the others responded,

"Eagles," it sounded less like a cheer than a reminder. Coach Rock didn't seem to mind the disorganization too much, but you could see the veins bulge from the forehead of one of his assistants, Coach Calloway, who played in the South Ward Little League as a kid and seemed intent on reconstructing his memories of 1960s order and discipline.

Derek knew none of his teammates and did not join their antics. He carried himself with a detachment that made him seem world-weary and wise. It was often hard to tell if he was enjoying himself. He kept to the perimeter of team gatherings, scrutinizing them with dark, wide-set eyes magnified behind thick glasses, looking way too jaded for a boy who still carried remnants of baby fat around his belly. Derek didn't talk much, but when he did, he chose his words carefully. The other kids figured he was just shy, but Rodney knew better. Derek's remoteness reminded Rodney of himself, and he wondered what it concealed.

Derek's mother, Gail, and his father, Derek Sr., were drug addicts who met while they were both in court-ordered rehab in the mid-1990s. Derek Sr. had a wife and three daughters at home at the time, and Gail was married but separated, with four young children being cared for by relatives. They carried on a secret affair that continued after they left rehab—he graduated, she quit—and soon she got pregnant. For months, she spurned his pleas to either get clean or have an abortion, and when she gave birth in September 1997, baby Derek began trembling from the effects of cocaine and heroin withdrawal. He was placed in the neonatal intensive care unit, and the hospital refused to let Gail take him home. Derek's father asked to have him, but child-welfare workers turned him away when they learned of his drug history. Gail's sister, Mary, who at the time was raising her three young children by herself, volunteered. For three months, Mary cradled Derek through his nightly trembling spells until they gradually diminished. Gail didn't see Derek until he was nearly a year old, when she showed up at Mary's with baby clothes, cuddled with him for a few days, then left, presumably for the streets. Gail saw Derek every so often but did not attempt to claim legal custody of him. Derek's father eventually won visitation rights but, although he had stopped doing drugs, he continued selling crack and ended up serving a brief stint in prison. He was released in July 2000.

Derek may have seemed brooding and quiet, but beneath the surface was a hair-trigger temper he couldn't control. He held anger inside like the air of an expanding balloon, and when the stress got to be too much he burst. And then, just as suddenly, the fit subsided and he regressed to a state of near stupor, while the people he'd raged at wondered what had just happened. But Mary believed she knew the cause. While there was no conclusive research proving that babies who were born addicted to drugs later developed behavioral issues, the obstetrician had warned her to look out for trouble.

The first signs emerged soon after Derek's third birthday, when he became defiant, hyperactive, and unable to sleep. At nursery school, he threw things, kicked classmates, bit teachers. In Derek, Mary claimed to see traces of Gail, a headstrong bruiser who "took no junk," but she also recognized that he needed professional help. She took him for counseling, where therapists noted that he didn't smile or laugh, couldn't look them in the eyes, and didn't sit still. He seemed overly concerned about getting hurt, interpreted innocuous situations as threatening, struggled to express himself, and had trouble reading others' social cues. Mary enrolled him in a program that specialized in treating children with behavioral problems.

When Derek was five, Mary began looking for a proper place for him to attend kindergarten. Months before the start of the school year, she submitted a formal request to have a Newark Public Schools child-study team evaluate him. She called several times to follow up, but no one ever got back to her. That summer, she received a notice that he'd been assigned to a mainstream classroom. Furious that she'd been ignored, she tracked down the school principal and told her story. "If he's not unconscious and he's not bleeding, don't call me," Mary said. "I don't care if he tears up this whole classroom. And if you kick him out of school, I'm going to sue you."

The first day of kindergarten went fine. On the second, Derek flipped out, tossing a desk and frightening the kids and his teacher. The school called Mary and asked her to get him, but she refused to come until the end of the day. This happened a couple of more times until the school finally agreed to bring in the child-study team. Derek was assigned to a special-education classroom and prescribed a low dose of Ritalin. Recalling the experience years later, Mary still seethed. "The education system *sucks*," she told me.

Derek calmed a bit, in part because of the Ritalin but also because Mary had found something just as useful: the drums. Derek *loved* to bang on things—anything—and Mary discovered that if she set out pots and pans on the kitchen floor and let him play, the frequency of his tantrums decreased. At school, Derek made some encouraging progress, but he still struggled to pay attention and didn't get along with other kids.

While Derek was in grammar school, his father began petitioning the court for partial custody. Since getting out of prison, he'd cleaned up and found steady work, and was now living with his sister. Mary was dubious of Derek's father, but she did not oppose the request. She did not want Derek growing up not knowing his dad. "I don't try to keep nobody from their child," she told Derek's father. "And if you feel you can get through to him, so be it."

They went to live with Derek's father's girlfriend in a studio apartment in Paterson, a depressed former factory town a few miles upriver. That lasted about a year. When Derek's father dumped the girlfriend, she began calling Mary with stories about how Derek wasn't being properly fed or clothed and didn't have a bed of his own. Mary wasn't sure whether to believe her. But eventually the girlfriend made good on a threat to call the state Division of Youth and Family Services. A caseworker came to check the apartment out and found it too small for a child. Derek's father was given a few weeks to find a bigger place. He missed the deadline, and Derek was sent back to Newark, where his grandmother Irene offered to take him in.

Derek appeared indifferent to the daily dramas that disordered his world; he recounted them cautiously and articulately, making it easy to forget that he was only ten years old. "The DYFS people showed up and pulled me from the room. I didn't know why. I just liked the attention," he told me. He said he wasn't resentful about his nomadic childhood; this was just the way it had turned out, and it didn't do any good feeling sorry for himself. But still, it would have been nice not to have to wonder where he was going next. "I just want a place to live and to be loved," he said. "I'm like, whatever, as long as I have a home, a family that cares, a roof over my head."

The ball field was one place that didn't seem so unpredictable. An older half brother had taught Derek baseball when he was five, and he'd been playing ever since. He understood the game's rules and rhythms and found comfort in its rituals: batting practice, fielding drills, dress codes, the focus on teamwork and fair play. The beauty of baseball, Derek said, was that any team, even the longest of long shots, could beat any other, no matter how far behind they'd fallen. In other sports, the clock ran out, but in baseball you could be on your last strike and still come back to win. That was important to remember, playing for the Eagles. Everyone expected them to fail. Coach Rock said he liked being underestimated because they could sneak up on people. Derek liked that idea.

Neither Mary nor Irene lived on Elizabeth Avenue; their homes were on the other side of Interstate 78, which sliced through a particularly ominous section of the South Ward. They forbade Derek from walking the streets alone, but they both worked and could not coordinate their schedules to get him to and from the ball field every day. Derek missed many of the Eagles' early practices until Rodney offered to let them drop him at his place early and pick him up late. The boy and his coach waited together in the approaching twilight, Rodney showing Derek how to grip a curveball while clouds of gnats bobbed around their heads. "He's a babysitter, coach, and everything else," Irene told me.

The first time Derek showed up at Rodney's, he told his coach, "*Assalamu alaikum.*" Derek was not Muslim but had somehow figured out that Rodney was. Rodney, confused, paused before realizing that the boy was goofing with him. "*Wa alaikum assalaam,*" Rodney replied, smiling. It seemed odd for such a young boy to wield a deadpan sense of humor. But he soon got used to it, and it became part of their routine. He bought Derek sandwiches and snack cakes at the bodega next door. They talked mostly about baseball, but Derek also shared some of his personal story. The basic details were familiar enough to Rodney; a lot of boys in the neighborhood lived in similar circumstances. It pleased Rodney that Derek trusted him with such information, but he didn't pry for more and didn't offer advice. He just listened and told Derek he understood what he was going through. They began to bond over those conversations. "He's a great person," Derek told me later. "He teaches me about baseball, but not only about baseball, about life. When we do bad, he blames it on himself. And he always tells me to keep trying." Not long after the start of preseason practices, the coach of a rival team, a much better team, tried to lure Derek over to his side. But Derek declined. The Eagles needed him. That mattered more than winning.

Practices were fitful. The Eagles considered the new field their home turf and expected to use it for practice every day. But once the season began, the field became busy with games, and the Eagles usually got booted before they could hit a rhythm. One day, after they'd been sent packing, one of the boys, William, hollered to the coach of another team that was preparing to play that evening.

"Hey, Coach, wanna scrimmage?"

The coach shook his head.

"Man, I want to scrimmage," William said, sighing. "I'm bored."

DeWan turned to Rodney with pleading eyes. "We can't practice?"

"We'll be able to practice tomorrow."

"I came out here for nothing? I want to practice, to get better."

"You'll get better."

Their only other option was a trek deeper into the park, where there were a half-dozen all-dirt diamonds, but they were out of Rodney's— and many of the kids'—geographical comfort zone; the surrounding neighborhood was more desolate and considered more dangerous. So Rodney instead led the Eagles, his chair jerking over rocks and lumpy grass, to a clearing beyond the left-field fence where people often walked their dogs. One player stood beside him while he threw grounders and pop-ups. Most had weak, erratic arms, their return throws bouncing short of him and clanking against the frame of his electric-blue battery-powered scooter.

He knew how pathetic they looked. Many parents thought they were wasting time and money that could be better spent on a summer basketball league or preparing for the Pop Warner football season. If the Eagles didn't exist, no doubt some of his kids would find something else to do. But not all of them. *I can't make this work,* Rodney told himself. Then, he decided, *I have to make this work.*

The Elizabeth Avenue Eagles played their first game in late April against the Black Sox. Minutes before the opening pitch, Kelley, the league president, showed up with a bag of cheap white T-shirts with red numbers on the back. These would be their uniforms until the official ones arrived. They played like they looked: a bunch of misfits. They booted grounders, staggered under fly balls, lobbed throws into the stands, and flailed at pitches over their heads. The reality of their ineptitude came crashing down on them. They yelled at each other. They accused the umpire of cheating. They lost, 13–2.

Rodney watched from inside the dugout gate, eyes obscured by his flat-brimmed Yankees cap, his long frame crammed into his scooter. He was in many ways still the stoic recluse I'd met on the platform outside his apartment building three years earlier, breaking his silence only to make a lineup change or to reassure a player who burst into tears or looked ready to slug someone. After the last out, he gathered them at the pitcher's mound. "We just need to practice more," he said. "We'll get it right." But privately Rodney wondered how in the hell they were going to last the season.

The next afternoon, the Eagles returned to the field rambunctious and ready to learn, the humiliations of the night before forgotten. The sight rejuvenated Rodney and restored his confidence, at least temporarily. "I'm just happy these kids are doing something," he said, a reminder aimed more at himself. "As long as they're active, I'm happy with that."

The kids were raw, but they were not without talent. Most important, they wanted to play. When their tempers calmed, Rodney could tell that they enjoyed being together. He could see it in the way they shouted "Eagles" and in the eager looks on their wind-chapped faces. He could see it in the way they strutted around the neighborhood in their generic numbered T-shirts, even on off days. He could see it in Derek's creased-brow concentration. He could also see it in the way DeWan, at third base, took grounders to the chest without complaint and in the way he returned smiling to the dugout after striking out, his jaunty demeanor and goofy dance moves lightening the mood.

Kids kept coming to him asking to join the Eagles. When he told them he needed their parents' permission, a doctor's note, and the $25 registration fee, many turned glum. "My mom can't bring me," they said. Or, "We can't afford to pay." Rodney told them to meet him at the field anyhow, and he'd find a way. And so the roster of misfits grew. "How can you tell a kid he can't play?" Rodney told me. "What if he's shot and killed the next day hanging out on the street? I couldn't deal with that."

CHAPTER 8

Game two began with Kaneisha, Thaiquan's stepdaughter and the Eagles' only girl, misjudging two fly balls, allowing their opponents, another newly created team called the Black Crackers, to take an early 2–0 lead. "She's killing us out there," groaned Coach Calloway, the disciplinarian assistant coach. "She's trying her best, and I love her for it, but her glove is questionable." Calloway was in his fifties, thickly muscled with a stud earring in his left ear. He now lived in the suburbs and said he wanted to give back to his hometown. But the city, and the league, had changed a lot since he left. Today's players lacked discipline and respect for the game. He was trying to instill it the way it had been instilled in the sixties. But to the kids, Calloway was a militaristic relic who barked orders, made them run sprints, and abided no backtalk.

He called time and told Kaneisha to switch places with the left fielder.

Kaneisha smiled and jogged to her new position, her fluffy ponytail bobbing behind her. She was a quietly tough sixth grader, taller and more physically developed than other girls her age, with a demure, almost polite laugh and a voice she rarely raised, except to cheer. That was the part of the game she liked most: chattering for her teammates. The part she loathed was the fear she'd disappoint them, or, worse, cause them to lose. Although Kaneisha could catch and throw at least as well as many of the boys, she was still a girl, and she knew that she was being judged as one. So if the coach told her to move, she did.

A moment later, Versace, the outfielder with whom Kaneisha had switched places, darted toward the dugout, shouting, "I gotta pee!" His big brother, Kemar, the starting pitcher, covered his eyes in mock horror as Versace sprinted to the Porta-John. Someone cackled: "What, we have to order some Depends now?"

"Hey, yo, take that finger out of your mouth!" The shortstop, Jalil, was sucking his middle and ring fingers, an oral fixation he'd had since infancy. He was eight years old and barely four feet tall and belonged in the pee-wee division, not on the Eagles. But he'd been one of the first kids to venture onto the new field after it had been completed last autumn, and he insisted on playing for Coach Rock.

Opposing pitchers were unable to throw low enough to meet Jalil's strike zone, so he could be depended on to walk on nearly every at bat. Batting leadoff, he squatted as low as he could, his oversize helmet making him look like a life-size bobblehead doll. When the Eagles came to bat in the bottom of the first against the Black Crackers, Jalil walked on four straight pitches, stole second and third, and then scored on a weakly hit ground ball. When he arrived in the dugout, his teammates wrapped their arms around him and lifted him off his feet, banging his helmet so it rattled around his skull.

The Crackers' scrawny pitcher threw meatballs, so just about everyone got a hit, and the Eagles pulled ahead. Now, instead of getting angry about their errors, they laughed. A bushy-haired outfielder named Mubarrak smacked a single, and when the next batter made contact, he forgot to run. Kaneisha put her helmet on backward but was corrected at the last minute by her younger brother, Nasir, a beanpole of a boy who played first base. An inning later, celebrating a teammate's clean handling of a ground ball, Nasir forgot to cover the bag, allowing the runner to reach base safely.

The Eagles ran the score to 12–2. After the last out, someone said, "Yo, 'Sace, show them how to do those flips." Versace, the team clown and gymnast, ran across the infield and launched into a string of aerials and semis. Then the Eagles took a victory lap around the bases, each of them sliding into home. Someone came up with the idea of dumping Gatorade over Coach Rock's head, but the street vendor didn't have any. In the dugout, they formed a circle and cheered. Everyone put their hands in. "Let me tell you something," Coach Calloway said. "We may lose one or two, but we're going to win quite a few." The kids shrieked: "Yeahhhh!" Rodney was still uncomfortable with the emotive aspects of coaching, especially the motivational speeches. He sat just outside the perimeter, allowing a grin to wrinkle his face.

Two days later, the Eagles faced the Philly Stars, one of the league's best teams. The first three of Rodney's batters struck out, and when they took the field, one of them, Delonte, glowered as he walked to his position. A timid and well-mannered kid with almond-shaped eyes, Delonte had soft hands and quick feet but could not handle baseball's high rate of failure. Rodney had been meaning to talk to his mother but feared a confrontation with her boyfriend.

The Philly Stars scored twice early, but the Eagles tied it in the second with an RBI double from Derek. Then they went cold, striking out six consecutive times in the third and fourth innings. Delonte went down swinging again and burst into tears. "I quit," he said in a quavering voice. His teammates surrounded him and urged him to stay, but Coach Calloway was fed up. "He's a cancer to the team," he said. "If he decides he doesn't want to play, he doesn't have to play."

The score remained tied in the bottom of the fourth inning, when Kemar, the pitcher, tired and walked several consecutive batters. William, the catcher, lifted his mask and looked at Rodney. For weeks he'd been begging for a chance to pitch. Rodney called for a time-out and told William to take the mound.

William was the Eagles' other Little League veteran and considered himself the team captain. He was ten years old, already barrel-chested, with a tiny stud earring in his left ear, and took command of his teammates through a torrent of insults and demands: get me my helmet, run a lap, do stretches, get outta my way. He hollered at everyone to move faster but was unable to complete a lap around the field without doubling over. He lived in Carmel Towers, the high-rise at the corner of Elizabeth and Meeker Avenues that was generally considered

Weequahic's roughest building, outside of the projects. Their tenth-floor apartment overlooked an asphalt lot strewn with plump plastic trash bags that people had dropped from above; over the years, his family had seen just about everything fall there, including cats, pit bulls, and, at least once, a man high on crack.

All the Eagles hated to lose, but it affected William the most. He watched his teammates' acts of incompetency with scolding eyes, a hand on his hip. William's father, a former drug dealer who raised him on baseball, told him to count to five when he got angry and reminded him that losing was a part of the game. But his dad wasn't around today.

The Philly Stars knocked back-to-back hits. William lost his cool and his control. His pitches bounced on the turf and sailed past Derek, now playing catcher. William yelled at the umpire. He barked at his teammates. He tossed his glove. The Philly Stars danced off the bases, practically doing a conga line between first and home. William looked about to cry. Calloway turned to Rodney. "We gotta pull him, Coach."

Rodney nodded. As Calloway approached the mound, William slammed the ball to the turf. Calloway tried to lay a palm on William's shoulder, and William recoiled, bunched his hands into fists, and blurted, "You wanna fight?"

"You're coming out," Calloway said.

"I'm getting my brother to kick your ass," William screamed.

"You're out of the game," repeated Calloway, wrapping William in a bear hug. William struggled to free himself and kept shouting at Calloway, who shouted back. Rodney rolled to the mound and pulled William away. "Where do you want to play?" Rodney asked. "Catcher?"

"No, he's out," Calloway protested. "If you don't take him out, *I* quit."

Rodney turned back to William and put an arm around him. "Calm down," Rodney said. "Bear with me. I need you. If you quit on the team, you're going to quit on me."

William nodded and went to Derek for the catcher's gear. Calloway stormed off the field. "I'm done," he bellowed. "When a player threatens a coach to get his brother to kick my behind . . . I don't need this. I quit. Oh no, I can't have this." He flopped down on the bench like one of his pouting players.

"Coach," a voice said. Calloway turned. On the other side of the fence was Darnell Chase, a respected Pop Warner football coach and father of Mubarrak, the outfielder who'd forgotten how to run the bases. Darnell was burly, with a goatee, and wore a Yankees cap and a leather Oakland Raiders jacket. "You got to remember that we're trying to show them better," he said. "These are some hard kids. I coach football and they tell me the same thing. But you can't give up on them. They're used to people giving up on them. Yes, you're being disrespected, but you can't walk away. When you calm down, you'll see it."

Rodney ordered Derek to the mound and returned to his post near third base, fuming. William was out of line, but Calloway had to realize that respect came slowly, and not by force, at least not with these kids. If he was too harsh, then he'd give them an excuse to leave, and what would happen to them then? What if he let William leave the field full of rage? It was safer to err on the side of leniency.

The Eagles lost, 12–4. Rodney gathered them at the mound, unsure of what to say. He felt responsible for every error, every run, every fight, every groan of disappointment from parents in the bleachers. He looked at his team. One boy wore his glove on his head. Jalil knitted his hands behind his neck and contemplated something in the sky. William gazed scornfully into the distance, cap twisted sideways. Mubarrak picked at a fingernail. Derek glared. DeWan looked at his coach expectantly. "C'mon," Rodney said. "Hands together." He raised his right palm. Several small hands grasped his. "We're not giving up. Eagles on three." Their response was subdued, spiritless.

Later, Calloway came to understand why Rodney kept William in the game. But he could not deal with what he called "the element"— the anything-goes street mentality that undermined Little League's rules and customs. He could not be part of a team that did not properly discipline its players for things like threatening a coach. He decided not to return. "I know times have changed, but in order to build character, which has everything to do with discipline, certain things cannot be allowed in organized sports," he told me when I caught up with him at a Dunkin' Donuts across town. "There has to be structure, a chain of command. There is no structure there."

A quirk in the Eagles' schedule paired them against the Philly Stars again the following week. The Eagles struck out fifteen times and committed even more errors. The umpire called the game on account of darkness (the field's new lights had yet to work) with the score 13–4. "Oh, now the game over, ha?" a mother yelled. "Now the game over, 'cause you're cheatin'!" One of the players picked up on that and echoed her: "Now you done cheated!"

Afterward, the Eagles sat around Rodney, staring at the turf.

"Next season get some better players, yo," one said.

"Yo, don't get mad, man, y'all did good," Rodney said. He tried to remain upbeat, but his words felt forced. "We just need some pitching. I fault myself for that. So don't be down on yourself."

"It's not your fault," DeWan said.

"It's the umpire's fault," said William.

"No, look, we need more practice, we gotta get more practicing in. Y'all good, don't worry, you did good."

"It wasn't even dark," someone whined.

"That's just part of the rules until they get the lights on," Rodney said. "They don't want nobody out here to get hurt."

"They be cheatin'," one of the boys blurted.

"No, listen, listen," Rodney said, growing frustrated. "We need more practice and we need some more pitching. That's it. After we do that, we're gonna be better than who we are."

"But we one and *three*," Versace said, triggering another cascade of grievances.

Rodney shut them up with a loud "Ay!"

Kelley, the league president, came over to give them a pep talk. She reminded them that while the team had been created overnight, it would take much longer for them to play like one. Winning required patience and hard work, she said. They needed to settle into their positions, learn each other's strengths and weaknesses, get comfortable. She told Rodney that he ought to distribute copies of the Little League pledge, which was inscribed on the back of all rule books and in some parts of the country was recited before games. In it, players commit themselves to God, country, and fair play and vow, win or lose, to "always do my best."

Rodney doubted the talk would inspire them. They were not playing in Toms River or Millburn, well-endowed suburban programs that treated baseball as a way of life, its rules and codes of sportsmanship— and goal of reaching the Little League World Series—drilled into children's heads from a young age. His team didn't even have real uniforms. He returned to his apartment, still thinking about his lame postgame pep talk. He'd been unable to console his players, and in their persistent squabbling he could sense their hope draining away. He could sense that parents were getting impatient; he overheard some grumbling that their kids ought to be playing elsewhere. "I'm doing the best I can do," Rodney told me. "People just got to be patient with me, because I'm damn sure trying."

The next day at practice, Rodney announced that he'd come up with a new rule. "No more arguing," Rodney said. "That arguing has us all discombobulated. All right? No more, no more, no more. It's over, all right? That's from now on." He repeated it, over and over, day after day, until he began to notice something change.

CHAPTER 9

DeWan slumped groggily into the front passenger seat of a rented red Ford Focus and watched with half-open eyes as the car rolled out of their neighborhood. It was just before dawn on the last Saturday in May; his mother was at the wheel and his little brother was dozing in the back. They coasted through the torpid streets of the South Ward's industrial periphery, and in a few turns they were merging onto the southbound lanes of the New Jersey Turnpike. His mother stepped on the gas. In the rearview mirror, the contours of Newark's downtown skyline faded into shadow. Up ahead, a massive fluorescent "A" blinked atop the Anheuser-Busch brewery. They sped past it, the airport landing strips, the utility plants and oil refineries oozing waves of heat. DeWan's mother slipped a worn CD into the stereo, and he immediately recognized the sauntering piano riff that opened Chris Brown's first album, a family favorite. The music coaxed them along. They were alert now, feeling the rhythm, singing together: *Gimme! Gimme! Gimme!*

DeWan smiled. This was fun, crooning and bobbing their heads in the passing lane, leaving the city behind on the start of a spring weekend, just like any other road-tripping American family. But this was no ordinary drive, and as they continued south and the landscape grew lusher and leafier and more unfamiliar, a giddy brew of suspense and anxiety bubbled through DeWan. In a little more than an hour, they would arrive at the gates of a distant prison, where they would surprise one of the inmates with an unannounced visit.

The prisoner's name was Kareem. He was DeWan's stepfather, a drug addict who had spent much of his adult life behind bars. Kareem was nearing the end of a four-year sentence for burglary and narcotics offenses, and if things went well—if he did his time, finished rehab, graduated to a halfway house, found work, kept curfew, and didn't piss off his parole officer—he would be released sometime the following year. He had been away for so long that DeWan barely remembered what he looked like, but the boy was willing to give his stepfather a pass if he would commit himself to a new life with them. In DeWan's mind, Kareem's successful return would mark a change in the family's fortunes. "My mother just needs a husband, and I need a father, to get us all back in balance," DeWan once told me. "When a father comes home, that's when everything is straight and neat and what they're supposed to be." For DeWan, that meant having someone to help him grow up to be a man. Despite all of the heartbreak and disappointment Kareem had caused them, he was, at this point, DeWan's best hope.

Whether Kareem actually returned home to them was still an open question: DeWan's mother, Joicki, wanted to take Kareem back but wasn't yet sure she could trust him. This visit was a test, in a way, to see if Kareem meant what he said about wanting to be a real father to DeWan and his five-year-old biological son, Kareem Jr. But DeWan was so intoxicated by the possibilities that he couldn't consider it not working out. As their rental car lurched past hissing tractor-trailers and beach-bound SUVs, DeWan indulged himself in a shotgun-seat daydream about all of them at home together, eating and laughing and doing the things that normal families did.

DeWan saw every day how difficult it was for his mother to raise two boys on a teacher's salary—working long hours, preparing meals, and performing countless other tasks to make sure he and little Kareem got what they needed. She wanted to buy a house in the suburbs, where she thought they'd be among more ambitious people and her sons would have a better chance of moving up in the world. But she couldn't take the risk alone.

Joicki was in her early thirties, with dark, assertive eyes and a voice that carried the commanding boom of a veteran teacher; when you heard it, you turned and listened. She preferred understated clothing and jewelry, such as thin gold-link necklaces and small stud earrings, and wore her hair in short, narrow dreads, similar to DeWan's. She prided herself on the fact that she'd always been able to provide for DeWan and little Kareem. It was a grind, but they never wanted for necessities, and although their two-bedroom apartment felt tiny at times, it was homey. She stocked the bookshelves with literature, reference books, mathematics flash cards, and classic board games like Twister and Operation. She decorated the walls like a classroom, tacking up the boys' artwork alongside a laminated poster of multiplication tables and construction-paper cutouts of inspirational words in glittery paint: HOPE in red, PEACE in gold, BELIEVE in silver. "In a world where you can be anything," read an inscription hanging from one wall, "be yourself."

Joicki grew up on Elizabeth Avenue, a few years behind Rodney. She stood out at an early age as a driven, obedient student and was a favorite of her teachers, who steered her into gifted and talented programs; because of that, the kids picked on her and called her "white girl." To make it through adolescence, she developed what she called "a tough-girl persona." She hung out with kids in the projects, learned to swagger and brawl, and became, in street parlance, "thorough"—someone not to mess with. Joicki slipped adeptly between worlds—black and white, street and school—but eventually she was unable to decide where she really belonged. "I didn't like that about myself, but I had to be that way to survive," she told me. "It worked. But I never wanted to be that thorough, that hood."

That conflict still tore at her. She was now, by most appearances, a professional, educated, churchgoing single mother whom some still called "white girl." But at the same time, she could still fight rough and party, and every so often she felt herself wanting to let go. Whenever those thoughts crept into her head, DeWan seemed to sense it. He'd come to her and say, "Mom, I had a bad day. I need a hug." The feeling usually faded.

DeWan loved his mother dearly. He felt he could tell her anything. She encouraged him to, because growing up in a household full of secrets—her mother never even told her who her father was—had made her resentful. DeWan told her when he got in trouble in school, about the girls who chased after him, about the drug and gang lingo he heard on the street. One day he came home from school and asked what a "clip" was.

"Why do you want to know what a clip is?" Joicki said. "There's only two clips I think you could be talking about. One is ten bottles and one is bullets."

"I don't know," DeWan said. "I just heard someone talking about it."

Joicki waved it off. "That's drug addict, murderer stuff."

Like most boys his age, DeWan was fascinated with what Joicki called "the thug life." It was nearly impossible not to be because it was so deeply entwined with their neighborhood: the thugs, or emerging ones, were on every corner, in every classroom, in the park, and in the lobbies. Joicki knew that world intimately and swore that her son would not become part of it. DeWan was thoughtful, self-aware, sensitive. He admonished her when she cursed or "talked hood," reminding her, "Mom, we need to speak proper." He liked to dance and sing, and paid a lot of attention to the way his hair looked. He posed for pictures shirtless, flexing his arms and flashing the coy grin, sloped nose, and soft, parabolic eyes that would probably make him a lady killer one day. She still called him "Puda," the pet name she gave him as an infant and had been picked up by everyone who knew him. He had no choice but to accept it, but when I asked what he wanted me to call him, he replied, without hesitation, "DeWan."

Joicki wanted DeWan to be able to traverse the cultural gap from the inner city to the rest of the world, so she saved money for enrichment programs and summer camps where he could learn to feel comfortable among middle-class suburban people. But she also needed to prepare him for the realities of being a black man. No matter how well he assimilated, people would find a reason to underestimate and undermine him. That was why the choices he made now, even the ones that seemed inconsequential, would have a lasting impact on his life. His best strategy, Joicki advised, was to remain true to his values and remember that he had the ability to choose between right and wrong. "Just know that if you run the streets or join a gang, you're not going to live that long, or you'll go to jail where they're going to tear you up," she told DeWan. "Now, if you want to go to college, well, then, you can have a wife, children, a business, that Hummer you want, and you'll live the good life. It's up to you. It's your life."

DeWan always listened to his mother intently and took what she said to heart; he wanted nothing more than to please her. But lately he hadn't been himself. He was unable to focus in school. He came home and gave her attitude. He talked back. They argued. DeWan vaguely sensed that something about him was changing; he described the feeling as "hittery-jittery." At one point, he suggested he might be going through puberty. Joicki refused to accept that as an explanation, not because she didn't believe him but because she had no idea how to handle it. Despite their frequent talks, Joicki knew she could never truly understand what it was like to be a boy growing up in the South Ward of Newark.

Sometimes, Joicki went to Rodney for help. They were old friends, and she saw how much her son looked up to his coach. DeWan didn't know how Rodney had ended up in a wheelchair and didn't know about the life he'd lived before his injury. DeWan's unblemished image of Coach Rock wasn't entirely true, but Joicki preferred it that way. "We don't—well, DeWan doesn't—see Rodney do what he sees all the other men in this neighborhood do," Joicki said. "He's not out smoking Black and Milds, he's not out smoking weed, he's not cursing, he's not disrespecting women. He's not in jail. He's not begging. He's taking care of his business. He has his own apartment. He brings that positive male presence to DeWan."

She began sending DeWan to hang out with Rodney after school. DeWan would show up at Coach Rock's door, drop his overstuffed book bag on the living room floor, and join him on the sofa to talk while half-watching television. "You got to do your homework or you'll end up out there on the corner," Rodney told DeWan, who nodded along. "You gotta take school seriously. You gotta watch out who you hang out with and stay active. If not, you're going to be a statistic, quick." Rodney saw a lot of similarities between DeWan and himself at ten years old: the strong mother, the distant father, the untapped athletic potential. "If I'd-a went on a different road, it would have worked out better," he told DeWan. "But I took my talents for granted. Don't take yours for granted. If you go to school and go to college, you have a shot of doing what you want to do."

One day DeWan asked Rodney to buy him a new glove. He'd been complaining for weeks about his raggedy blue hand-me-down mitt, which an uncle had given him. The webbing was falling apart and the pocket was worn so thin that ordinary fly balls hurt DeWan's hand. His teammates said it looked like it was made out of someone's old jeans. Rodney had heard the teasing and agreed to help.

On Memorial Day, Rodney and DeWan set out on the downtown bus for Modell's, where DeWan chose a $29.99 closed-web Mizuno Prospect Series glove, brown with black and white stitching and a Velcro wrist clasp. Rodney told DeWan to pick out batting gloves, too, and while Rodney waited at the register, DeWan tried on a pair. He posed in front of a full-length mirror and took an imaginary swing, pivoting on his left foot and ending with his hands up near his left ear, just like he'd seen on TV. "I look like Derek Jeter?" he asked.

Outside, DeWan lagged a few feet behind Rodney, the fingers of his batting gloves flapping from the back pocket of his jeans. They made their way through a phalanx of street vendors selling incense, oils, bootleg DVDs, hair care products, and T-shirts. He slipped the mitt onto his left hand and stared into it, caressing the stiff new leather. At the bus stop, Rodney asked to see the glove, pinched the webbing between his thumb and index finger, and told DeWan how to break it in by sticking it under his mattress overnight.

The bus dropped them off near the field, where some kids were playing pickup. DeWan asked Rodney to teach him how to pitch, so Rodney got a boy to catch while the others crowded around. DeWan rocked back on his right foot, wound up, and threw home. The ball sailed wide. The boys ducked as it clanged into the chain-link fence. Rodney told DeWan to calm down and focus on the target, and his next pitch slammed into the catcher's glove with a crack. The boy holding it winced and flapped his left hand to shake away the pain. "Puda, that's good, baby," Rodney said. He turned to the wide-eyed kids behind him. "He got a nice little arm, right?" The boys pumped their heads.

Rodney went home with an unexpected sense of satisfaction. "When you're helping somebody, giving them something, it does something to you," he told me.

DeWan told his mother about his day. "Mom, he's like a real role model."

"Yes," Joicki replied, "he is."

But she knew that DeWan needed more than Rodney and the Eagles. That was on her mind one afternoon when DeWan and little Kareem accused her of sending Kareem to prison. It wasn't true; she and Kareem fought a lot, but it was Kareem who'd sabotaged himself by getting high and breaking into people's homes. But Joicki suddenly saw how acutely her sons felt Kareem's absence. "Okay, you know what?" she said. "You guys want to go visit Daddy? You want to see him? Because you need to see someone to talk to."

The trip required her to break a long-standing vow to herself that she'd never let her sons see the inside of a prison. In their neighborhood, it seemed, the people who got the most respect were those who were the hardest and most violent, and prison was a rite of passage. Having a father behind bars only made the place more appealing, indoctrinating them with the notion that getting locked up was just part of what you did when you were black and from the inner city. In Newark, it was not unusual for a family to have multiple generations of men in jail. The pull of prison, it seemed, was contagious, and Joicki did not want the virus to infect DeWan or his brother. But given the circumstances, she'd make an exception.

The boys whooped for joy when she told them they were going to visit Kareem, and since then DeWan had been unable to think of much else.

After years of separation, DeWan's lasting memory of Kareem was how "shady" he looked in the days before his last arrest: eyes buggy, clothes filthy, hair knotty, cheeks hollow, T-shirt jerked to one side as if he just woke up. Joicki wanted a less frightening image to be lodged in his mind, so before the visit she called DeWan to the computer and typed Kareem's name into the New Jersey Department of Corrections website. Up popped a mug shot and a long list of crimes—"Burglary . . . Burglary . . . Burglary . . . Burglary . . . Burglary . . . CDS/Distribute Drugs on School Property . . ."—and about ten aliases. DeWan skipped over the words and focused on the picture of a smooth-skinned man with plump cheeks, full lips, longish ears, and a scant goatee. He didn't look unhealthy or unhappy. Maybe it was true what Kareem told DeWan's mother, that he was done with the drugs and was ready to come home.

DeWan thought about that picture again from his seat in the rental car. He wondered how Kareem would react to seeing him. DeWan tried to calm himself but could not. Soon they would be sitting next to each other, and DeWan wanted to have something ready to say, to break the ice and make the visit go smoothly. There was so much he wanted to tell Kareem: about the Eagles, about school, about girls, how badly they—he—needed him. DeWan was afraid of fumbling his words and ruining the moment. He tried to come up with talking points, then decided it didn't much matter. The important thing was to see that Kareem had changed and become a better man.

Joicki was still trying to mend her own relationship with Kareem. They'd been childhood sweethearts and had once planned to have ten kids together, but from the start they were an odd couple: Joicki took college-prep classes at her magnet high school while Kareem stole cars, robbed homes, and developed a taste for heroin, cocaine, and prescription pills. He was in jail for her graduation ceremony and remained there when she moved into her freshman dorm at Rutgers. She always visited him, always reserved a spot in her heart for him, and always waited for him to return. "Every time he was back, whatever I was doing, whoever I was doing it with, all of it stopped and it was just about him," Joicki told me. "It was like he'd never gone away." When Kareem was sentenced to his first term in state prison, she was devastated. She thought she was never going to see him again, and that feeling of finality led to her romance with DeWan's biological father, a handyman, martial arts instructor, and entrepreneur.

She got pregnant as she prepared to enter her sophomore year at Rutgers, and just before she was to give birth he left. They tried to reconcile a few months after DeWan was born, but Joicki could not forgive him for leaving her, and they fought over how to best care for their son. They separated, then battled over his wishes to see DeWan. Once, when DeWan's father refused to return DeWan to her, she called the police, a move that drove a permanent wedge between them. "I can't say that I fully put my all into the situation after that," DeWan's father told me. "I wasn't about to fight the government and the child's mother. However she wanted to raise him, that's her doing and I never interjected on any of the things—education, health care—that a father should."

When Kareem heard that Joicki had given birth, he went berserk, assaulting other inmates and getting placed in solitary confinement. But later, brooding in his cell, he came to realize that if he was to ever get Joicki back, he would have to accept what had happened and embrace the baby. After he was released from prison in 2001, he tracked her down and they got back together. They married that year and, not long after, Joicki gave birth to another son and named him after Kareem.

It wasn't long before the marriage began to crumble. Kareem went back to drugs. He stole and pawned many of Joicki's most valuable possessions, including her wedding band. She kicked him out, though he did not go far. He lived in abandoned houses, in the hallways of the Seth Boyden projects, in an empty bread truck around the corner from Joicki's apartment.

Sometimes Joicki would be walking with her sons and point out a Dumpster. "Look at Daddy's house."

They didn't understand her sarcasm and took her literally. "He lives there? Really?"

"Yeah," Joicki would say. "You know, if you do drugs you'll live in that same place and you'll smell like garbage."

Other times, Joicki took her sons to see Kareem and found him on the street, looking cadaverous. "There's your father," Joicki would tell them. "Say hi." She would let the boys go to him, and they would grab on to him like he didn't stink. Then she pulled them away. Kareem, weeping, looked at Joicki and thought, *Why are you bringing them to see me looking like this?* Joicki felt guilty but said she wanted to show her boys the unvarnished truth, a lesson in how easily things could go bad.

Kareem got arrested again, this time for breaking into a house while high, and was sent to Riverfront State Prison in Camden, just outside Philadelphia. He wrote Joicki a letter in which he apologized and asked her forgiveness. When she wrote back months later, it was to tell him she wanted a divorce. Kareem pleaded with her to reconsider, but in February 2008, as a gift to herself on her thirty-second birthday, she planned a visit to Riverfront in which she would bring the papers and demand that he sign. On the way down in a rental car, Joicki prayed for guidance and the strength to go through with it. She pulled into the prison parking lot, gathered her things, and realized that she had left the papers at home. She wondered if it was a sign from God.

Kareem was shocked at how thin and stressed-out Joicki looked. She had cut her hair short and bleached it blond, and had been doing a lot of partying. This was the woman who usually showed no vulnerability, whom he had never seen cry. He told her he was ready to turn himself around, get sober, and be a real husband and father. "I'm done with drugs and I'm done with running," he told her. "I'm tired and I'm ready to live my life with my family." Joicki said she'd think about it.

She returned to Riverfront twice a month for a series of confessionals with Kareem, in which they came clean about the things they had done behind each other's backs. They agreed to rebuild their relationship from scratch. On those long drives back and forth to the prison, she prayed she was not making a mistake. Between visits, Kareem wrote her letters, encouraging her to grow her hair out naturally and "start new." In March, Joicki went to a jewelry store and bought herself a new ring, a reminder of her renewed commitment to him, and to herself.

* * *

Exiting the turnpike on the final leg of their journey, Joicki checked the time and concluded that her superior driving had them well ahead of schedule for the eight thirty a.m. visitors check-in. A few minutes outside of Camden, they pulled off Route 38 in the suburb of Cherry Hill and stopped at a Dunkin' Donuts. Over hot chocolates, she coached DeWan and little Kareem on what to expect at the prison. She explained how they would line up at the entrance, where guards would make them take off their jackets and belts and turn their pockets inside out. She described the gymnasium where the visits took place and how they would probably have to wait a while before the guards let Kareem come in. She urged them to behave. "You have to follow instructions because you don't want Mom to wild out and go to jail," she said.

At nine a.m., the three of them waited in chairs arrayed in groups of four on the gym's hardwood floor. Sunlight streamed in through blinds covering a dozen barred windows, while nine industrial-size fans hummed from the ceiling twenty feet above. The gym was more crowded than DeWan expected, with dozens of faces, mostly black or brown, watching the entrance. It hurt to think about how things might have been if Kareem hadn't ended up in jail. A dad should want to be home with his family; he should want that so bad that he'd be willing to give up drugs. But DeWan didn't harbor any ill feelings toward Kareem, or his mother, who was always apologizing about how things had turned out. Right now he was just happy they were getting another chance.

The doors swung open and the prisoners began to emerge, scoping out the room for their wives, girlfriends, children. Kareem stepped through the threshold wearing his "states": khaki shirt, matching pants, and new white sneakers bought in the prison commissary for $20. He was five feet ten inches tall, with a trace of a mustache, a soft jawline, dark eyes, and a flabby torso. He looked different from what DeWan remembered. Not strung out or edgy. He looked . . . normal. Like a dad.

His nervousness vanished. DeWan reached from his chair and waved.

CHAPTER 10

The Eagles were antsy. All of them had arrived at the field on time—a rarity— for their three p.m. mid-May matchup against the Black Barons, a well-drilled team from the Seth Boyden projects. But the game scheduled before theirs was running long, and the Eagles were distracting themselves in a raucous tangle of school yard amusements: a shrieking round of pickle, a sprawling game of full-contact tag, a rock fight involving an aluminum bat. They weaved among clusters of parents, while some of the more serious kids, Derek among them, stopped to study the Barons, who had paired off in neat rows to play catch. Wherever they were, all the Eagles kept their peripheral vision open for signs— a car pulling into the parking lot, an adult holding a package—of the long-delayed arrival of their uniforms. Word had spread that today was the day.

Rodney found their rambunctiousness reassuring. The Eagles had just suffered through two consecutive blowout losses, including the nasty clash between Coach Calloway and William, and Calloway's subsequent departure. They couldn't get through a game, it seemed, without fighting and screaming at each other. Rodney had issued an edict barring these intra-squad squabbles, telling them that they were never going to enjoy themselves, let alone win, if they kept turning on each other when things got rough. The kids had agreed to the no-arguing rule, but that had been at practice. Today was their first opportunity to prove they could keep their composure with a game on the line.

At three twenty, the kids sighted Kelley, the league president, drag-ging two bulging garbage bags. They fell in behind her, craning their heads for a peek as she made her way to the right-field bleachers. Kelley turned the bags over, and out fell bright clumps of golden stir-rup socks and caps, and black mesh shirts that said EA NEWARK EAGLES across the front in shimmering golden type. The kids jumped on the pile like a pack of hyenas, and when the frenzy ended, they stood admiring themselves in jerseys that were comically gargantuan, dangling to their knees, or lower, short sleeves flapping at their wrists. "Make sure your hats are on forward and your shirts are tucked in," Kelley instructed. One of Rodney's assistants, Reggie, whose oldest son, Kemar, was the starting pitcher, and whose youngest, Versace, was the acrobatic outfielder, reminded them of Rodney's new mantra. "Nobody arguing with anyone today," Reggie said. "I don't care what the next guy does, you cheer them on. Someone strikes out, you say, 'Get 'em next time.'" The field was now ready for them. "Two laps!" someone shouted. The Eagles sprinted single-file down the third-base line and along the outfield's edge, knees bouncing, shoulders pumping, chins high. Thaiquan, father of Nasir and Kaneisha, applauded them. "Look like a team, feel like a team!" he sang. He looked at me, smiling. "Man, they look *good*!"

I'd been spending time at Thaiquan's side lately. He'd turned out to be one of the most involved of the Eagles' parents, slipping into the dugout for pep talks or to help with equipment, and volunteering to coach first base when Rodney's assistants weren't around. Most of the people in the bleachers were members of his family; they arrived for every game in Thaiquan's Chevy Venture minivan, pouring out of it like a troupe of circus clowns. I began joking with Thaiquan that they were taking over the stands, like a gang. "Yeah, we roll deep," he would say, laughing. We mostly talked about sports and parenting, but when I told him I'd been a crime reporter for the last few years, we began sharing stories. Thaiquan followed the criminal underworld through the paper but also through friends who were still involved in it. Many others were dead or locked up, and when something reminded him of them, he hung his head and fell quiet. Brothers were turning on each other, killing one another, going to prison and leaving their families behind, he said; it was like a modern-day slave system, and they didn't even realize they were part of it.

Young black men today had no appreciation of the sacrifices of earlier generations of African-Americans, Thaiquan said. He knew, because for a long time he'd been one of those guys. His deepest fear was that his oldest son would become one of them, too. That was why Thaiquan watched games with such intensity, shouting at Nasir to concentrate in the field and to lay off bad pitches. Thaiquan knew this sometimes rattled his son—Nasir often played with one eye on his father—but Thaiquan was unapologetic; he was on a crusade to keep his kids focused and out of harm's way. "It's an uphill fight. That's why I'm an aggressive parent," Thaiquan told me. "I try to keep them sharp on all angles. I pray, man, I really hope they don't fall victim. 'Cause, shit, I was in the streets like everybody else. Been to prison. Ain't nothing I'm proud of. I tell my son, 'That don't define your manhood. That don't make you no man. That's dead time.'"

Despite the morale boost that came with the new uniforms, the Eagles got crushed by the Black Barons, 12–4. A few days later, they lost a one-run heartbreaker to the Black Yankees, a team made up of neighborhood castoffs from Rodney's surge of preseason recruits. But in those two losses I noticed a self-possession among the Eagles that hadn't existed before. They'd picked up universal Little League banter, filling up the idle moments between plays by chanting "Nobatterno-batternobatter!" "Easy out!" and "Rally, rally, pitcher's name is Sally!" They slapped each other five. They passed around packets of sunflower seeds, methodically sticking them into their mouth, one by one, and spitting out the shells. They made plays that would not have seemed possible a week or two earlier—a perfect relay from Nasir in center field to DeWan at third that caught a runner trying to stretch a double into a triple; William driving a fastball to the warning track, the deepest ball hit by an Eagle in a game so far. At Peshine Avenue School, they stopped each other in the halls to relive triumphant moments and to speculate about their next opponent. Most important to Rodney, they did not throw tantrums or bicker. If he saw a scowl or heard a curse, he grabbed the perpetrator's jersey, pulled him close, and urged, "You're doing great. *C'mon.*"

The rekindled spirit spread to the fans. Mubarrak's mother blasted an air horn during big plays, and Reggie's wife, a former cheerleader, assembled a gaggle of small girls into an improvisatory pep squad, leading spectators through call-and-response chants, their beaded braids fanning the air as they hopped to the beat. They shouted the first lines, and the Eagles barked in answer, their buoyant rhythm kept in time with the scratchy stomp of sneakers on asphalt. Their voices reverberated off the band of trees beyond the outfield fence.

> *Everywhere we go.*
> *People want to know.*
> *Who we are.*
> *So we tell them.*
> *This is E.A.!*
> *Mighty, mighty E.A.!*

Joicki told me she believed baseball brought a little more peace to the neighborhood, sucked a bit of danger from the air. The field was a safe haven, a place where people set their differences aside to watch kids play ball. Young men from the streets lined the fences and shouted, "Eeeeeeaaaaaayyyyyy!" in gruff, singsong voices. "Rock has brought the children together, and as a result of the children being brought together, all of our thugs, so to speak, are being brought together," Joicki observed.

Rodney could feel the momentum turning. The Eagles were still in many ways a pack of misfits, but they were *his* misfits. His team. His responsibility. After the narrow loss to the Black Yankees, Rodney looked at me and frowned, as if he were going to cry. Then his long face bunched into a smile. "Interesting, right? They're getting better. They're having fun. They're listening to me. We're past all that bad stuff in the beginning."

The following week, the Eagles clubbed three inside-the-park home runs to beat the Black Senators, 16–2. Then they rolled over the Black

Crackers by the same score. Kaneisha, Thaiquan's daughter, who'd been riding the bench most of the season, shocked everyone, including herself, by hitting the ball. She swung blindly, like she always did, but this time she connected, the ball caroming off the bat with a flat *boink* and dribbling into right field. The boys whooped in astonishment, and the coaches shouted at her to run. Panic shot through her body as she broke to first, bat still in hand, everyone cheering. She arrived safely, and later, when she returned to the dugout, her teammates showered her in high fives.

Kaneisha was one of the best-dressed Eagles, her jersey always carefully tucked into her pants, her socks tight and straight, her ponytail popping perfectly from the back of her cap. She got along with all her teammates. She laughed at all their jokes. She joined them in victory laps around the bases and yelled "Eagles!" as loud as any other. She'd become something of a den mother, chiding them for cursing or quarreling, and reminding them what Coach Rock told them about being their own worst enemies. Her teammates never outwardly questioned her place or showed her any disrespect, but until that day she had never fully felt like she was a part of the team. After that hit she *belonged*.

Kaneisha's younger sisters joined the Eagles' postgame celebration, running dizzy curlicues in the outfield. Her brother, Nasir, finished a lap around the bases and slid across home plate, left foot tucked under his right thigh, and for a few moments did not move, just grinned. After the game, Thaiquan took Kaneisha and Nasir to Modell's, where they picked out two pairs of solid football-style socks, one gold and the other black, which they split up: from now on each would wear a gold on their left leg and a black on their right. When Thaiquan unloaded them outside their home on Peshine Avenue, the kids on the block ran up to admire them. They begged Thaiquan to take them to the field next time. "There's something about the uniform that stands out to people, especially when they see you going faithfully every day," Thaiquan told me. "When people see you doing stuff like that, it brings a certain respect to you."

The two consecutive victories were followed by a pair of lopsided losses in early June against the Black Barons and the Black Sox, but even those defeats were rowdy and fun. Just before the start of the Black Sox game, a bunch of Eagles gathered in left field to shag flies. Instead of taking turns, they wrangled for each pop-up, their faces twisted in terror and delight as the ball arced impossibly high into the cobalt sky, then plummeted toward earth. Just before impact, a floret of gloves reached up from their tangled bodies, all eyes flinched shut. When the ball landed—more often on the turf than in someone's glove—the kids shrieked with laughter. It was a pure baseball moment that Rodney hoped the kids would remember when they grew up—not necessarily the specific event, but the feeling of exhilaration, of expectation, of possibility.

After the loss, the Eagles shook hands with their opponents and took off around the bases, just as they'd done when they won.

That left one game on the regular season schedule, against the Black Yankees, their Elizabeth Avenue rivals. In the days leading up to the Saturday afternoon rematch, Rodney began to rethink his self-soothing catchphrase, "As long as they're having fun and not on the street, I don't care if we win or lose." Now that the Eagles were having fun and playing like a team, was it too much to want to clobber the Black Yankees? He didn't think he could handle getting beat by them again. At practice that week, Rodney begged his team for a win. "I need this one," he told them. "Real bad."

On Friday evening, Rodney arrived at the park for practice, and his players surrounded him. "Where's Mubarrak?" someone asked. The bushy-haired outfielder, who'd forgotten to run to second base early in the season, had since become a regular starter and rarely missed a practice. Rodney had hoped his absence would go unnoticed. He didn't want to have to explain.

"He ain't gonna be here," Rodney said. "He got family problems."

"Something happened to his father," a gossipy kid volunteered.

"I know! I know!" another offered. "He got killed!"

"Damn . . ." someone said.

"For real?" another asked.

Rodney nodded weakly. Darnell, Mubarrak's father—the well-regarded Pop Warner football coach who'd urged Coach Calloway not to leave—had been stabbed to death in his bedroom before dawn that morning. Mubarrak, his older brother, and his mother were home at the time; Mubarrak had called 911. Police were now holding Mubarrak's mother for questioning and had placed Mubarrak and his brother in the temporary care of the state Division of Youth and Family Services. His mother insisted that she had nothing to do with it, telling detectives that she'd heard a commotion and the sounds of someone running from the house before she and her sons found Darnell's bloody body. She suspected that his murder had something to do with Darnell's fierce defense of their home against the encroaching crime on their block: two houses near theirs had been overrun with drug dealers, and there had been two shootings on property adjoining theirs in the past year. The police would eventually release her without charging her with any crime. She would collect Mubarrak and his brother, and together they would sleep in a bed at her parents' house, knives hidden under the mattress. Detectives warned them not to call Darnell's cell phone, but the boys did it anyway, just to listen to his voice on the outgoing voice-mail message.

Rodney heard the news of the killing a few hours after it happened, and it haunted him all day. He'd known Darnell since childhood and had played semipro football with him in the early 1990s. Ever since Darnell had stepped in to calm Coach Calloway after his showdown with William, Darnell and Rodney had been discussing the best way to discipline players. Darnell understood Rodney's concern that a tough-love approach would backfire; he, too, advocated a gentler touch. "You're doing a good job," Darnell assured Rodney.

Rodney didn't want to discuss Darnell's murder with his team. He didn't think it was his place. Besides, he still envisioned baseball as a means to escape that kind of stuff. He changed the subject to tomorrow's game against the Black Yankees. Neighborhood bragging rights were at stake, he told them, so they needed to focus. "C'mon, I need for y'all to play good because I need this one," he said. Then he told them to take the field, hoping they'd forget about the world outside the foul lines, at least temporarily.

* * *

The Eagles took a 6–4 lead into the fourth inning against the Black Yankees before Kemar, the pitcher, began to tire. Rodney called time and introduced a secret weapon: a tall, left-hander named Daniel who'd signed up a few days earlier. Warming up on the mound in a white T-shirt with the sleeves rolled to his shoulder blades, Daniel looked like a miniature Randy Johnson, taking long strides to the plate and uncorking zippy fastballs.

"Where'd you get the fake birth certificate?" the Black Yankees' coach howled. "That's a grown assed man!"

Mothers behind him chimed in. "He was at the prom last week! You know it, Rock!"

"Ask Kelley," Rodney replied. He had already gotten the league president's approval for a late addition to his roster.

Daniel struck out the side, and an uncharacteristic arrogance took hold of the Eagles in those final innings.

"Yo, next year we're going to be undefeated," DeWan said. "How much you wanna bet?"

"E.A.!" Kemar barked.

"All day!" his teammates called back.

The Eagles widened their lead, while Daniel struck out the side in the fifth and sixth for the win. The team erupted. Versace dashed through the infield and reeled off a string of backflips. The others sprinted around the bases, slid into home, and rolled around on the turf. Rodney bought a round of celebratory soft-serve ice-cream cones from a Mister Softee truck. He reminded them that every team would be included in the league's postseason tournament, so as long as they kept winning, their season would continue.

Eventually Rodney found himself in the dugout alone. I walked up to him and together we watched the kids celebrate. "They looking good," Rodney said. "It makes me feel good. You saw how they looked in the beginning. I guess I'm doing my job, especially with the kids who didn't play no organized ball. I did a good job, right?" I told him he didn't need me to answer that question. All he had to do was look at the field.

Then Kelley interrupted with news that the league had run out of money. Every year, it relied on a $5,000 grant from the city, but the latest one had not materialized. Kelley didn't even have the $600 she needed to pay umpires for the play-offs. If she didn't come up with the cash in the next couple of weeks, the tournament would be canceled.

Rodney's smile faded, and he began to roll home. For three months, the Eagles had given him a reason to wake up every morning. They made him feel good about himself. He'd grown accustomed to seeing them at the field every day, waiting for his instruction. He thanked God for bringing them to him. And now, suddenly, it looked like it was over. It wasn't fair.

At home, Derek yanked off his uniform, showered, and quickly changed. His half sister was celebrating her infant son's birthday in Jersey City today, and many of his siblings, aunts, uncles, and cousins were expected to attend. Everyone on his mother's side would be there— everyone, that was, but his mother. Gail was clean now, after a successful stint in rehab, and she had recently given birth to another child, a daughter, who had severe mental and physical disabilities. Caring for the baby gave Gail new purpose. She even promised Derek that one day she'd bring him home with her. They'd never lived under the same roof before, and Derek knew better than to expect that to change, but he allowed himself to dream about it anyway.

Then, in May, Gail had gone to the hospital for gallstone surgery and ended up with an infection. Now doctors had her on a morphine drip and had inserted tubes that pumped what looked like black liquid from her stomach. No one told Derek what was wrong, and when he went to visit her, she acted like it was no big deal. Derek, wanting to believe her, played along, even when she began retching into a little pink bowl.

"Ewww," Derek said, scrunching his face.

"Shut up!" his mother replied, forcing a smile.

He'd left the hospital that day thinking, *She'll be fine*.

At the party in Jersey City, Derek played with his cousins for a while, but he felt tired and uninterested. He walked to a window and watched the sky darken. Lightning flashed beyond the rooftops, and he counted a few seconds before thunder rattled the glass. Rain began lashing the street. The house phone rang, and Derek's half sister picked up. A grave look washed over her face. Gail was dead.

While the rest of the family convulsed, Derek sat on the sofa, unmoving, unable to speak. His grandmother picked him up, and she took him back to Newark. She wept as she drove, while Derek stared out the window. Later, he would not be able to recall what was going through his mind at the time, other than a sense of suspended animation, as if he'd gone numb.

The next day, Sunday, Irene called Rodney, still in tears. She wanted to get Derek out of the house, away from his grieving relatives, and asked if she could drop Derek off at his place. The request surprised Rodney, but he immediately agreed. He couldn't pretend to understand how Derek felt; the thought of losing his own mother terrified him. But he wanted to comfort Derek. That was his goal with all of his players: to try to put a smile on their faces and to make them feel good about themselves, at least for a little while. But as familiar as he was with the cascading tragedies of neighborhood life, he hadn't expected to be consoling two players who'd lost parents in less than a week.

"You know I lost my mom, right?" Derek said when he showed up at Rodney's door.

"Yeah, I know, Derek," Rodney said. "It's going to be okay, though. You gotta be strong. How are you feeling?"

"All right," Derek replied. "We just gotta go through the procedures, you know, with the funeral and stuff."

Derek didn't seem to be grieving much. He seemed to be holding it in. Rodney didn't push. Instead, they went about their routine. Rodney gave Derek snack money, and Derek returned from the bodega with an armload of Zebra Cakes and a pastrami sandwich. Rodney gave him a new baseball, and they went to the ball field. Though the play-offs had been postponed, many of the Eagles still returned every day; they didn't know what else to do. Rodney and Derek watched them play pickup and talked about Derek's prospects as a pitcher next year. Rodney asked him if he wanted to join his teammates, and Derek nodded. Back on the diamond, Derek seemed to regain his equilibrium. His body loosened. Rodney thought for a moment that he saw Derek smile.

Later that week, Kelley found money to pay umpires, so the play-offs were back on. The Eagles drew the Black Yankees in the best-of-three first round. By then school had ended, and several kids left town. That included DeWan, whose mother had sent him to an arts camp in Washington, D.C., and Nasir and Kaneisha, whom Thaiquan had taken to Atlanta to visit family. Rodney barely had enough to field a full team, but on game day only seven Black Yankees showed up, and the umpire called a forfeit.

Two days later, my article documenting the Eagles' season ran on the front page of the *Star-Ledger*. On Elizabeth Avenue, Rodney could not travel past his lobby without someone congratulating him. "Keep it up," they told him. "Don't let nobody stop you." The online version of the story collected a string of gushing comments from around the country.

> "Go Newark!!! GO Kids!!!! GO Coach!!!!! I am proud to say that I was born and raised in Newark!!!!"
>
> "Keep up the great work. There needs to be more like you in the world."
>
> "It's time for our country to wake up and help other non violent ex-cons become members of society. If you pretend they don't exist then they are going to act that way."
>
> "My daughter plays on a competitive softball team in Colorado. In the heat of battle, we as parents, spectators, coaches, and players forget the true spirit of the game and how lucky we are. I will think of your fantastic attitude on the field with these kids and the wonderful things you do for them every time my daughter takes the field."

In the *Star-Ledger*'s newsroom, I received a stream of e-mails and phone calls from people asking how they could donate equipment or cash. I asked Rodney what he wanted me to do with these offers, and he suggested that I send them to Kelley, the league president. He knew better than to collect the donations himself; as soon as word got out, people would suspect that he'd been in it for his own profit. "I don't want to touch that money," he said.

A producer at *ABC World News* came across the article and sent a crew to film the Eagles play the Black Barons in the second round of the play-offs. With the cameras rolling, Daniel, the newly signed fastballer, held the Barons to three runs, and the Eagles rallied in the fourth and fifth innings to take a one-game-to-zero lead. A couple of nights later, anchorman Charles Gibson introduced the piece. "Here is a story that is hard to resist," he said. "It involves a bunch of kids given little reason to hope, little chance of winning. And then, well, you can guess where this is going. And we go tonight to the hard streets of Newark, New Jersey . . ." The clip ended with the Eagles going crazy on the field, led by Versace flipping across the turf. That night and through the following day, relatives and friends called Rodney to congratulate him, to say how proud they were. A new wave of donations poured in.

The Barons evened the series, and in the weekend tiebreaker they took a narrow lead into the sixth inning, leaving the Eagles with three outs to mount a comeback. The first two batters struck out, bringing up William, the combustible boy who'd clashed with Coach Calloway in the season's second game. In the weeks since that blowup, I'd noticed that William had become the Eagles' undisputed captain, dutifully leading them through warm-up calisthenics, standing at his coach's side to help with fielding drills, the first to shout out encouraging words to slumping teammates. With Rodney's help, William had come to realize that his teammates looked to him for cues on how to behave on the field, and he'd worked on controlling his anger. He hadn't conquered it, not by a long shot, but he'd definitely learned to conduct himself with more composure. It seemed fitting that he now came to bat as the Eagles' last hope.

This was the moment Rodney had in mind when he told the kids that if you believed in yourself and worked hard, there was always a chance to win. He wasn't ready for the season to end. A few short months ago, he'd sat in the same spot, looked at his blundering team, and wondered if this was all some deluded fantasy that would end in humiliation. He'd considered calling time-out and pulling them off the field. But the Eagles had made him feel like he did when he was a kid just falling in love with the game. This time, Rodney had to suppress the urge to call time-out just to make the moment linger.

William took a called first strike.

Rodney thought about the long, hot weeks still ahead—the most dangerous time of year in the South Ward. It seemed wrong to let the players disperse into the neighborhood just as the summer was getting started. Rodney was sure he'd kept some of them off the streets—the same streets where he'd ended up in the summer of his fourteenth year. Who knew where they'd end up now? He couldn't bear the thought of not seeing them every day. It suddenly occurred to him that this was what it meant to be a coach.

William swung and missed. Strike two. He squinted and leaned over the plate, wiggling his bat. The Eagles lined the dugout fence, bouncing on the balls of their feet, screaming for him, begging him to get a hit, to give them a reason to return to the field tomorrow.

The third pitch came, and William lunged at it, head down, grimacing as the bat looped through the strike zone. He pivoted around on his left foot, bringing his face to his teammates in the dugout. He clenched his eyes in disgust. Rodney looked down for a moment, then wheeled to William and wrapped him in his arms.

CHAPTER 11

On a balmy Monday night at the end of June, more than five hundred people crammed into the pews and balcony of Metropolitan Baptist Church in the Central Ward. They were teachers, principals, guidance counselors, and custodians, but mostly parents, all anxious to get a public look at the man who had just been appointed to lead the city's embattled school district. Anticipation hung in the air as one dignitary after another praised the new arrival: Clifford Janey, a sixty-one-year-old African-American from New England who had recently lost his job running Washington, D.C., public schools. That Newark, a city with a chronic suspicion of outsiders, was rolling out the red carpet for a man who spoke with a Boston accent revealed volumes about the desperate state of affairs. Before ceding the podium to Janey, the stream of politicians, pastors, and educators reminded him that Newark's future as a viable city hinged on a well-run school system, and they were all investing a great deal of hope that he would rescue its forty-two thousand students from the educational trash heap. The speakers included Mayor Booker, who had privately opposed the selection—he wanted to shape school policy himself—but was powerless to block it because the district had long ago been taken over by the state.

Finally, Janey faced the crowd. He wore a sharply tailored suit and had a graying beard and curly tufts of frosted hair that ringed a bald spot in the middle of his head. A careful and deliberate thinker, Janey had evidently done his homework about Newark and crafted his remarks to show that he understood that the city was at a crossroads, politically and spiritually. He said he identified with Newark's "feistiness, its fire, and its unflinchingness" and wanted to be part of the "undoing" of people who dismissed the city as a lost cause. He cited as inspiration Paul Robeson, the New Jersey–born athlete, actor, and civil rights activist, whom he quoted as saying that the measure of a leader was in "the way and extent that that person gives back to the community." Janey said he was reminded of Robeson's words after reading an article about a baseball coach.

> I believe his name was Rodney Mason, who began to do some work with the Little League, a boys and girls Little League. He's in a wheelchair now. He too went through some hard times. But he found a way to give back. . . . This was not a story about adversity knocking on the door. This was a story about adversity staying on your back, and how you would perform in that context.

The speech was not broadcast on television, and Janey's remarks about Rodney did not make the paper. But Newark was, in essence, a small town, and it did not take long for word to reach him. He was posted outside Zion Towers when one of his neighbors, a teacher who'd followed the Eagles' story, stopped to congratulate him. Rodney asked what for. She said she'd been in the audience at the church. "Janey made a great speech about you," she said.

Rodney's heart went skippy. First the article, then *ABC World News*, and now a public shout-out from the superintendent of schools. He couldn't understand why people responded to his story so enthusiastically. It was heartening to know that they believed in him. It would be nice to harness the goodwill in such a way that allowed him to make a living working with kids. But how? He didn't have any real skills, let alone a plan. It had been thirteen years since he'd earned a legitimate paycheck. He was still a hustler by instinct and believed that if he could just get a chance to meet Janey and explain to him what he wanted to do, the superintendent, having praised him in a speech, would have no choice but to give him a shot.

"Just call him up," I told Rodney when he asked my advice. It was easy for me to say; cold-calling public officials was part of my job. More times than not, they called me back. Rodney, on the other hand, worried that people like Janey still saw him as an ex-con looking for a handout. He'd dealt with government agencies before and knew he was easy to blow off. But that wouldn't happen if I stepped in on his behalf. He asked if I'd call for him.

I wasn't sure what to do. Seeking a favor for someone I wrote about was not considered appropriate behavior for a newspaper reporter. But I'd grown fond of Rodney and wanted him to succeed. How could I not help him? I dialed Janey's office, and soon we had an appointment.

On the day of the meeting, I picked Rodney up and we drove to district headquarters, where we waited at a polished conference table with Janey's spokeswoman, the district's athletic director, who knew Rodney from his baseball days at Shabazz High School, and a recreation coordinator. Janey walked in a few minutes late, wearing a white and black herringbone suit with a lavender shirt and art deco cuff links. Skipping small talk, he turned to Rodney and asked how he could help.

For all the hope he'd invested in this moment, Rodney had done little to prepare. It had not occurred to him that he ought to bring a résumé or a proposal or even a description of the kind of job he wanted. "I just want to be able to continue what I'm doing with the kids," he said. Janey didn't answer for a moment, thinking. I began to worry that if Rodney didn't speak more in support of himself, his opportunity would slip away. I debated again whether to chime in. I'd already crossed the line from neutrality, so what difference did it make now? The silence was killing me.

"If you don't mind my saying," I blurted, "Rodney could use a job. We heard about your speech and assumed you were moved by his story, and figured that you might be willing to give him a chance. Rodney believes his future lies in mentoring young people, and perhaps you could find a place for him." Janey nodded and said he wondered if there was a school near Rodney where he could work with troubled students. Rodney said there was—Peshine Avenue School. Janey told his aides to get in touch with the principal. He said it would be easiest to hire Rodney as a contractor, but before he could go on the books he had to submit to a background check.

Janey already knew from my article that Rodney had been to prison. Perhaps he wasn't familiar with state laws barring convicted felons from certain public-sector jobs. The problem was particularly acute in Newark, where there were thousands of men stuck in the underworld economy because of their nonviolent criminal records.

As we left the superintendent's office, Rodney's gut sunk. But he had no one else to blame. "I put myself in this situation," he said as we drove back to Elizabeth Avenue. "I went out there and sold drugs. I went out there and got locked up. Sometimes I'm like, damn, I wish I never sold drugs and got a charge on my back. But it's something I gotta work through, and hopefully someone will look past that and hire me."

I learned later, when I went back to interview Janey, that he was, in fact, deeply concerned about the problem because it disproportionately affected African-American men. "If Rodney and others have purged themselves of the demons that drowned them, there ought to be some second-chance legislation to allow him to be a whole individual," he told me. "I'm not saying we should look the other way at criminals who have no place in our schools or society. But if a person is fully committed to redemption and we allow periods of time that measure the quality of those redemptive efforts, they should get a second chance. Why should they be sentenced for life?"

From Mayor Booker's perspective, the summer of 2008 was shaping up to be a good one. The city was on pace to hit its lowest year-end murder total in modern history. He'd become a bona fide national political star, a symbol of the next generation of black leadership, mentioned in the same breath as presidential candidate Barack Obama, for whom Booker was stumping across the country. Booker's travels also took him to colleges and think tanks, where he made rousing public policy speeches and attracted the attention of celebrity philanthropists—Bill Gates, Oprah Winfrey—who donated money for his causes back home. Among the most ambitious was a multimillion-dollar renovation of city parks, including the trash- and drug-littered baseball diamond at

St. Peter's Recreation Center that had once been the Jackie Robinson South Ward Little League's home field. But it seemed that whenever things were heading in the right direction, something horrendous happened. This time it was a thirty-five-hour span in late July during which three people were killed and four more injured in shootings around the city. Among the victims was a ten-year-old boy who was riding his bike from a summer football camp at Weequahic High School and unknowingly pedaled into a fight between two young women. As the boy coasted through the intersection of Hansbury and Mapes Avenues, a few blocks from the Eagles' new ball field, one of the women ducked into a car, and a moment later a man emerged with a gun. He began firing at the second woman, who escaped. Caught in the fusillade, the boy toppled from his bicycle and landed in the street, bleeding from the neck.

Dozens of people gathered at the crime-scene tape, while police and news helicopters thumped overhead and firefighters washed the blood from the pavement. Print reporters and TV crews scoured the crowd for the predictable reaction: *No one is ever really safe around here . . . It could have been anyone's kid . . . The mayor has to do something.* Suddenly, a sinewy, middle-aged man in a red T-shirt stepped into a group of journalists—including a documentary film crew—and launched into a rant that cut right to the city's anger and frustration. He was addressing the media, but he might as well have been speaking to the people across the country who still saw Newark as a degenerate village of murderers and marauders. "Yo! Get the fuck out of here!" the man shouted. "Y'all have no other reason to come over here, only for some stupid shit. Go find a *good* story. Go find a *happy* fucking story. Go to the park. There's kids playing in the park. Go take *that shit*. Get the *fuck* outta here. Go catch people having a good time . . . All y'all motherfuckers focus on is tragedy. Go find some black people having a *good fucking time*, right *here*, right *now*." It was tempting to interrupt the man and tell him about my article on the Eagles, but I don't think it would have calmed him or changed his mind. Besides, he was right to be angry. Uplifting stories about Newark—outside of profiles of Booker—didn't appear very often, and when they did, they were typically told as shimmering contrasts to the darker backdrop of despair. I was guilty of this as much as anyone. The articles I'd written about Newark that challenged the stereotypes were far outnumbered by those that perpetuated them.

Rodney saw the shooting on the news and later learned that the victim was a friend's nephew and one of the dozens of boys who'd swarmed Rodney before the start of the Little League season. Rodney had liked what he'd seen in the boy, whose name was Tajzir. He had good athletic ability, even if he hadn't played baseball before. But there were so many other kids, and Rodney lost track. After a while, Tajzir stopped coming, and Rodney forgot about him.

Rodney wondered if there was anything he could have done to help Tajzir. But even if he had kept him on the Eagles, that wouldn't have prevented him from attending football camp that Monday afternoon, or leaving when he did, or taking that route home. If anything, Tajzir's shooting was a reminder of the limit to the protection Rodney or any other coach or parent could offer a child, even on their own street in the middle of a summer's day.

A couple of days later, Tajzir's uncle called Rodney and told him that his nephew was paralyzed. The boy was despondent, about to be transferred from the hospital to Kessler Institute for Rehabilitation, where Rodney had been treated. The uncle pelted Rodney with questions. What was going to happen at Kessler? Could Tajzir expect to walk again? If not, what would his life be like? What would he have to look forward to?

The uncle asked Rodney to visit Tajzir, hoping that he would calm the boy's anxiety. Rodney didn't like returning to Kessler, but he went anyway. He told Tajzir that he was in the right place and that the best thing he could do was put all his energy into physical therapy. Rodney could see the fear in the boy's eyes and knew what he was thinking. But there was little Rodney could say to make Tajzir feel hopeful about the life that lay ahead of him. Rodney was still trying to figure that out for himself.

For days, Rodney and I tried to figure out how to obtain his background check. Everywhere we went—the county courthouse, school district headquarters, state offices—we were given conflicting explanations of where to go and whom to pay. We drove from one government building to the next in my two-door Honda Civic, Rodney's wheelchair disassembled in the trunk and his knee knocking against the stick shift. At each stop, we encountered ragged sidewalks and curbs without cutouts that required blocks-long detours just to cross a street. Rodney didn't complain, but I grew increasingly aggravated. This was just one early step in Rodney's job search, and I wondered if he would have even bothered to take it this far if he did not have someone helping him get around. Most people, disabled or not, probably would have given up.

Our search finally ended near where it started, in a building around the corner from Janey's office. After I went online and used Rodney's credit card to pay a $41 fee, we scheduled an appointment for him to submit an electronic fingerprint. When that was done, Rodney was instructed to wait for a response in the mail. By then, he had gone to see the principal of Peshine Avenue School, who knew him from the article and offered him a room in the basement where he could spend an hour or so during the school day with some of her most truculent students. He'd start as a volunteer, then begin earning a salary after the background check came through. Rodney returned to the school the next day and met a half-dozen boys who had been kicked out of class. He told them his story and played a DVD produced by one of his antiviolence activist friends. He asked them about themselves and their families and what they wanted to do when they got older. They listened and seemed to relate to him, and Rodney left thinking it had gone well.

On December 20, Rodney opened his mailbox and found an envelope from the New Jersey Department of Education's Criminal History Review Unit. He clawed it open.

Dear Mr. Mason,

A fingerprint search conducted through the New Jersey State Police and the Federal Bureau of Investigation . . . has revealed the following information in the attached Addendum A.

Pursuant to the above-cited statutes, you are permanently disqualified from employment in any position with a school or other educational institution under the supervision of the Department of Education or with a contracted service provider under contract with said school or educational facility. You have 30 days from the date of this written notice of disqualification to challenge the accuracy of your criminal record . . .

Rodney stopped reading. He flipped to the attached pages, which documented his three past drug convictions: the 1986 traffic stop near the George Washington Bridge, the 1987 traffic stop in Newark, the 1989 taxi bust that sent him to prison. In the eyes of the state, those convictions, two decades old, made him a permanent danger to schoolkids. "I kinda knew it," Rodney told me. "I just thought I could go down there [to Janey's office] and fill out an application. But when I found out I had to get a record check, I said to myself, 'Once they find that shit out . . .'" He paused. "Anyway, I guess it's out of Janey's hands now."

The Peshine principal told Rodney he was free to continue volunteering at school, but Rodney didn't bother. He didn't want to cause a fuss. He stayed home and never went back.

CHAPTER 12

While the Eagles were finishing their season in June 2008, DeWan traveled to Washington, D.C., with his mother to attend theater camp at the Duke Ellington School of the Arts. The camp, an intense four-week program that culminated in the production of a musical, was his mother's idea, something she hoped would nourish his talent for dancing and singing while getting him away from Newark for a while. It cost a couple of thousand dollars, and Joicki paid for it out of a savings account she'd set up for such expenditures—things that were important but not essential. She took satisfaction in achieving a level of financial discipline that allowed her to do such things for her sons; it was analogous to her ability to compartmentalize the contradictory aspects of her own personality. They arranged to stay at a relative's house for the month, and during the car ride down Joicki told DeWan, "Look, I'm not paying all this money for you to go down here and not represent. You're going to represent. You're going to get the lead part."

DeWan did not want to leave his Newark teammates to battle through the play-offs without him, but once they arrived in Washington, he embraced his mother's challenge. He had a gift for shining in new and difficult situations. His life was loaded with letdowns, but he didn't stay discouraged very long. His capacity to forgive and recover, to dust himself off emotionally and avoid long stretches of anger or sadness, made him appear mature beyond his years. A flair for drama was a key component of that resilience, played out in countless moments throughout his day: goofing off in school, adjusting his gait on the street, wiggling his hips in the dugout, imagining his family whole again. It may have been a coping mechanism, but DeWan was only beginning to understand it. "When I get mad, I need to express it out in acting," he told me. "I can act real good and I have another personality I can express."

DeWan turned out to be one of the smallest and youngest kids at camp, but he was not intimidated or nervous. On the first day, instructors held placement auditions to pick out the most talented of the three dozen children, and DeWan landed on a short list for the lead in *Magic in Me*, the story of a child wizard struggling to discover his special powers. The role required acting, singing, dancing, even a little rapping. Carol Foster, a veteran theater producer and the camp's director, watched DeWan that day and knew he was going to stand out. "After you've done this for close to forty years, you automatically know who has the energy and enthusiasm for what you're doing," Foster recalled. "You know it's there. And that was my first impression of DeWan. He had the personality and the presence that we needed for that part. From day one I knew he was that part."

DeWan's fellow campers were mostly middle-class African-American kids from the Washington suburbs, although some were from the inner city and a few were white. They called him "New Jersey." They said, "You're from Newark? How did you pay for this? Did you go on scholarship?" When DeWan told Joicki this, she said, "There's a scholarship? Damn!"

The campers brought DeWan with them on trips across the city on the Metro, where they spontaneously broke out in song, and reminded him to check in with his mother. DeWan's ability to fit in with these kids may have been more important than the camp itself. "I didn't see that little 'hood boy anymore," Joicki told me after they returned. "He was really picking up their mannerisms. That was something that I wanted him to do. Because being from an urban area and then going to suburbia is like two different worlds."

On the last day of camp, with parents in the audience, the kids took the stage for a onetime production of *Magic in Me* in its entirety.

DeWan, in a costume of oversize shorts, a T-shirt that said WIZARD, and a sideways baseball cap, delivered a near-flawless performance as Do-Nothing Dale. Afterward, Foster told Joicki that DeWan could pursue a career in the arts and offered to help find him more programs in the Newark area. "He really needs to do something with it," Foster said. "Even if he keeps it on the back burner. DeWan is one of those kids, whatever he puts his mind to he's going to do well with. If he just focuses on it."

But when the school year started a few weeks later, DeWan picked up where he'd left off in the spring—as a class cutup. He tried to rely on his charisma, but school was not a stage. He often ended up in the hallway, standing outside the door of the class he'd just disrupted. Nearly every day, Joicki got a call from one of his teachers saying he'd skipped homework assignments. By the end of the first trimester, he was failing four subjects. Joicki blamed herself for letting him get away with too much. "As the mother, I'm saying, 'What's wrong? What am I doing? Is everything okay?'" Joicki told me during one of our many conversations in her Elizabeth Avenue living room. She projected herself as an iron-willed and imperturbable single mother, but the more we talked, the more evident the fissures in this veneer.

Despite the fact that she had attended Newark public schools and now worked in one, Joicki had decided to keep DeWan out of the city system. She didn't object to the quality of the education as much as the lack of safety. She gave me regular updates about the unmoored kids at Malcolm X. Shabazz High School, where she taught English: how they threatened and occasionally assaulted staff members, how they ran wild through the halls during class time, and how many of their parents had already given up disciplining or encouraging them. She tried to make her classroom a sanctuary, but it didn't matter how good an individual teacher was; no child could learn amid such chaos.

Joicki had started DeWan at a parochial school on Elizabeth Avenue, but it went out of business after his third-grade year. Researching her options, she heard about TEAM Academy, a new charter school housed in a former Catholic school building on Custer Avenue, just a few blocks up the hill from their home and kitty-corner from Peshine

Avenue School, which most neighborhood children attended. Because charter schools were publicly funded but independently run, Joicki was under the mistaken assumption that her son had to be in the city system to be considered. So, against her better judgment, she enrolled DeWan in Peshine, one of the city's worst elementary schools. He did well, but at the end of the year, his favorite teacher told Joicki: "Get him out of here. He doesn't belong here." Joicki entered DeWan in the lottery for TEAM Academy, and his name came up. When she stopped by Peshine to pick up DeWan's transcript, the principal asked her not to take DeWan out; there were plans under way to improve the school. Joicki listened politely and then went ahead with the transfer.

Newark's notoriously inept school system, seized by the state in 1995, made the city a fertile testing ground for the charter-school movement, which operated outside district bureaucracy and labor-union contracts. Mayor Booker was an enthusiastic supporter of that movement, touting charters' innovative teaching techniques as one way to turn things around in a city where, despite spending $22,000 per pupil, only about 40 percent of third graders read and wrote at proper levels. Only one in ten Newark children attended charter schools; Booker wanted to more than double that number.

DeWan was now in his second year at TEAM, which was run by young graduates of Teach For America. When I first requested to spend a day there, I was not only welcomed but invited to return whenever I wanted. (By contrast, I'd been trying for months to get into Peshine.) TEAM's principal, Sha Reagans, grew up and started his teaching career in Harlem. When he came to Newark, he assumed the kids would basically be the same as those he had taught at home. In some ways, they were; most arrived at least two years behind in reading and math and came from homes where parents were either absent or too busy to help with homework or enrichment activities. But Sha was shocked at how much more isolated the Newark students were. Because Newark did not have an extensive public-transportation system, kids rarely ventured out of their immediate neighborhoods. Few had ever been to New York City or understood that it was just a few miles away. Many did not know how to behave in a restaurant. One teacher was asked if it was necessary to take a plane to Great Adventure, an amusement park that was an hour's drive south. This lack of exposure to the outside world stunted their sense of independence and amplified the stress put on them by the neighborhood's dysfunction, Sha said. I was reminded of that a few months later when I was cruising the halls and came upon an exhibit of students' artwork, the result of an assignment that asked, "What would you say if you had everyone's attention around the world?" One watercolor piece was dominated with what looked like a black, menacing eye and the words, DRUGS RUIN FAMILIES. Another poster, decorated with hearts and circles in thick blue crayon, said, I WISH THAT THERE WOULD BE NO MORE DRUGS BECAUSE IF YOU'RE REALLY HIGH YOU END UP HURTING SOMEONE. On a third, a student had drawn bars of bright pastels and scrawled over it, I WISH I COULD GO BACK TO THE PAST AND STOP MANY DADS FROM DYING.

TEAM's teachers approached their jobs like they were performing education triage; they based their curriculum on the premise that if their students weren't performing at their proper levels by eighth grade, they wouldn't stand a chance in high school, let alone college or the real world. At TEAM, the school days were longer and classes continued deeper into the summer. A strict code of conduct was drawn from the mantra, "Make a big deal out of small things so big things don't happen." Seemingly minor transgressions landed students "on the bench," a form of social isolation in which violators wore yellow mesh pinnies and were not allowed to speak unless called on. At the moment, DeWan was spending a lot of time on the bench.

Although TEAM billed itself as a new paradigm in urban education, it could not protect students from the world outside its doors. Every year, several got beat up or robbed walking to or from the Custer Avenue building. The most adaptive kids learned to avoid trouble by engaging in what was known in linguistics as "code switching" as they transitioned between class and the street. Because DeWan played sports and was adept at code switching, he didn't run into much trouble with bullies, but the streets still unnerved him. One afternoon in late October, a string of five gang-related drive-by shootings rocked Newark in ninety minutes, leaving two dead and two injured. The attacks were splashed all over television and the papers, prompting suburban high schools to refuse to send their football teams to Newark. Rumors spread that gangs were preparing a massive wave of violence on Halloween. Parades and extracurricular activities were canceled and school attendance plummeted. Mayor Booker insisted that Newark was becoming safer and more vibrant, but DeWan was scared to go outside. Joicki tried to assure him that the shootings had nothing to do with him and the way they lived their lives. "You're not a part of that world," she told him.

It was difficult to find the right balance of boosting DeWan's confidence and teaching him life's hard truths. Joicki helped DeWan with homework—sometimes doing it herself—and challenged the teachers who disciplined him harshly. But she worried that she was making him lazy and complacent. "He's still a black man and society will still kick his behind," Joicki once told me. "I don't want him to get stuck in this mind-set that Mommy is going to be here and take care of everything."

Another day, our conversation at her apartment was interrupted by a phone call from one of DeWan's teachers. After Joicki hung up, she called DeWan, who was doing homework at his grandmother's apartment on the other side of the building. "Yo!" she barked into the phone. "Why did you get all worked up and throw your book bag in class and act like a nigger? Leave that lady alone. You're scaring her. You gotta carry yourself correctly, so I won't have to wild out." Another time, Joicki told me how DeWan had come home and said a boy from Carmel Towers, where she'd grown up, had taken his cell phone. Joicki went to the building with DeWan, got some friends for backup, and confronted the boy's mother. They scuffled, and DeWan started crying. Someone called the police, but they let Joicki go after she acted "all polite and innocent." She recounted the episode matter-of-factly, but she seemed proud of having gotten one over on the mother and the police. DeWan, on the other hand, was dismayed. He hated when his mother acted like that and was always extracting promises from her to stop. These were the times when DeWan worried about her.

Joicki went back and forth with the staff at TEAM about DeWan.

When they threatened to make him repeat the sixth grade, Joicki told them to do it because maybe it would teach him a lesson, but the school backed down. She suggested that they test him for a learning disability, and the teachers refused, saying they were sure he didn't have one. Finally, she recommended that DeWan get some counseling. They agreed and set up an appointment with the school's social worker, Phaedra Ruddock.

Ruddock's basement office was a popular hangout for kids who needed advice or to blow off steam or finish homework. A former dancer in her mid-thirties, she was slender with straight, shoulder-length black hair and was perpetually cheerful. She saw seams of goodness in the most obstreperous students and genially corrected their behavior. The first time I showed up at TEAM Academy, DeWan introduced me to his classmates and teachers with a variant of "I told you so," as if they hadn't believed what he'd said about a reporter writing a book about him. Ruddock overheard DeWan and reminded him how unseemly it was to boast. DeWan, looking chastised, stopped. He was sensitive about his reputation as dramatizer.

As she got to know DeWan, Ruddock found him intelligent and courteous—not the type at risk of getting into fights or joining a gang or hurting someone. He seemed to always be looking for a way to stand out, and too often he did that by goofing off. But despite his impulsive, immature behavior in class, DeWan in private conversation was remarkably self-aware, a deep thinker. His teachers believed that if he focused his talents in the right way, his potential would be limitless. Joicki told Ruddock, "You know, he can sing and dance. Is there anything here that he can get into like that?" Ruddock, it turned out, was organizing a school production of *West Side Story*. She had already held auditions and cast most of the parts, but she promised to find DeWan a place.

Ruddock assigned DeWan to a minor character with a couple of lines. At his first practice, DeWan didn't simply remember the words; he *acted* them in a way that took her by surprise. She gave him some verses from a song, and he belted them out without hesitation. She threw him into a dancing scene, and he picked up the moves effortlessly. Ruddock gushed, "How could you hide this from us?" DeWan soon had a lead role, as Riff, leader of the Jets. He memorized his lines quickly and added his own improvisational flourishes. "He has that *it*," Ruddock told me. "Charisma. The ability to interest the crowd. I can't teach that to those kids. He already has it."

DeWan's spirit seemed to lighten, and that didn't only have to do with the recognition of his acting talents. It had been months since his first visit to see his stepfather, Kareem, in prison. The meeting had left DeWan ecstatic, and ever since he'd envisioned Kareem's return as a magical moment that would bring order to the house and allow him to focus better at school. Now, finally, DeWan had a date to mark on his calendar. On November 25, Kareem would be released from Riverfront State Prison and transferred to Logan Hall, a halfway house about a mile from their apartment, in an industrial zone near the railroad tracks. Kareem would have to spend nights there but would be otherwise free during the day to find work and visit Joicki and the boys.

A few weeks before the big day, Joicki took DeWan and his brother to see Kareem at Riverfront one last time. Afterward, I asked DeWan how it went. "We talked about how I need to change my attitude, and when he comes home things aren't going to be messed up and out of place," he reported. Kareem also came clean about his own mistakes, like stealing, drinking, fighting with his mother, and not being a good father. "He said he was not going to do that anymore," DeWan told me. He expected Kareem to keep his word.

CHAPTER 13

When he was a young boy, Thaiquan's mother married a New Jersey Transit bus driver, and for the first time he could remember, there was a man in the house. His father was an alcoholic, and had never really lived at home, so Thaiquan had been raised exclusively by women—a durable, resourceful mother and a pair of plucky grandmothers. But then his mother found a good man, or so they thought. Her new husband was a blue-collar guy who took pride in rising early, putting in a full day behind the wheel of a diesel-spewing bus, and returning home to his family. He knew that Thaiquan had few, if any, men to serve as proper role models, so he singled him out for lectures on the values of school-work, team sports, and the realities of growing up black in the inner city. He had a habit of dispensing little nuggets of wisdom, which Thaiquan didn't always understand, but they somehow got lodged in his head anyway: sayings like, *Everything in life recycles itself.* When Thaiquan asked what it meant, his stepfather explained that trouble had a way of repeating through generations, and if you came from a succession of "pimps and hustlers," you'd probably become one, too. He meant it less as a divination than a warning: Thaiquan needed to watch himself.

Five years into his marriage, Thaiquan's stepfather got hooked on drugs and was fired, leaving Thaiquan's mother, a counselor for devel-opmentally disabled children, as the sole breadwinner. Instead of doing homework and playing ball, Thaiquan had to babysit his little sister. He grew increasingly angry and rebellious. He dropped out of school, started dealing drugs, and, at the age of twenty, fathered a son. When he got arrested and was sentenced to three years in prison, his stepfather's aphorism began to seem prophetic. Thaiquan wondered if he had not only doomed himself but also his little boy, Nasir.

One day, while waiting to be transferred to a correctional facility in rural New Jersey, Thaiquan's biological father showed up for a visit. They'd had a scattered relationship in the intervening years but had reconnected in earnest just before Thaiquan's imprisonment. The old man had found Jesus and stopped drinking and was now trying to repair past damage. He showed up in a black suit that hung from his gaunt frame, a Bible in his weathered hands. He told Thaiquan that there was still time to change. "I know you have to jail, but what happens when you leave here?" he said. "You go back to the streets? You have a son now. Don't get caught in the web. Don't get stuck in the cycle."

Thaiquan shrugged off his father's plea; he didn't see the point in taking advice from the man who was responsible for setting this terrible course in motion. But his father persisted. He returned several times over the next few months. Sometimes he brought baby Nasir. During one visit, he told Thaiquan that one of his grandmothers had predicted that he would end up in prison for the rest of his life. His father still knew what buttons to push, and Thaiquan felt a sudden rush of shame. If the women who'd raised him lost their faith in him, no one else would have any, either. Thaiquan shook his head at his father, gave him that prison stare, but inside he was wounded and scared. *Nah*, he thought. *This ain't what I'm going to be. You watch and see.*

But that resolve weakened by the time he was released. He fell in with his old crew, who welcomed him with a blunt, a beer, and a standing offer to rejoin them. On the way to a club, the police stopped them and found a gun in the car, and Thaiquan was sent back to prison for violating parole. Alone in a cell again, he spent a lot of time thinking about his father. He was struck by an old memory, one of the few childhood experiences with his dad worth remembering. It was the summer Thaiquan was twelve. His father picked him up in a ragged Pontiac Bonneville and drove him to Yankee Stadium. When they arrived in the Bronx, it started to rain, and they took cover near the food stalls where fans wolfed down hot dogs and beer. Thaiquan's father didn't buy him anything, but it was his first baseball game, and they had seats along the third-base line. The sumptuousness of the grass, the buzz of the crowd, the *enormity* of the place, made Thaiquan's skin tingle. Then the sun came out, and the Yankees took the field. Mattingly. Winfield. Henderson. Baseball immortals, almost close enough to touch. He and his father stood together and cheered. He couldn't remember anymore if the Yankees won or lost, but that didn't matter. Thaiquan sent his father a letter recalling that afternoon. "I have a vision," he wrote, "that one day me, you and Nas will go to a baseball game together."

After his release, however, Thaiquan went back to the streets; he still could not resist the sense of freedom or the easy money. He knew it was a mirage, but the switch in his heart remained unflipped.

Then he found Shamira. Or, to be more precise, rediscovered her. She was curvy and dark-complected, strong but warm, a striver but also easygoing. He'd nursed a crush on her since they were kids, and now, years later, she had a young daughter named Kaneisha and was pregnant with another. Neither girl's father was around, so Thaiquan asked Shamira out. She'd grown up around dealers and addicts and knew what Thaiquan was up to. She made it clear that if there was any future for them, he'd have to get out of the game. He moved in with her but continued to deal a bit on the side. And then, one frigid December day, he got a call from the brother of Nasir's mother, who complained that he was taking care of Nasir more than she was. "I can't do this anymore," the brother said. "Come get your son." Thaiquan borrowed a car, brought Nasir to Shamira's, gave him a bath, changed his clothes, and did not look back. "That," Thaiquan told me, "was the beginning of my journey into real fatherhood. Once I had Nas in my grasp, I was like, *I definitely gotta do it by the books*. There was no other choice."

Thaiquan's transformation was slow, aggravating, and exhausting. It meant turning his back on his friends and "getting on the slow grind." He went to the Division of Motor Vehicles and applied for a state identification card. He arranged for Nasir to be covered by Medicaid and took him to a health clinic, where he was given eight shots to make up for missed immunizations. He worked out a weekend visitation schedule with Nasir's mother, and when she resisted, he filed for shared custody. With help from a cousin, he got a job registering patients at the emergency room of Irvington General Hospital. Every week, Thaiquan brought his paychecks home and handed them over to Shamira. Lying in bed at night, he realized that while his pockets were lighter, for the first time he felt good about where his life was going.

In 2004, three years after he started the job, the hospital announced it was closing. Thaiquan was laid off, but he got picked up as a security guard in its waning days. Shamira, who worked as a clerk at Beth Israel Medical Center in the South Ward, heard about an opening in its emergency room, and because the two hospitals were owned by the same corporation, Thaiquan was allowed to transfer there. A few months later, Thaiquan and Shamira married, creating what he called "a ready-made family" that would grow to include two daughters of their own. His father attended the wedding ceremony and seemed surprised that Thaiquan had paid for it legitimately. That hurt Thaiquan's feelings, but it also made him proud.

Thaiquan continued to dream about returning to Yankee Stadium with his father, but his father died of emphysema and congestive heart failure before they could. Over the years, Thaiquan would return to that lost opportunity for inspiration, a sort of touchstone for his own journey into parenthood. He wanted to be the kind of father who would not look back with regrets, one whose kids could use him as an example, not an excuse. "If I close my eyes today, you could never grab the crutch that my father didn't teach me shit, my father didn't do shit for me," Thaiquan told Nasir. "You could never say my father wasn't there for me so I had to go banging."

Thaiquan became consumed with atonement and making sure his kids avoided the innumerable pitfalls of an inner-city childhood. He wept, raged, wallowed, and, when things went his way, allowed a reluctant smile. The more I got to know him, the more deeply I admired him. I began to see him as the kind of man DeWan and Derek wanted, the one Rodney had never known.

After school ended in the summer of 2008, Thaiquan took the family on a road trip to visit relatives in Atlanta. Nasir and Kaneisha were disappointed to have left Newark while the Eagles were still battling through the play-offs, so Thaiquan thought the timing was right to make a new memory. He bought tickets to see the Braves play the Philadelphia Phillies at Turner Field. They passed the statue of Hank Aaron on their way into the ballpark at twilight, replica batting helmets on their heads and souvenir tomahawks in their fists. When they emerged from the tunnel beneath the stands and saw the perfectly manicured turf and the endless tiers of seats, Nasir and Kaneisha's eyes popped. Thaiquan knew how they felt, and he hoped they wouldn't forget it.

Back in Newark that autumn, Nasir asked Thaiquan if he could spend more time with his mother. Thaiquan was torn; he did not want to prevent Nasir from having a relationship with her—she was legally entitled to visits, anyway—but at the same time he worried about her influence. She let Nasir roam rough neighborhoods with his older cousins, one of whom, a young woman, had recently been shot on her doorstep by a gunman aiming at another member of her family. The woman wasn't seriously hurt, but Nasir could have easily been in her place.

The way Thaiquan saw it, this was the most pivotal time in his son's life. Nasir was a seventh grader at Peshine Avenue School and would soon begin his precarious passage into adolescence, when his behavior and academic achievement would influence much of his future, starting with whether he ended up at a general population high school, like the notorious Malcolm X. Shabazz, or one of the city's magnet schools, where the cream of Newark's public school students matriculated. Thaiquan lectured Nasir on the importance of being a *student-athlete*, because if you got good grades and did well on the ball field, you could really go places. "The world is yours," he told his son, "but you got to want it." Thaiquan watched with growing alarm as his son reached the age of many young recent murder victims tallied in the newspaper: a fifteen-year-old linebacker and honor roll student gunned down as he walked home from his girlfriend's, an eighteen-year-old former wide receiver for Weequahic High School shot around the corner from their house, a sixteen-year-old Shabazz halfback stabbed during an after-school fight, the four college-bound friends shot in a school yard last year. But Nasir didn't seem to grasp how high the stakes were. He often returned home from a visit to his mother seeming to think he could do whatever he wanted. Thaiquan sometimes left angry messages on Nasir's mother's voice mail. "I'm not going to let you take his future from him," he said. "I'll die first or spend the rest of my life in prison before I let you rob him of that." He tried to convince Nasir that "going up and down the street, cussin'" was nothing to aspire to and that his cousins would probably drop that lifestyle in a heartbeat if given the chance. "They want to switch positions with *you*. They think *you're* living large over *here*, man. And *you* want to switch positions with *them*? I don't understand it."

Kaneisha, meanwhile, grew envious of Nasir's new arrangement with his mother. Her biological father had never been around much—he had several children with women other than Shamira—but Kaneisha yearned for some kind of connection with him. Shamira seemed willing to allow it, but Thaiquan didn't like the idea at all. Some of his mistrust had to do with his experience with Nasir's mother, but it was more than that; Thaiquan saw himself as the only dad his children should need. But Thaiquan also knew that he could not deny Kaneisha a few weekends a year with her birth father. He'd promised himself when he married Shamira that whatever he did for Nasir he would do for Kaneisha. When Nasir signed up for baseball, so did Kaneisha; when Nasir got a new pair of sneakers, so did Kaneisha; when Thaiquan took Nasir to a ball game, Kaneisha came along. Besides, Kaneisha was growing up. She was no longer the meek girl who'd first stepped onto the field with the Eagles. She'd become more demanding of herself and others, more outspoken, and more responsible. She pushed her little sisters to do their homework, scolded them when they misbehaved, and completed her own household chores without complaint. She'd made new friends and joined the Pop Warner cheerleading squad. One afternoon, Thaiquan looked out the window and noticed Kaneisha playing catch with Nasir. He flinched at how hard Nasir was throwing the ball at her, but Kaneisha was holding it down, gamely stabbing her glove at every offering, even those that bounced in front of her face. The girl had heart.

Kaneisha had been classified as a special education student as a young girl, and ever since, Thaiquan and Shamira thought her teachers had failed to push her enough. Accordingly, Kaneisha never showed much academic ambition. But lately she'd been talking about becoming a pediatrician, or a nurse. She was now in eighth grade, the time when she was supposed to begin thinking about what high school she wanted to attend. Thaiquan and Shamira didn't want her to go to Shabazz, which, besides its reputation for rowdiness and underachievement, did not offer any vocational courses in nursing. They were concerned she would be overwhelmed, especially in the special-education classrooms, where many of the most "unteachable" students got dumped. They did not want her sequestered, labeled, and undervalued any longer. "That's what they want to do to black kids, classify them and put them on medication," Thaiquan said. "We ain't doing that." They met with Kaneisha's child-study team at Peshine Avenue School, and one of the members suggested the Academy for Vocational Careers. Shamira and Thaiquan balked. It was infamous for harboring kids who got kicked out of regular schools for behavioral problems. But it was either that or Shabazz—Kaneisha had no chance of getting into a magnet school, and a girl her age was unlikely to hit the charter school lottery. Even after all he did for them, Thaiquan still felt he was leaving his kids' fate to chance. That sense of powerlessness tormented him.

Thaiquan and Shamira grudgingly picked Shabazz, but with a caveat: they wanted Kaneisha to be placed in mainstream classes. They sat her down and told her the plan. "Ain't nobody else on this earth believe in you," Thaiquan said. "I'm telling you, *we* believe in you. And I *know* you can do it. It's time to step up to the plate."

"I'll try," Kaneisha said.

Thaiquan so badly wanted to believe that he'd broken the cycle, unloaded his stepfather's burden, and was no longer bound to a life of unfulfilled promise and failed expectations. He wanted to know that he was leaving his children a legacy that would allow them to flourish. But he wondered if he could ever be sure of that, or if the struggle would ever end.

CHAPTER 14

Not long before Halloween, Derek packed his things again for what was sup- posed to be a temporary move. His mother had died four months ago, and now his grandmother Irene was going into the hospital for surgery to remove a benign tumor on her spine. It would be a week or two before she was back on her feet, so she sent Derek to stay with his aunt, Mary, who lived in a railroad apartment with her three grown children and year-old granddaughter. The apartment was in a perpetual state of disarray—baby toys and laundry bags sat in piles around the place, along with discarded furniture and other household odds and ends. Derek slept on a couch amid the clutter and added his clothes to the mix. Mary's kids, who'd helped her care for Derek when he was an infant, agreed to look after him while their mother was at work.

Irene's surgery went fine at first, but as she was preparing to check out of the hospital, she began to feel woozy. Her doctors discovered that she'd developed an infection, which in turn led to meningitis, a dangerous inflammation around the spinal cord. They readmitted her and found a blood clot in one of her legs. Once the infection cleared, she was transferred to a rehabilitation facility a few miles outside Newark, where she faced weeks of physical therapy before she'd be able to walk.

In order to care for Derek, Irene had given up plans for a quiet retirement from a human resources company in the suburbs. She had straight black hair that fell to the tops of her shoulders and wore silver hoop earrings that bounced as she walked. She was sixty-three, but when I visited her at the rehab center, she appeared to have aged years: her body was bloated, her hair hung in thin clumps, her cheeks and jawline sagged. She was too weak even to sit up in her bed. She was on painkillers and became increasingly disoriented and distressed at not being able to return home for Derek. "I need to get on my feet again so I can concentrate on bringing us back together," she said. "But right now I'm helpless."

As her absence dragged on, things at Mary's grew tense. Derek refused to do what his older cousins told him. He cursed them out, locked himself in their bedrooms, spent afternoons in the park behind their apartment building, and lied about where he'd been. Mary's son, Ozias, let Derek play video games with him, but when Derek lost he threw violent tantrums, trying to kick the television and rip the console apart. It was all Ozias could do to keep from beating him up. He'd call Mary at work and say, "Mom, come get him, because I do *not* want to go to jail."

Mary was the family's rock. Sturdily built, with a dry caustic wit and a burdened gait, she worked two jobs—days at the Newark Preschool Council and nights and weekends at Macy's in the Short Hills Mall—and was everything that her younger sister, Gail, Derek's mother, was not: temperate, dependable, focused. Mary knew Derek's moods better than anyone because she'd raised him from a newborn and had cradled him in her arms during his first three months while he trembled from drug withdrawal. She had little patience for his refusal to answer to anyone. "You are a *child*," Mary told him. "And when I'm not home, your cousins are in charge, whether you like it or not." But he didn't want to accept that. When he was angry, Derek would reflexively draw his hands up, like he wanted to fight. Mary would lean over him and boom, "If you *ever* try that, I'm going to treat you like these kids on the street and I'll forget you're my nephew."

One afternoon, Mary's daughter Alnisa was helping Derek with his math homework. He wanted to stop, and she pushed him to continue. He got angry and started arguing with her. They shoved each other. He grabbed a knife from the kitchen, muttering vague threats.

Alnisa had lived with Derek on and off since she was a girl and was used to his tantrums, and although she'd never seen him do something like this, she knew enough to stay out of his way and let the fit pass. Soon enough, it did. The episode left her less scared than angry. And sad. She felt bad for Derek. She wished things were different for him. She loved him. They all did. But when Mary got home that night, and Derek acted like nothing had happened, she knew she had to do something before he hurt someone or himself.

Mary couldn't leave Derek in her house anymore, but she also couldn't quit her night job to look after him. And there was no telling when Irene would be well enough to come home. She saw only one option. Mary called Derek's father and told him to come get his son.

The new arrangement wasn't going to be easy. Derek's father was a plumber by trade, but he wasn't in a union, so jobs were hard to come by. He was currently working a job at a Whole Foods Market that didn't pay much and living with his sister in Passaic, a small, rusty city that served as an industrial satellite of Newark in the early years of the twentieth century. Still, at first, Derek and his father seemed happy to make up for lost time. They talked a lot, went out to eat together, and went to the library so Derek could research book reports for his new school.

When Irene found out Derek was going back to his father, her heart sank. In her opinion, Derek's father had caused his son nothing but heartbreak and disappointment. If she had it her way, he'd never see Derek again. But she was powerless to intervene. In January, her insurance coverage ran out, and the rehab facility sent her home in a wheelchair. She got a hospital-style bed set up in her living room and arranged for a physical therapist to visit her a few times a week. Mary stopped by just about every night and took her to church on Sunday, but she was, for the most part, stuck in a claustrophobic apartment at the coldest, darkest time of year. Sometimes she wept uncontrollably. Derek called her every day after school to check in on her, and as her depression deepened, he asked his father to let him keep her company on weekends.

He agreed. And so, every Friday Mary picked Derek up in Passaic and dropped him at Irene's. Derek pulled up a chair to his grandmother's bed and flicked on the television. They watched the Sci-Fi Channel, replays of old baseball games on the MLB Network, and pro wrestling. Derek cooked her spaghetti and cleaned for her. Sometimes, when Irene was feeling particularly weak, he would unroll a sleeping bag beside her bed and tell her to call out if she needed him, though most of the time he was snoring too loud to hear. When none of their favorite programs were on, Derek retreated into the rear bedroom and worked on mastering the video games he'd received for Christmas. With the blinds pulled across the windows, time crept unnoticed until Sunday evening, when Derek threw his few things into a small bag and went back to his dad's. Irene saw no trace of the volatile boy who'd frightened Alnisa the previous fall.

I stopped by one gloomy February afternoon to catch up. Irene was in her wheelchair, watching reruns. She greeted me with a hug, then jabbed a thumb toward the end of the dim hallway. A late winter dusk was falling over Newark, the last shreds of pale light fading behind the low-slung brick buildings of Hawthorne Avenue, one of the city's most notorious drug trafficking areas. On days like this one, when night came early and the only outside sounds were the bleating of sirens and car alarms, Irene's overheated apartment felt like a bunker.

Derek sat at the foot of a rumpled bed, the iridescent glow of a video game reflected in the lenses of his chunky-framed eyeglasses. He leaned forward, lips pursed, statue-still save for his thumbs, which frantically pounded the buttons of a Sony PlayStation 2 control pad. It had been several weeks since I'd seen or spoken to him, and encountering him now in the creeping dark, walls flickering with the television's light, enhanced my enigmatic impression of him. Derek wasn't outgoing or self-assured like DeWan. In fact, he more resembled Rodney, or how I imagined Rodney had been at his age: hard to read, slow to trust, prone to long spells of silence broken by laconic conversation.

He seemed so engrossed in his game that I feared I'd startle him, but as I entered the room he called out, "Hey," without looking from the screen. The computer-generated squawk of a stadium crowd filled the room; an organ wheezed through the "charge" cheer as Derek's avatar belted a double into the right-field gap. A roar crackled from the tinny speakers. I sat beside him to wait.

An ambulance whined past. In the living room, a preacher on television was telling viewers that Jesus was more important than money and fancy cars and other earthly pleasures. The inning ended, and Derek paused the game and stuck his hand out to shake.

I asked him how things were going. He shrugged. "All right."

I asked him if he liked it in Passaic. He shook his head.

I asked him why. He said his father and his aunt both worked long hours, and so he often ended up in the house alone. "I heard you have to be at least a teenager to be in the house by yourself," he said.

He told me that he wanted to come back to Newark so he could take care of his grandmother and rejoin the Eagles in the spring. I asked him if he'd run that by his father, and Derek said that he'd tried. "He doesn't really talk to me that much," Derek said. "He just kind of walks away."

I brought up the Eagles, and Derek's eyes brightened. He pointed out three scuffed baseballs on the dresser, near an opened bag of sunflower seeds, and an aluminum baseball bat in the corner that one of his half brothers had bought him. "I have a passion for baseball," he said proudly. He used to get made fun of for that—kids at school called him gay. Then, when he joined the Eagles, things changed. He became indispensable, one of Rodney's veterans. Coach Rock had become a kind of father figure, during the season at least. They'd spent entire days together, up in his apartment and down at the field. By contrast, Derek's father went the whole season without attending one of his games. When Derek's mother died, returning to Coach Rock and the Eagles lifted his spirits. He didn't even feel bad when the Eagles lost the heartbreaker to the Black Barons in the second round of the playoffs. "As Coach Rock said, you can't win all the time," Derek said. "All you have to do is try your best and never give up."

As spring approached, Derek's father abruptly announced he was going to Oklahoma with his new girlfriend to find work. Unbeknownst to his family, she was a crackhead, and he'd relapsed with her. He told

Derek he wanted to take him along, and Derek, charged for an adventure, got ready to leave. But without Mary's consent, a judge would never let them leave the state together. Besides, Derek was about to graduate from sixth grade. His father's twenty-seven-year-old daughter, Latoya, offered to let him stay with her in a nearby public housing complex until he finished the school year.

Latoya and Derek's father were a study in contrasts. She was a single, working mother with soft facial features and determined eyes; he was thick and muscular, with a shaved head, thin mustache, and a ponderous, hapless air—Derek joked that he looked like Damon Wayans—and always seemed to be working his way out of a self-created jam. Latoya was stern and sensible; Derek's father's behavior was erratic and unreliable. And while she still lived in the same building where she was raised, he kept moving, trying to outrun his past. Derek's father promised to send for him when he got settled, but even Derek had a feeling something would go wrong. He just shrugged and packed his things again.

Latoya lived with her five-year-old daughter in a tidy two-bedroom apartment with new furniture and a galley kitchen whose windows overlooked the Passaic River. Since her daughter already occupied the second bedroom, Latoya told Derek he could sleep on the sofa or the floor. Derek set his bag of clothes down inside Latoya's front door, looked around, and said okay.

Though they were siblings, Latoya and Derek hardly knew each other. She was more than a decade older, her only memories of him dating back to when she was fifteen, when her father brought him home as part of a custody arrangement. Since then, Latoya had heard only secondhand stories about Derek's itinerant life. She pitied him; it was no way for a boy to grow up. But he appeared to tolerate it. As she watched him unpack, she reminded herself that they had at least one important thing in common: they both knew what it was to suffer from their father's wanderings.

Before leaving town, Derek's father signed him up for Little League. His new team played on a pebbled, all-dirt infield in Passaic Stadium, an aging athletic complex at the edge of town. Derek got there by walking along an industrial road that hugged the river. Driving to one of his games, I spotted him on the sidewalk, a lone figure in a black-and-gold uniform, bat bouncing on his shoulder. I gave him a lift, and when we showed up at the field together, his coach asked if I was his case worker. I corrected him, and the coach asked what Derek's "story" was. "He's a foster child, right?" I told him it was more complicated. "Derek's a good player," the coach offered, "but he has some anger issues. If he gets hit, he wants to go after the pitcher. And he always wants to come at the ump. I have to tell him, 'You can't do that.'"

Derek's new team was far more experienced and organized than the Eagles, and his role was limited to reserve outfielder. He shagged flies during warm-ups, then took his place on the bench. After the game, I drove him to Latoya's. On the way, he told me he still wanted to return to his old team in Newark. But there was no way to know when, or if, he'd move back. He couldn't predict where he'd be weeks from now. Latoya had just told him that she couldn't promise him a spot in her living room past the summer because she'd already offered her sister a place to stay. His grandmother Irene had submitted an application for an apartment at a senior citizens building that did not allow children as tenants. As for Derek's father, he'd stopped calling home, and no one knew where he was or how he was doing. I asked Derek if he was worried, and he shook his head. "Nah, everything will be fine." I thought maybe he was just telling me this to mask his true feelings. But it occurred to me that he didn't have much choice than to answer that way. It was futile for him to think much about the future. By necessity, he took a short view of life.

CHAPTER 15

Rodney arrived an hour before game time, rolling over a rutted asphalt path, dodging fallen tree branches, his body bouncing in his scooter as if it were an off-roading ATV. He parked himself along the left-field foul line, near where a collection of cackling kids, some in stocking feet, others shirtless, played pickup. He looked for the Eagles among them, counted heads with his index finger, and frowned: just a handful, nowhere near the nine he needed. Almost all of his players from 2008 had returned to him this season, and with a year of experience and physical growth behind them—and the addition of some new talent— the Eagles could feasibly rank among the Jackie Robinson South Ward Little League's top squads. Today his team would open the 2009 season against the Philly Stars, but it was almost six p.m., and he didn't have enough to field a team.

He jerked the bill of his Yankees cap low over his eyes and scanned the park. It was an unseasonably warm Friday evening in early April, darkened by a thick lining of low, shifting clouds. Three young cherry trees swelled with cottony blossoms beyond the outfield fence. A couple kissed on a bench. Men walked their pit bulls through an adjacent meadow. Drivers idled in a nearby parking lot. The crackle of a ball game seeped from a dashboard radio; a silky 1970s R & B tune bounced from another. A police cruiser crawled alongside a group of boys, who prepared themselves to be patted down; parents had complained about the smell of pot during T-ball games.

Rodney turned back to the field. The scoreboard flickered half-numbers and zeros, and the turf was strewn with a year's worth of accumulated debris. Dried leaves, cigarette cartons, used juice boxes, empty doughnut wrappers and Cheez Doodles bags lay in small, wind-swept drifts along the edges of the chain-link fences. A six-pack of Keystone beer lay drained and discarded near the home dugout. A burly father with a week's worth of facial stubble pointed out a used condom and shook his head. "This is shameful," he said. "I'm embarrassed to say I live in Newark." Rodney nodded in commiseration. Still, it was baseball season, and he felt a stab of anticipation, a hint of new possibilities.

Since the disappointing letter from the state Department of Education, Rodney and I had talked at great length, and in intimate detail, about his life: his boyhood, the mystery surrounding his father, his introduction to the drug trade, his time in prison, the shooting, his conversion to Islam, and his desire to make something new of himself. Our conversations prompted intense spans of self-reflection, as Rodney relived memories that he would have preferred to keep buried, and confronted unpleasant questions about his inability, or unwillingness, to take advantage of the openings that the attention surrounding the 2008 season had brought him. He'd turned down an offer by the league to become its new president—an unpaid position for which he was in fact poorly qualified and would have required him to give up coaching—and had stopped looking for work. I reminded him of what he always told his players: never give up. He assured me that as long as he kept "doing positive," things would work themselves out. Somehow.

Just before the start of the season, one of Rodney's doctors had invited him to speak to a class of inner-city students at an after-school program at a suburban synagogue. I had driven Rodney there, and we'd waited in an all-purpose room with banquet chairs and temporary walls that unfolded like the bellows of an accordion. A long time had passed since Rodney's last public speaking event, but his nerve returned when the sixth graders walked in the room and he recognized several faces from his neighborhood, including William, the tough-talking captain, who'd nearly come to blows with an assistant coach last year. "I better represent!" Rodney said to me.

He started off by telling the kids about the day he was shot and finding out that he'd never walk again.

"You was cryin'?" a boy asked.

"I *was* cryin'. I was crying like a baby."

"You fall a lot?" another boy asked.

"All the time." Rodney lifted himself out of his seat and set himself on the ground, his legs splayed limply in front of him. The children hushed. Rodney grabbed his chair and heaved himself back onto the seat, seemingly without effort. "This is what I do every day," he said. "All day, every day."

Then, almost reflexively, the children began volunteering their own tales of grief. One girl told a story about her mother getting shot in the foot by a stray bullet while picking up a nephew at school. A second girl mentioned the killing of her stepfather a couple of weeks earlier. A boy said his aunt had just died of an asthma attack. Another blurted, "I know a guy who was shot. He lost a lot of blood."

Rodney nodded. "There's so many negative things out there in city of Newark and in this world," he said. "The most important thing for all you kids here is to put God first and let him steer you into the positive path. Without that you're vulnerable to any and all things."

He went on: "I'm just blessed to share my story with y'all and tell you the dos and the don'ts. The dos is make sure y'all put God first and let him lead y'all to a positive look on life in general. And the don'ts is don't get caught up in gang violence and drugs and stuff like that or you could end up like this."

The doctor, standing in the back row, said Rodney's story reminded him of one of Dr. Martin Luther King Jr.'s speeches, titled "Unfulfilled Dreams." "It touches on being on the right path," the doctor said. "You may not get to the end of the path, but as long as you get to that path, that's what's important. There's always a decision you can make, right or wrong, and in your heart you probably know what is the right decision, and that's what I think Rodney is saying: to make that right decision."

A white teenager, one of the program's tutors, raised her hand. "Did you have any role models, then or now?"

"When I was like y'all I was reaching out to a lot of people, but ain't nobody reach out to me," Rodney said. "The only person I reached out to who reached back was God. That's my role model. Before I got shot, I didn't see God as much as I do now. That was a wake-up call."

"Where do you think you'll be in five to ten years?" the girl asked.

"Hopefully I'll still be involved with kids, steering them in a positive way. I just want to stick around and try to help as many kids as I can so they won't end up in the same situation I found myself in."

I'd heard him say this many times before. It was about as much detail as I ever got from Rodney about his plans for the future. Admirable, but also uncertain. I worried that without a detailed plan, he'd inevitably drift back to his old resting spot on the platform outside his building.

I'd never heard of "Unfulfilled Dreams," so when I returned home that evening I looked it up. King had delivered the speech in March 1968, a month before he was assassinated, and he seemed to know he had a short time to live. In it, he examined the battle between good and evil in everyone's souls, including his own.

In the final analysis, God does not judge us by the separate incidents or the separate mistakes that we make, but by the total bent of our lives. In the final analysis, God knows that his children are weak and they are frail. In the final analysis, what God requires is that your heart is right. Salvation isn't reaching the destination of absolute morality, but it's being in the process and on the right road.

Reading the speech caused me to reconsider my concerns about Rodney. I had no idea if he'd ever be able to make a completely new life for himself, but at least he was on the right road. And his heart, as far as I could tell, was in the right place.

* * *

"Hey, Rock, we gonna have to forfeit the game?"

Rodney glanced at his cell phone, which rested faceup in his lap. It was now 5:54 p.m.—six minutes before game time on opening day. The Philly Stars were in the visitors' dugout, lining their bats and helmets in a neat row against the fence and spreading out to play catch. He'd gotten accustomed to last-minute scrambles, but this was ridiculous.

"Coach?"

It was Delonte, the boy who'd pouted and sobbed through much of the 2008 season. He was among the handful of Eagles who'd arrived on time, and he was raring to play. He wore a white tank-top undershirt, gray baseball pants, and a new fade-style haircut.

"We gonna have to forfeit?"

"Why?" Rodney asked.

"Ain't nobody here."

"Nah, it'll be all right."

But privately Rodney wondered if it would. Everyone expected him to do something special again, something better than last year, to prove that he'd deserved all the publicity and donations. Yet in some ways he felt as if he were back where he started. Practices were still chaotic, with kids often looking as if they had just wandered off the street—ripped jeans hanging low off their butts, unlaced high-tops, no glove. They volleyed fat-and-ugly jokes, did handstands, slipped away to the corner bodega without asking permission. Once again, they had no uniforms—Rodney had failed to collect them from his departing players at the end of last season, and most had gone missing, and the league refused to supply new ones until everyone paid their $25 registration fee. Rodney still struggled with how to discipline the kids—to many of them, he remained "Uncle Rock," the reserved but kindly neighbor who handed out money for snacks and never raised his voice. And he still could not persuade them to show up on time.

The Philly Stars fanned across the field for pregame warm-ups. Just then, a pack of boys from Carmel Towers emerged from the trees along Elizabeth Avenue, led by Versace, the handspringing outfielder.

Thaiquan's minivan pulled into the parking lot, and a flock of children piled out, including Nasir and Kaneisha. Rodney shouted for everyone to gather around him and began to sketch out a lineup. Every few seconds, he looked up to check who was there. The players took his hesitation as an invitation for suggestions.

"I'm batting first."

"I'm batting second."

"You didn't even come to practice."

"Yes I did."

"Who pitching?"

"I am."

"Pooh is."

"Pooh don't even be here."

William was currently stuck on a downtown bus on his way back from buying turf shoes at Modell's. DeWan was also absent, but with an excuse: the aspiring actor was in New York with a teacher to see *Fiddler on the Roof*. A few weeks earlier, he'd missed practice for a Broadway revival of *West Side Story*, the same play he was rehearsing at school, and proclaimed it "beyond good." Also missing was Derek, who was living with a sister in another city.

A tall, thin boy named Ibn, who'd played for the rival Black Yankees last year, raised his hand. Ibn claimed to have abandoned his former team because they'd lost all their star players. "I know how to pitch," he offered.

Jalil, the finger-sucking infielder who'd started last year as a second grader, clambered onto Rodney's scooter.

"Get down, man," Rodney pleaded. He caught the umpire looking at him expectantly and flashed his palm. Five minutes.

"Why can't what's-his-name play first base?" Jalil continued, still clinging to the scooter's handlebars.

"Get away from me, man," Rodney said. He ducked under the brim of his cap and kept writing. He wished the chattering would stop, for just a minute.

"Somebody gotta play third," Jalil pressed.

"I'm gonna pitch," Ibn said. "I know how to pitch."

"*I* know how to pitch, too," Jalil said.

"So what base I'm playin', Rock?" Versace asked.

"I don't know, man, please . . ." Rodney said. He scrawled a "P" next to Ibn's name.

"That's a P?"

"Yeah, that a P."

"Yah!" Ibn held his glove tight to his chest and beamed.

"Not Ibn!" howled a tall, pear-shaped boy named Jeffrey who'd defected with Ibn from the Black Yankees. With William missing, Jeffrey would be catching today. "Let Jalil pitch."

"Can I pitch if he get tired?" Jalil asked.

"I could pitch," Nasir offered.

"Let Nasir pitch!" Versace said.

Rodney hit reverse on his scooter's joystick and pulled away. "Y'all go warm up."

The Eagles paired off to play catch. There would be no pregame drills because Reggie, Versace's father and Rodney's only returning assistant coach, had not yet arrived with the equipment bag. Bahir, a new boy from Carmel Towers who wore his hair in neck-length braids, caught sight of a group of older kids walking toward the field from Elizabeth Avenue. "That a crew," he announced, breathless. He pointed at a skinny boy walking a few paces ahead of the rest. "That dude? Him and them strapping. I saw some dude swing at him, *shoooo*, he duck and, *pow*, came back up . . ."

"Don't worry about that, man," Thaiquan said. He'd joined the Eagles in the dugout, offering to help Rodney get things together. "That's a dead issue. Worry about the game."

Reggie slinked through the gate, chest heaving, equipment bag over his shoulder. Jeffrey strapped the catcher's gear over his ample frame and squatted, his butt crack exposed. Ibn took the mound for his practice pitches, throwing sidearm with a jerky windup. Each toss dribbled from the webbing of Jeffrey's mitt and dropped at his feet. The umpire called for play to begin.

The Philly Stars started the top of the first inning with a long string of base hits, walks, and stolen bases; anyone who made it to first advanced at least to third. Rodney replaced Ibn with Jeffrey and moved Nasir, who'd never caught before, behind home plate, where he had to be shown how to put on the chest protector and shin guards. The whites of Nasir's frightened eyes were visible through the grill of the face mask. Between pitches, he turned sidelong at Thaiquan, who barked at him to toughen up. But that just made Nasir more jittery. He dropped one pitch after another, sending in more runs. When the half-inning finally ended, the Eagles were losing, 8–0. They went down in order in the bottom of the first. William and another new recruit, a versatile athlete named Abdul, showed up mid-game, but it was too late to undo the damage. In the bottom of the fifth, the umpire called the game at 13–3, citing the league's mercy rule. Everyone took a knee at the mound.

"See what happens when you don't come on time?" Rodney said.

"Why we always doin' wrong?" Bahir asked.

"We'll get them next time," William said.

"Hold your heads up!" another boy said.

"That's right," Thaiquan said. "Hold your heads up."

"It'll be all right," Rodney told them. "You just gotta remember to have fun."

A week later, the Eagles redeemed themselves with a 12–1 drubbing of the Black Sox at the newly refurbished artificial-turf diamond at the St. Peter's Recreation Center, the result of Mayor Booker's new effort to spruce up Newark's dreadful ball fields. Nearly everyone took part in the hitting onslaught, and there was no whining or crying from those who didn't contribute. That included DeWan, back from Broadway, who, after striking out for the second time, complimented the pitcher's "nasty breaking ball." He slapped his teammates on their butts, praised their "sexy hits," and introduced a new cheer: "I see a H-O-L-E hole out there, so hit the ball out there!" Delonte caught a liner over his head, snow cone–style, at second. Zahir, another new boy from Carmel Towers, hit an inside-the-park home run. Nasir smacked a liner to left field that bounced over the fence for a ground-rule double. As the Eagles widened their lead, someone broke out a packet of sunflower seeds. Everyone grabbed a handful, popping them between their teeth, blowing the shells through puckered lips, and letting them flitter to the dugout floor.

That game was followed by a rematch with the Philly Stars, which the Eagles lost, 4–3. Against the Black Barons a few days later, DeWan led off with an inside-the-park home run down the right-field line, and his teammates mobbed him in the dugout. "You lookin' pretty, baby!" Versace said. William added, "That's the first time I seen Puda hittin'!" DeWan grabbed my notebook, found a blank page, and scrawled on it in block letters: "DeWan hit an in-side the park home-run (got 2 rbi's)." On his next at bat, as his teammates chanted "Aero, Aero, Aero-postale" in honor of his favorite clothing line, DeWan raised his hands to his chin, stuck his butt out, jabbed his left shoe into the dirt, and wagged his heel in the air. "Puda," one of his teammates yelled from the bench, "stop trying to look pretty and hit the ball!" The next pitch drilled him in the head. DeWan dropped to the turf, and the pitcher edged closer to see if he was all right. DeWan bounced to his feet and stuck out his hand to shake before heading to first. Everyone applauded. Then Ibn, looking like he'd just rolled out of bed in a white under-shirt and baggy polyester basketball shorts, knocked DeWan in with a double.

The Eagles won, 11–4, the start of a winning streak in which they also beat the Black Senators, the Black Sox, and the Black Crackers. After each victory, the Eagles shook hands with their opponents, then ran around the bases and slid into home, smiling gleefully. Versace did his flips. Moms in the bleachers shouted, "Rock, Rock, yeah, yeah!"

Three weeks into the season, the Eagles finally got their 2009 uniforms—burgundy with white piping and EA EAGLES in white across the chest—which Rodney and Reggie had customized with the players' names. The league would protest, but team spirit was more important: the perennial underdogs were now in striking distance of first place.

"People still be doubting me, but I just keep moving along," Rodney told me. "Sometimes I be lackadaisical, but that's what keeps me motivated, people doubting me. That and all my trials and tribulations. Right now, though? We on the road to the championship!"

CHAPTER 16

It should have been a day to celebrate.

On May 27, 2009, DeWan's stepfather, Kareem, checked out of his halfway house and, for the first time in years, went home a free man. In practical terms, his release didn't change things very much; he'd already been spending time with Joicki and the boys as part of the state Department of Correction's policy of gradually reintegrating felons back into their communities. But it was still an auspicious moment, symbolic of their renewed potential as a family, and a good reason, I thought, to stop by and see how the reunited clan was getting along.

But instead of coming upon a joyful scene, I found myself caught in the middle of a shouting match between Kareem and Joicki. He was at the computer, checking their bank account, grilling her about recent withdrawals, implying that she'd been wasting money on partying. She sat near me on the sofa, denying it and antagonizing him with laughter. That made him angrier; he called her "haughty" and accused her of lording over him her efforts to hold the family together while he was locked up. Occasionally, one of them asked me what I thought, and I insisted that it wasn't my place to take sides. At one point, little Kareem emerged from his room, did a silly dance, and, after failing to lighten the mood, retreated to his homework.

Finally DeWan breezed into the apartment wearing a burgundy TEAM Academy polo shirt and khakis. Rehearsal for *West Side Story* had run long, and now he was late for the Eagles' game against the Black

Senators. He called out, "Hey," lowered his gaze, and quick-stepped through the din, disappearing behind a closed door to change. If he was concerned about the fighting, he didn't show it. He began pulling off his school clothes as his stepfather stormed out of the apartment, slamming the door behind him. A few minutes later, Kareem stomped back in, muttering as he beelined for the bedroom. The apartment fell uncomfortably silent, as if everyone was taking a long, wary breath. DeWan reappeared, wearing gray baseball pants and a tank-top undershirt, still acting oblivious. He was anxious to get to the field, he said, because tonight would be the Eagles' first appearance in their new customized jerseys. He sat beside his mother and pulled on his stirrups, careful to make sure that the burgundy stripes ran parallel along his calves. I asked DeWan how he thought the team would look tonight, and he turned to me with that guileless, gap-toothed smile of his. "Beautiful," he said, drawing the vowels out dreamily. When he got up to leave, Joicki stopped him and pointed to his undershirt, known as a "wife beater." "I don't want the world seeing you like that," she said. DeWan didn't protest; he knew she was right. He switched shirts, hitched his glove's Velcro clasp around his belt loop, grabbed his bat, and scooted out.

Kareem emerged from the bedroom and announced that he was going to watch DeWan's game. That left me alone with Joicki.

"So," I said, clumsily, "how's it going?"

Joicki sank back into the sofa and chuckled. "Well, you see with your own eyes." I noticed that she had reorganized and tidied the apartment, something she seemed to do during times of stress. "But really, it's going well. Ironically, today we're beefing when it's supposed to be a real happy day. But we'll get past it." She nodded at the door, where DeWan and Kareem had just departed. "*They're* close."

I already knew from talking to Kareem and DeWan that they were eagerly rebuilding their relationship. The process included a new household routine that began at five thirty a.m., when Kareem woke up DeWan and cued up Evanescence's "Bring Me to Life" on the computer. They dressed and ate breakfast together, and at seven o'clock the boys left for school while Kareem headed across the street to catch the first of two buses that took him to work at a telemarketing firm in the suburbs. He returned home around the same time as Joicki, and they often walked up Custer Avenue to fetch DeWan from school. After dinner, DeWan and little Kareem spread out on the living-room floor to finish their homework, and Kareem flipped on the television and waited for one of them to ask him for help. DeWan cherished those moments because they were just as he'd imagined in the months leading to Kareem's release: everyone together, hanging out, just like any ordinary family.

DeWan was also seeking Kareem's advice on a myriad of teenage boy issues, the two most pressing being girls (he'd struck up a little romance with a classmate) and fashion (he'd adopted the skater look: Vans, skinny jeans worn below the waist, and brightly colored polos). Kareem explained to DeWan the dangers of teenage sex and wanting to fit in. He urged DeWan not to forget two things that his mother had tried to instill in him: belief in God and the power to make the right decisions for himself. "I like having another person to encourage me and tell me right from wrong," DeWan had told me. "I mean, I already have my mother, but now she doesn't have to worry about doing this and doing that. It's great to have my father. He's going to take care of us."

Joicki, however, was stopping short of making a full emotional investment in Kareem. Maintaining a sense of independence and control protected her from the inevitable disappointments. But DeWan feared her attitude would undermine their chances of success. He made unsolicited comments to her, like, *Mom you know we love this relationship*, and, *I know you're not going to do anything to mess this relationship up*, and, *Daddy loves you*. "I don't know what makes him say that," Joicki told me from her perch on the sofa, chuckling. "I wish he wouldn't say it. I wish he would just be on my side. He values family, though, and relationships, and stuff like that, DeWan. He wants to see us work."

She had to admit that, so far, Kareem *was* doing well. This was the longest he'd been clean and out of jail since his teens. He was earning the largest paychecks of his life and planned to go back to school to become a drug counselor. He still saw Joicki as his soul mate and claimed to have never been happier. "I know that when I'm with Joicki I'm totally better, and I know it's mutual," he'd recently told me. "I'm not saying we're perfect, but we got a straighter path because we got a goal to get to." Earlier that spring, Joicki had hosted a "poetry cafe" for her English students, and Kareem asked if he could read something he'd just written. It was a deeply confessional piece that revealed his internal battle with his dark side. He called it, "Who Am I?"

Remembering the moment made Joicki smile wistfully. She'd always said that Kareem was smarter than she was, and a much better writer. Too bad that talent had mostly gone to waste.

Kareem had spent a lot of time behind bars analyzing his life, and he traced his descent into addiction—which started when he was ten, smoking weed and sipping forty-ounce bottles of beer during grammar-school lunch breaks—to his mother's drug abuse and the fact that he didn't meet his father until he was eleven, a year before his death from alcoholism. Kareem felt a responsibility to keep DeWan off the streets. "I'm telling Puda things that no man ever told me when I was little," he'd explained a few weeks before his release from the halfway house. "Asking questions like, 'What do you want to be when you grow up?' Like, 'What inspires you today?' Like, 'Why do you do the things you do?' I'm just giving him what I thought I should have got when I was young. I love Puda like he's my son. I don't make a distinction. I believe he feels the same way."

Joicki believed it was having an effect. "I see DeWan asking Kareem things and waiting for Kareem's response," she said. "And since Kareem's been home, DeWan has been more honest with me and more comfortable expressing his emotions and feelings." She recalled watching from the bleachers when DeWan got knocked in the head by a pitch. "I was like, *hell, no* . . . And then when he got up and shook the pitcher's hand and walked to first base, I was *so proud*. That was a defining moment for me. I was *so proud*."

A similar transformation was happening at school. Before Kareem's return, DeWan had been failing almost all of his classes, including reading, which particularly galled Joicki because she was an English teacher and had devoured books when she was his age. But DeWan had since rallied; his latest progress report showed four As, two Bs, and a C.

DeWan's social worker at TEAM Academy, Phaedra Ruddock,

confirmed that DeWan was showing new life at school. She knew all about Kareem's arrival, but she also saw another factor at work: DeWan had become the star of *West Side Story*. "No one knew this kid had that in him," she'd told me recently. She recalled accompanying DeWan outside after play practice one day to wait for his parents. They talked about DeWan's hopes for his family, and, as if on cue, Joicki and Kareem appeared on Custer Avenue, hand in hand, like new lovers. As they approached, Ruddock saw a huge grin break across DeWan's face. She recalled watching the three of them walk back down the hill, their silhouettes receding in the twilight, and thinking, *DeWan finally has what he wanted.*

Kareem returned to the apartment, where Joicki and I were still talking. He'd cooled off while waiting for DeWan's game to start and now wanted to wait for Joicki to join him. Joicki and I finished up, and the three of us, along with little Kareem, walked to the field. They took their place in the bleachers, and I took mine in the home dugout. Throughout the game, I heard their voices cheering for DeWan, together.

The next time I saw them was at the New Jersey Performing Arts Center, where KIPP, the charter school company that ran TEAM Academy, was holding a fund-raiser for potential donors. Ruddock had ditched plans to stage a full-length production of *West Side Story* because no one but DeWan had learned their lines well enough; instead, DeWan and a small group of boys performed one scene at the fund-raiser. As the gang leader Riff, DeWan swaggered around the stage with the sleeves of his white hooded sweatshirt rolled to his elbows, snapping his fingers, swinging his arms, and punching the air like a street fighter, leading the others in "When You're a Jet." The audience rose to its feet and roared. Joicki and Kareem looked at each other, beaming. "Pudaaaaaa!" they cried.

They were still rhapsodizing about the performance when I visited their apartment the following evening. DeWan, slightly embarrassed, lay on the floor, face in his homework. On TV, the detectives of *CSI* were tracking down a murderer using discarded food as forensic evidence.

Joicki and Kareem told DeWan he could pursue a career as an actor, but DeWan still had aspirations of becoming a professional athlete. They told him that was fine, but he needed to find something to fall back on if he got hurt or otherwise couldn't play. "I just want him to have a dream to shoot for," Kareem said, "something to fulfill and be successful at, and not to let his peers or negative thoughts lead him the wrong way."

When I caught up with Kareem a few weeks later, he admitted he'd stumbled and taken Ecstasy. "I got bigheaded," he said, "but we talked about it, and Joicki forgave me." They were now discussing plans to get their credit straight and buy a car, maybe a house. He wanted to get as far from Newark as possible, perhaps to North Carolina, while Joicki preferred somewhere closer, like suburban Montclair. Either way, the goal was to find a new, calmer environment where they could focus on what was ahead of them, instead of the past.

Soon they had more inspiration: Joicki was pregnant. A baby would help bring the family even closer and give Kareem another reason to become the father he knew he could be. They spread the news together, looking radiant, relaxed, hopeful. "Everything's been a blessing," Kareem said. "This is like starting over again. The only way now is up." When I saw DeWan, I asked him if he was ready to have another brother or sister in the house, and he looked at me as if to say, *Of course*. Because there was no better promise of a family's future. "It's gonna be perfect," he said.

CHAPTER 17

A new boy began hanging out in the Eagles' dugout. He didn't play, which was not that unusual, as Rodney had many young acolytes who, though not official members of the team, came and went as they pleased, happy to watch the big kids. But the new boy was different. He sat apart from the others and did not venture far from Rodney's side. Every so often, when the Eagles were in the field, he stood and practiced throwing or swung a bat, but as soon as the dugout became crowded again, he quietly returned to his seat. When the game ended, the boy and Rodney sometimes left together, and when they were alone, the boy called him "Daddy."

When I first overheard this, I was surprised, because Rodney was universally known to the neighborhood children as "Uncle Rock." I introduced myself. His name was Nashawn, and he was almost nine, with an open, solemn face. I later learned that he lived with his mother and younger brother in the apartment building next door to Zion Towers. They had recently moved from another neighborhood, and, not long after, Rodney started coming over to their apartment. In the beginning he came to see Nashawn's mother, but he ended up spending a lot of time with Nashawn and three-year-old Zion, watching TV and playing video games. Sometimes, Rodney took Nashawn outside to play catch. He was too young and too frightened of the ball to be an Eagle, but Rodney told him he could sit on the bench until he was ready.

Nashawn's mother, Naimah, was a preschool aide, a former model, and an aspiring jewelry designer who sometimes called herself Lady Na. She had an arresting smile, an up-sloped nose, a girlish, slightly nasal voice, and a body that had grown significantly curvier since her days of posing before a camera. Come-ons still followed her wherever men saw her: at work, on a walk to the bodega, Facebook. She radiated sexual confidence and accused Rodney of lying when he said he hadn't noticed her checking him out that spring. "I *know* I'm fucking cute," she said.

Naimah told me that when she first eyed Rodney sitting outside Zion Towers, she knew nothing about him or the Eagles; she just thought he looked handsome in his fitted baseball cap, dark blue jeans, and bright white T-shirt. She'd survived a string of treacherous relationships, which had resulted in a number of black eyes and bloody noses and a lot of trauma for her sons. To spare her boys more pain, she tried to prevent them from getting attached to any man in her life. In fact, she tried to avoid romantic entanglements entirely, telling herself she'd rather be alone than risk their getting hurt. That was her plan, anyway, before she saw Rodney.

She was furtively admiring him at the park one day in April when an older man, possibly drunk and calling himself "Doc," began hitting on her. Naimah tried to brush him off by saying she was already taken. By who? he asked. She pointed to Rodney, who sat nearby, in a scrum of children.

"Rock Bottom!" Doc called to Rodney. They were friends, apparently. Rodney looked over. "Rock, this female over here talking about you her husband."

"Who?"

"Right here." Doc pointed to Naimah.

Rodney rolled over to see what was up. Naimah was embarrassed but also glad to finally meet this man who, she now knew, coached Little League and seemed to be adored by all of Elizabeth Avenue. Batting her eyes, she asked about his team, and Rodney gave her one of the registration forms he kept in his bag. "Make sure you put your number on there," he said.

"Oh, I *will*," Naimah replied, grinning mischievously.

Rodney took that as an invitation to call her, so that night he did. Ostensibly, the point was to talk about Nashawn, but the conversation quickly progressed. Naimah asked if Rodney was hungry, and Rodney said yeah, so she met him outside his building with a plate of food she'd made. They talked some more. She invited him to come over sometime for dinner. "It happened kind of quickly," Rodney told me afterward. Some nights they stayed up late talking, falling asleep with their phones to their ears, like teenagers.

Naimah told herself that she might have finally found a good man: not only was Rodney good-looking and well-groomed, but he was also religious, loved kids, and doted on his mother. She disregarded her rule about new boyfriends and allowed herself to fall for him. She nursed him when he caught a terrible flu, threw a surprise forty-second birthday party for him at her apartment, and was the first to say, "I love you."

Rodney was also smitten. He'd always fallen for women quickly, perhaps too quickly. He'd had a couple of flings since his injury, but he'd never found anyone who truly cared about him, who made him feel comfortable with his broken body. He understood how difficult it was for women to accept the fact that he couldn't perform normally in bed, couldn't even control his bladder or bowels. Naimah was different. She not only tolerated it, she embraced it as something that made him unique. "That takes someone strong and understanding," Rodney told me. He was hesitant to share these feelings at first, but before long he told her he loved her, too.

As the romance with Naimah blossomed, Rodney and Nashawn developed a relationship of their own. Naimah didn't have time to try to keep it in check and was surprised when she overheard Nashawn refer to Rodney as his "daddy."

"Why are you calling him Dad?" Naimah asked.

"I feel comfortable with him. He treats me like he's my father."

"That isn't your father."

"Yes he *is*," Nashawn said, lips quivering. "Why you saying that?"

Naimah dropped it. She couldn't bear to disappoint Nashawn. He was a sweet, trusting kid but suffered from emotional problems related to acute lead poisoning diagnosed when he was three. He struggled to remember things, wept easily, and was classified as learning disabled. Naimah struggled to find the right setting for him; no school seemed able to meet his needs, and he'd already had to repeat grades. Nashawn's father did not come to see him. By contrast, his brother Zion's father returned just about every weekend to visit. Nashawn longed for the same.

The next day, Rodney was getting dressed at Naimah's and Nashawn asked, "Hey, Daddy, we going to the park?"

Rodney paused. He pulled Nashawn close. "You want to call me Dad?"

"Yeah, my mom told me it was all right."

"Okay."

Later, I asked Rodney how that made him feel. "I'm cool with it," he said. Then he smiled so broadly that three arched wrinkles formed above each of his eyes. I'd never seen that happen before.

Rodney had always wondered what it was like to be a parent; he thought it might make him feel more complete. After the shooting, a doctor at Kessler told him about a surgical procedure by which he could potentially father a child, but it was expensive, and he needed a willing partner. Since then, he'd assumed he'd never be a dad. Until now. He and Naimah began to discuss marriage and the possibility of Rodney becoming Nashawn's legal guardian. But there was another part of him that was nervous. This was the deepest relationship he'd been in since Prudence. Rodney remained leery of getting involved with women who had other guys in the background. Naimah tried to assure him that there was nothing between her and her sons' fathers, but Rodney still worried.

By the second week of June, the Eagles' record stood at 7-2, good enough to put them in second place. Some had added pieces of flair to their new uniforms, including DeWan, who wore fluffy white wristbands, and Nasir, who replaced his stirrups with solid burgundy football socks stretched to his knees. Others, however, still had to be reminded to hike up their waistbands and tuck in their shirts. On a Monday night they faced the Philly Stars, the only team to have beaten them. In the bleachers, Versace's mother handed out burgundy leis and glittery burgundy pom-poms from Party City and led a group of players' sisters in a round of cheers. She put one of the pom-poms on her head like a clown wig. The Eagles studied her for a moment, then turned to Versace. "You mother crazy!"

The Philly Stars were excellent hitters, and the Eagles committed several defensive errors that put them in a deep first-inning hole from which they never recovered. You could feel the energy drain from the dugout. At one point, Delonte sat on the bench, trying not to cry, when he heard his mother's boyfriend in his ear: "There you go again, acting like a bitch ass." Rodney wanted to stop it but was wary of upsetting the boyfriend. "It ain't the kid's fault," he told me in a sotto voice. "The man's all in his head."

Kaneisha slid next to Delonte. She still spent most games on the bench, overlooked by Rodney and the other coaches. Her heart was with the team, but her playing hadn't improved much. Her role, as she continued to see it, was to keep her teammates calm and composed. "Y'all need some anger management," she often told them. "You got problems." With Delonte she took a gentler approach, holding out a sack of sunflower seeds for comfort. Delonte declined.

The Eagles lost, 7–3, but rebounded a few days later against the Black Barons, their rivals from the Seth Boyden housing projects, behind a one-hit shutout by William. Then, in the season finale, the Eagles demolished the Black Crackers, 11–1. Like last year, every team made the play-offs, and the Eagles once again swept the Black Yankees in the first round. They faced the Black Barons in the second, splitting the first two games and, in another repeat of 2008, played a tiebreaker to determine who would advance to the championship round. At practice, Rodney urged his team not to let down their guard as they had last year. "We gotta jump on them from the start. And I don't want no tears. You strike out, you sit down and you get another at bat."

But at game time, only seven Eagles showed up. School had ended, and several kids had reluctantly left on family outings. DeWan was among the missing; Joicki was driving them to Florida to see her grandmother. He'd begged Joicki to let him stay, but she told him family was more important.

Derek unexpectedly showed up, telling Rodney he'd walked across town from his aunt Mary's to show his support. His old teammates slapped his back and hugged him; Rodney wished he could give him a uniform.

Rodney sent his players into the towers for their AWOL teammates. Someone brought back Jeffrey, one of the new kids, and at the last minute Delonte showed up, his face chalky with chlorine residue after a day at the city pool.

An air of defeat permeated the bench before the first pitch. When the Barons smacked a two-run home run, the visitors' bench erupted with a taunting rejoinder to one of the Eagles' signature cheers.

"EA!"

"Not today!"

The hangdog home team didn't bother with a response.

The Eagles managed a rally in the fifth inning that pulled them to within three runs. In the sixth, they put a runner on base with two outs, offering a sliver of hope. But the runner tried to steal second, and the umpire called him out. The Eagles surrounded the umpire and accused him of cheating. As the Barons threw their caps into the air in triumph, the umpire stormed off the field, shaking his head. "This is one of the worst cases of bad sportsmanship I've ever seen," he said.

Rodney pulled his players together at the mound. "No one cheated," he told them. "That's part of the game. We played hard. We competed, and that goes a long way. So don't ever look at someone else as better than you because you never know. Just *compete*." They put their hands together and shouted "Eagles" one last time.

Rodney turned to leave. A mother was still yelling at the umpire. Several players were milling around, sulking. William leaned against a fence, near tears. Nasir and Kaneisha sat in the dugout, speechless. Delonte was disappearing down the sidewalk for home. Their Little League careers were over.

I walked Rodney back to his apartment, wondering what he was going to do now. I knew that the letter from the state Department of Education still weighed on him; for such a tough guy, who'd survived so much, breaking into mainstream society still felt impossible.

"I don't know," he said. "I've been with these kids for four months, spending all my time with them, and now I gotta try to figure out the next step. I can't see myself doing nothing. I need to do *something*."

A few days later, on a Monday afternoon in July, a drive-by gunman opened fire into a crowd of people in front of Carmel Towers, the building where William, Versace, and several other Eagles lived. One of their neighbors, a thirty-five-year-old mother, was caught in the barrage of gunfire as she walked to the store, and she dropped in the street, dying instantly. Four others fell injured. Several additional slugs tore through the wall of a Head Start center on the first floor of the towers, one ricocheting through an office doorway and zipping past the heads of children playing in the adjoining room.

The mother's killing, and a second unrelated drive-by shooting across town two hours later, resulting in two more deaths, represented the kind of spasm of deadly violence that occurred every so often in Newark, making national news and undermining whatever strides the city had made in improving its public image. Since taking office three years earlier, Mayor Booker had hired a decorated New York Police Department commander to run the local police force, and together they'd overseen the installation of state-of-the-art gunshot-detecting cameras, expanded a cash-for-guns buyback program, and beefed up patrols on nights and weekends. Booker still rode with his own security detail, breaking up midnight gatherings at drug corners and stopping people to ask why they were out on the streets so late. He'd become obsessed with shooting statistics and took any available opportunity to remind people that gun violence, along with every other category of major crime, had declined since he became mayor in July 2006. His national image, meanwhile, was continuing to flourish: he traveled the country pitching Newark to philanthropists, high-tech companies, and Hollywood moguls, luring millions of dollars of investment to the city. "With community support," he'd said in his most recent state of the city speech, "Newark is quickly changing its reputation and becoming more and more a place inhospitable to the level of crime once associated with our city."

And yet these efforts did not seem enough. The dead mother was the third innocent bystander killed by gunfire since the start of summer and the eleventh shot in a half-block area surrounding Carmel Towers in less than a year. "So many people have been killed and hurt at the same building, and nobody does anything about it. Nobody cares," one of the mother's relatives told the *Star-Ledger*. Another resident told the paper that people were "angry and ashamed, but stopped believing things could change around here a long time ago." The politicians, he said in a thinly veiled reference to Booker, "say the right things, but nothing ever gets done." Ne Ne Jones, William's thirty-six-year-old mother, began sobbing when I called to see if they were okay. William wasn't outside at the time, and neither were any other kids, but Ne Ne saw that as pure luck. She'd always intended to escape Carmel Towers and now felt desperate to leave. "I don't want to be stuck in this building all my life," she said. "My kids are not happy here. William wants to leave, too. He's thirteen. He's still a kid. He needs a backyard. It's hard. We go to church. We pray. I just pray on everything. Because God's not going to put us in anything we can't handle."

Later that summer, comedian Conan O'Brien joined the long list of talk-show hosts who'd used Newark as a comedic foil when he mocked plans for a Booker-backed nonprofit to expand medical services to the poor. "The mayor of Newark, New Jersey, wants to set up a citywide program to improve residents' health," O'Brien announced. "The health care program would consist of a bus ticket out of Newark." Booker responded by uploading to YouTube a video in which he barred O'Brien from Newark Airport. "From now on, if people are going to make fun of our city, I'm going to step back at them," he explained afterward. For decades, Newark mayors had been defending the city against talk-show jokes, but none of them appealed to so many different audiences, or had as much access to social media, as Booker. The video went viral, and O'Brien took up the challenge. For several days, the mayor and comedian traded tongue-in-cheek jabs at each other. It ended when Secretary of State Hillary Clinton intervened with her own teasing video, calling for peace. O'Brien invited Booker to his studio in California, where, after cracking a few more Newark jokes, he announced that he would donate $100,000 to the mayor's nonprofit. The episode made good entertainment and burnished Booker's national image. But it also fed the critics who accused Booker of being more comfortable with the elites of Los Angeles and New York than with his adopted hometown, where unemployment had just hit a fifteen-year high.

Rodney was one of many people who watched the so-called feud unfold with dismay: more jokes, more pages to the Booker-as-savior story line, but little that seemed to impact life on Elizabeth Avenue. He'd once thought he believed in Booker and his vision of a greater Newark. But now he felt disillusioned. "Newark is like a lost city," he told me. "By lost I mean that Newark never really gets no type of exposure as far as anything good. People see the mayor and the violence, but they don't see the *real* Newark. I see myself as the real Newark. The stuff I'm going through, this is the root of what goes on in Newark. I say, fuck this shit with Conan O'Brien."

CHAPTER 18

Rodney winced into his battered sofa, trying to find a way to sit without pain.
The springs creaked. His body tensed. Resignation filled his face. "I'm
hurtin', Schuppe," he sighed. Outside his apartment's east-facing windows, a misty autumn rain swaddled Elizabeth Avenue. His body
throbbed in weather like this, made him feel like he was stuffed with
sand. His back screamed, his joints moaned, his eyes stung with sleep-
lessness. Everything ached, including his spirit.

For the last few months, Rodney had been using a refurbished
manual wheelchair as a replacement for his electric scooter, whose
battery was no longer able to hold enough charge to propel him up the
hills that separated him from Friday prayers, the ball field, Naimah's.
When he visited the medical supply store, they told him that Medicaid would only cover a loaner, and they gave him a chair pieced
together with spare parts, including two different-size tires—one with
thick treads like a dirt bike, the other one narrow, like a road bike. It
was hard to maneuver, and hell on his shoulders and arms. The supply
store was also failing to keep up with his orders for condoms and
urine-collection bags, and when Rodney ran out, he had to reuse
them, or go without, and every so often he'd look down at his lap and
realize that he'd wet himself. His piss had started to smell funny, making him suspect that he'd contracted a urinary tract infection. A pressure ulcer had developed on his rear end. His physician urged him to
stay out of his chair, but that meant lying in bed all day. He made an

appointment with his doctors at Kessler, whom he had not seen in years, but when he called the medical van company for a ride, they refused to come get him because, according to their records, his legs worked perfectly well. He laughed, bitterly.

Then came yesterday's news. A friend, an activist and former drug dealer named Yusuf, was shot to death late at night in the hallway of a high-rise apartment building notorious for narcotics trafficking. Rodney considered Yusuf a protégé; he was a teenager with a long criminal record when they'd first encountered each other at a mentoring program, and they'd bonded over their struggles. Yusuf aspired to become a filmmaker and website designer, and planned to incorporate his criminal past into an educational curriculum. His latest project was a series of interviews with thugs and ex-cons—"a firsthand account of the dangers of the drug and gang life," he had called it when Rodney and I had run into him a year ago. Rodney sat for one of those interviews, and later, when he got permission to work with troubled kids at Peshine Avenue School, he played them one of Yusuf's DVDs. It was raw and intimate—so intimate that it made Rodney worry for Yusuf's safety.

A week ago, Yusuf had stopped by Rodney's to discuss partnering on another project that would draw from their personal stories, and Rodney warned Yusuf that he remained perilously close to the gangs he filmed. "That shit is going to catch up to you," Rodney said. "You can't play both sides. You can't be what you are *and* be an activist. Motherfuckers are gonna think you're snitching." But Yusuf insisted that the best way to get his message across was to show the bare truth of how the groups operated. "That's how it has to be," Yusuf said. And now he was dead.

Yusuf's friends in the antiviolence movement said he had simply been in the wrong place at the wrong time and just happened to get caught in the middle of a gun battle that had nothing to do with him. But Rodney wondered.

A few days before Yusuf's murder, another friend, a woman he'd grown up with in Zion Towers, had passed away in her sleep, leaving behind a ten-year-old daughter. Both funerals were held on the same day and adhered to Islamic strictures, meaning no embalming fluid.

Despite the liberal use of incense and aromatic oils, the smell of their decaying bodies was thick and revolting, and for days Rodney's sinuses remained saturated with it. He told Naimah that he needed to be alone and shut himself in his apartment, where he contemplated life's capriciousness and wondered when all the death and sickness and sorrow would finally break him. "It seems like even when you start to do good, bad shit still happens to you," he told me. "I can't focus on anything else."

Rodney's impulse for withdrawal caused friction with Naimah. She tried to share his grief, but Rodney felt smothered at her place. Her sons, Nashawn and Zion, demanded more of his attention, and Naimah was now leaning on him for support. She'd been laid off from her preschool, was applying for food stamps, and struggled to pay rent; if Zion's father found out, he would surely try to take full custody. Though Rodney had made arrangements to list her as his home health aide—good for a few hundred dollars a month from Medicaid—she believed Rodney didn't try hard enough to find a job. Her nerves were frayed, and her frustration often flared over things she saw as potential threats, like when Joicki began coming to Rodney to talk about her troubles with Kareem. Naimah snooped through his Facebook page and text messages and found out that he kept in touch with lots of other female friends, including Prudence, the woman over whom he'd been shot. Naimah thought that was insane. "Rodney, I love you," she said. "*I'm* here with you *now*. You want to see if the grass is greener? Just be straight with me. I've been through it all with the fathers of my boys."

Rodney denied having feelings for any other women but hated to argue. "It's nothing, it's nothing," he said. "I don't want to talk about it."

They exchanged angry texts. Rodney stayed out all day, came in at night, watched TV until everyone was asleep, then slipped into her bed. Naimah once became so frustrated with his refusal to talk that she smacked him in the face. He lunged from his chair and grabbed her, and then let go. She called him a coward, but Rodney actually felt proud of himself; back in the day, he might have beaten her up.

Since the end of the 2009 baseball season, Rodney had been haunted by a creeping sense of purposelessness, of lost momentum. Sometimes members of the Eagles buzzed his apartment with no advance warning and piled into his living room. Some of them, including William, would be too old for Little League next year and would move on to another program. The others wanted to hear his plans for the coming season. Rodney was afraid of disappointing them. "I'm hooked on these kids," he told me. "Helping them, being with them. I'd like to stick with them all the way through college." The perfect job, he thought, would be to coach high school ball. But he doubted that would ever be possible after the Department of Education background check.

Another, more modest, idea was to hold a baseball clinic before the start of the season. But he had no money, no place to run it, no one to help him organize it. He mentioned it to his old high school friend Jeff, who told him to apply for a grant from a new philanthropic organization he worked with. Jeff e-mailed him an application, and Rodney asked me for help filling it out. It was immediately clear that Rodney had not bothered to work out any of the details, but together we answered the questions about staffing and budgets and mission statements as best we could, and sent it back.

As he waited for word, Rodney began to fear that he was running out of time. He saw Naimah and her needs as distractions. "This is just like when I got shot—I got involved in a girl and I got sidetracked," Rodney complained.

In December, Naimah left me a message saying she and Rodney were finished. When I called her back, she was in tears. She acknowledged that she had intruded on Rodney's privacy. But she also cooked for him, cleaned for him, invited his mother over for Thanksgiving, and brought food to his place when he needed to be by himself. Rodney took it all for granted. He told her he'd put an engagement ring on layaway, but she wondered if he did it not because he wanted to but because he thought he was supposed to. Naimah told me, "I'm seeing a side of him that I never saw before. It's affecting not just me, but my kids. Nashawn said, 'Where's Daddy?' and I told him he's not going to be here anymore. He started crying. He said, 'He didn't tell me!'" She cursed herself for failing to protect Nashawn from more heartbreak. "There's so much hurt now. Rodney's not progressing as a person. I tell him, 'You like that negative life.'"

She thought she had good reason to act the way she did. When she was growing up, her mother put her in the care of her grandmother so she could spend more time in the streets, getting high. Naimah missed her mother so much that she often barged into her room and found her cutting lines, or in bed with someone. Maybe that had something to do with her youthful attraction to bad men. After becoming a model, Naimah met a wealthy, older guy who lavished gifts on her, cheated on her, beat her—"just like Ike and Tina"—and got her pregnant with Nashawn soon after her high school graduation. The boyfriend left, and after Nashawn was born she met Zion's father, also abusive. "So when Rodney says, 'You don't understand, I got shot,' I say, '*Both* of us have had something deep happen to us. I've been beat up, been through hell and back. I don't look at you and say I've been through too much so I can't be with you. I'm showing you there's life after that.'"

The tension thawed a bit when Rodney went on Facebook and saw that Naimah had offered one of her girlfriends a plate of food for dinner. He sent her a message asking if she had room for him. He was half joking, testing to see how she'd respond. She invited him over. "We're trying to work it out," Rodney reported afterward. But back at Naimah's he still felt constricted. And they continued to fight over the same things: trust, jealousy, Rodney's inability to communicate.

"It's over," she told him during another quarrel. "Your heart isn't in this." He left, and she refused to take his calls. She asked for her keys back, but he wouldn't give them until she returned his computer. She had her mother bring it over, and the screen was cracked. Rodney accused her of breaking it on purpose.

With Rodney and Naimah each venting to me about the other, I did my best to bring them back together. I reminded Naimah that it had been ages since Rodney's last serious relationship, and he required patience. I urged Rodney to talk to Naimah. When Rodney balked, I told him that leading a fulfilling life didn't require him to cut himself off from meaningful relationships with women; in fact, such bonds could make his life richer. Rodney went back to Naimah, but when I visited a few days later, I found him alone in her bedroom while the rest of the family got ready for dinner.

"I'm just having trouble adjusting to the situation," he said. "I'm so used to being independent and having only myself to depend on."

"But you have people who *want* to take care of you," I said.

Rodney grimaced. "I just need to adjust. I'll figure it out."

The next time they fought, instead of leaving, Rodney talked it out with Naimah. He called me and exclaimed, "That shit works!"

On a Saturday night in mid-November, a couple of hundred white, wealthy residents of the Newark suburbs packed into a banquet hall for a charity fund-raiser that would underwrite efforts to help poor and underserved residents of the city. The banquet hall, called Il Tulipano, was in Cedar Grove, where many of Newark's Italians had moved in the 1950s and 1960s. Suburban Essex County was dotted with big, garish venues like this one, which hosted weddings, sweet-sixteen parties, retirement dinners, and other celebrations, often several at a time. Massive crystal chandeliers hung from the ceilings, murals of a generic Italian countryside covered the walls, and marble tile lined the dance floor. If you wanted to name the architectural style, you could call it Late Century Sopranos Kitsch.

Tonight's dinner and silent auction was hosted by Respect Challenges, a newly created nonprofit organization with a mission to "teach young people how to make healthy life choices through education," in part through grants to community groups. Rodney's friend Jeff served on the board of Respect Challenges, which had picked Rodney as one of a half-dozen grant winners. The recipients were invited to give short speeches about their proposals, and the amount each of them received depended on the generosity of the people in the room. With Rodney were representatives from a shelter for battered women, a group that prepared care packages for needy families, and another group that taught people how to pull themselves out of poverty. Together, the emcee said, they would "weave a tapestry of hope" in New Jersey's largest city.

Rodney rolled to the front of the room wearing a new brown wool knit zip-up jacket with matching pants, a brown and white argyle sweater, and a brown knit skullcap. He took a long moment to collect his thoughts while the room fell silent. "Yes, good evening, my name is Rodney Mason." His bass voice boomed from the speakers and resounded off the walls. "The video y'all getting ready to see is a video I did down on Elizabeth Avenue in Newark, New Jersey, coaching kids playing baseball. I let everyone know, but it ain't no secret, that there's so much poverty and violence going on down there, and I'm just trying to make a change down there. And it's all about coaching baseball. So far so good. It started out with four kids and it done branched out to at least fifty to a hundred kids now, and I'm still working down there. So what I'm trying to do now is do a four-week baseball camp a month before the season starts to get the kids ready to play baseball. Most of the kids I done helped and coached, they didn't know nothing about baseball at all. Since I've been coaching they're learning and I'm teaching them on the everyday basics. Thanks."

Then the lights went down for a screening of the *ABC World News* segment from the summer of 2008. Rodney sat to the side in silhouette as the audience watched, rapt, then burst into laughter when Versace sprung into his triumphant flips. When the lights came back on, everyone stood and clapped. Some whooped. A bolt of pride ran through me, giving me goose bumps. Rodney hardly broke a smile.

"Go Eagles, right?" the emcee said after the lights went up. "Rodney, it would be wonderful if you were able to extend and expand the work you're doing with those young boys. We hope to be able to help you with your baseball camp and see those young people learning life skills you're teaching them. So, thank you for your work, Rodney."

Rodney returned to the table, and several men lined up behind him to introduce themselves.

"I need you to make me a wish list," one told him.

"My son has a $250 metal bat that he doesn't use," another said. "What can I do with it?"

A third stepped up, telling Rodney that he knew someone who could donate equipment. A fourth stuck his hand out to shake Rodney's, but when Rodney grabbed it, he found a wad of bills in his palm. "A little something to help you out," the man said. Then they posed for a photo together, moneybags flashing whitened teeth and Rodney looking bewildered. Later, as he was leaving, another man rushed up and said he coached a Little League team in the suburbs and wanted to meet the Eagles. Only as Rodney got into Jeff's car did his poker face soften and he let himself savor the moment. "Damn," he told me, "I think I really did something with myself."

When he got to Naimah's, he told her all about his big night, and she congratulated him. She would have liked to have been there, to cheer for Rodney and boast that he was her fiancé. But Rodney hadn't invited her.

CHAPTER 19

The Aspen Place public housing complex, built in the 1950s, comprises a half-dozen apartment buildings, each eight stories and shaped like a T, clustered around a rectangular parking lot on the eastern edge of Passaic. From the windows of the project's upper floors, you can make out some of the blackened-brick carcasses of cotton and wool mills, rubber plants, and paper manufacturers that once drove the local economy. The apartments in the back of the low-rises, at the stem of each T, overlook Route 21, a narrow highway that hugs the river and emits a perpetual rush of speeding engines and whooshing air that seeps through walls and windows and fills living spaces with an ambient drone. Spend enough time there and the sound dissolves into the back of your mind and becomes a kind of white noise that, in Derek's case, lulled him to sleep each night as he lay beside his father in his sister Latoya's living room in the autumn of 2009.

This was not exactly what Derek envisioned when he anticipated reuniting with his dad, who'd just returned from a cross-country search for work that ended with him strung out and homeless. Since his departure last spring, he'd made Derek many promises—first, to bring him along; then to send for him once he got settled; and finally, after the trip began to go awry, to take Derek on vacation when he made it back. He now vowed to find a construction job and save enough cash to rent "a nice little apartment" where each of them would have their own room, unlike the last time they lived together, when they'd shared a bed. No one saw much reason to expect that this latest pledge would turn out any different from the others. Derek knew not to get excited, but he nevertheless nurtured a spark of possibility that this time his father would prove the doubters wrong.

Derek had returned to Latoya's after spending the summer in Newark with his grandmother Irene, who was preparing to move into a senior citizens center that didn't allow children as tenants. Irene still could not get around well, so Derek ended up stranded most days in her apartment. The indoor routine that seemed so agreeable last winter—watching cable, playing video games, cooking for Grandma, and cruising the Internet for a rock group in need of a drummer—became, in the summer, torturously monotonous. The only times Derek was allowed out of the house was for church on Sundays, a day at a water park with his older half brother, and a sultry afternoon watching the Eagles get knocked out of the play-offs. Derek and Irene argued over her refusal to let him go outside on his own. The breaking point had come in August, when Derek flew into a rage, cursed her out, and threatened to burn her with a hot iron while she sat in her wheelchair. She called the police, but by the time they arrived Derek had calmed down and acted as if nothing had happened. The officers seemed uninterested in filing a report, but Irene was too shaken to remain home alone with him. She called Derek Sr., who'd gotten home days earlier, and told him it was his turn again. Broke and jobless, Derek Sr. had no choice but to bring his son back to Latoya's. He applied for welfare benefits in Derek's name and tried to pick up where they'd left off five months earlier. They played catch and talked about girls and sports—"the basic father-son thing," Derek told me—and at night, as Derek lay on Latoya's sofa, his father, on the floor, would tell Derek that he was finally going to make things right.

Derek began seventh grade at Lincoln Middle School, a century-old building with sixteen hundred students, most of them children of Latin American immigrants who, by all appearances, were the single demographic and economic force keeping Passaic functioning. The school district was one of New Jersey's poorest, in the same state-aid category as Newark's, with all but a small percentage of students qualifying for free or reduced-price lunches. Derek was among the hundred or so black kids at Lincoln, which presented somewhat of a culture shock. But Derek tried to adapt. He signed up for the school band, gamely ate the curious-looking empanadas in the cafeteria, and fulfilled a promise to himself to make one new friend on the first day of school: a white Hispanic boy named Noel who played guitar and piano and shared Derek's desire to start a band.

As the new boy, Derek tried to assimilate the best way he knew how: by goofing off. He made dumb jokes, drum-rolled his fingers on desktops, and ignored much of what his teachers tried to tell him. He often arrived at school without pencils or pens or notebooks, and needed constant prodding to follow directions. Soon he was among a small group of boys who played the dozens, slapped and tripped each other in the aisles, and chattered and chuckled until they got kicked out of class. Sometimes, Derek landed in the office of the vice principal, who placed him in a "behavioral modification program"— detention, basically—where he sat in a room with other troublemakers to catch up on his work. It didn't help. Twice, the school called his father to meet his teachers. During the conferences, Derek Sr. seemed genuinely concerned—he told Derek he expected better and made him promise to try harder.

His teachers puzzled over him. He wasn't a mean or malicious boy but saw misbehaving as the most effective way to make an impression. He was clearly intelligent: he read as well as just about anyone in class and showed spunk in his writing. But he seemed unwilling to put in any effort in the subjects he found difficult. He turned in assignments half-done or claimed that he'd lost them. When a teacher told him that he'd received an F, Derek replied, "Oh," and didn't ask why. His math teacher, Naomi Glugeth, feared he had a learning disability and noticed that he wore dirty and ill-fitting clothes. She kept him after class one day to try to figure out what was wrong, and Derek told her about his mother's death and the circumstances that had led to his moving in with his sister and dad. Glugeth empathized but told Derek that it did not give him an excuse to make trouble. "Life isn't fair," she told him, "but do your best anyway. When life hands you lemons . . ."

"I know," Derek interrupted. "Make lemonade."

Despite his solicitous appearances at the parent-teacher conferences, Derek Sr. was rarely around at home, where Derek needed him. He disappeared for days at a time, and when he returned it was usually before Derek came home from school. Women called for him at all hours, and Latoya got so aggravated that she canceled her home number, got a new one, and put a block on it so only people she knew could get through. She wondered what her father was doing with the welfare money he was receiving in Derek's name. "I'm personally going on the assumption that he's using it to buy alcohol," she told me. Latoya picked up the slack, pressing Derek on his homework and trying to punish him when he didn't come straight home after school. But Derek did not consider her an authority figure. She was his sister, not his mother, and refused to listen. Derek admitted to me that he was "a little bit mad" at his father and was directing his anger at Latoya.

Drums were his escape. He hadn't learned to read music, and never had a lesson, but he'd been banging on drums since he was a toddler and emulated his cousin Ozias, who played in Newark gospel bands. He obsessed over YouTube videos of his favorite musicians: Aaron Spears, a gospel drummer, and Joey Jordison of Slipknot, a metal band from Iowa whose members dressed in grotesque costumes and played songs with titles like "Psychosocial" and "Pulse of the Maggots." With his snare and drum pad back in Newark, Derek practiced the only way he could: palms slapping his lap, feet tapping the floor, beat-boxing the sound of cymbals. His incessant patter drove Latoya and his teachers crazy. While they rolled their eyes or pleaded with him to stop, Derek drifted off into his own world, mouth slack, eyes dreamy.

Whenever he could, Derek hung out in the Lincoln Middle School band room, where he thrilled other students with solos that mimicked the intense, double-bass style of Spears and Jordison. After school, he walked home with Noel, and they jammed in his room. At night, the boys spent hours on the phone, Noel noodling riffs on his end while

Derek pounded out beats on Latoya's kitchen tabletop. They pulled out notebooks and came up with lyrics—*Chasing a dream is like chasing a star, when you're almost there it seems like it's far*—until Latoya's cordless phone ran out of power. For Derek's birthday, Noel gave him a black Slipknot shirt, which became part of his rock-and-roll uniform, along with a rhinestone stud earring in his left ear, a pair of faded acid-washed jeans with drumsticks poking from a back pocket, and black and white Nikes. He described everything he liked as "freaking awesome," a phrase he picked up from a Slipknot interview he saw online.

In his regular updates to Irene, Derek told her everything was fine. But Irene didn't believe it. She'd never trusted Derek Sr.; he was, in her view, not a real parent, "just the sperm donator." And she hardly knew Latoya. She suspected them of feeding Derek a diet of TV dinners and Chinese takeout and failing to keep him dressed in clean clothes. She had Derek return to Newark for a weekend, where she did his wash and took him shopping. Like Latoya, Irene wondered what Derek's father was doing with the welfare money.

In December, Latoya kicked Derek Sr. out of her apartment, hoping it would compel him to sober up. She called DYFS to put the situation on record and the local welfare office to have his benefits canceled. But that put her in a jam. She could not afford to continue taking care of her daughter and Derek by herself. She and Irene and Mary came to an informal agreement in which she would continue housing Derek for the remainder of the school year, and Irene would let Derek sleep on her couch on weekends and holidays. In each apartment, Derek stored a few sets of clothes and some other personal things in a lidded plastic bin six cubic feet in size. Derek didn't complain about his predicament—he said he was just hoping "to go with the flow"—but sometimes he let himself think how nice it would be to stay in the same home for more than a few months at a time. To have his own bed. To stay in the same school. To make friends and keep them. Those were luxuries he'd never known. Still, he refused to blame anyone, at least not aloud. "Everyone has problems," he told me.

As Derek's weekday parent, Latoya began fielding the distress calls from school. Sometimes she had to leave work in the middle of the day to talk to Derek's teachers about how he'd missed another assignment or disrupted class. Derek was failing three subjects—math, science, and language arts—and he was sent to Saturday school to avoid having to repeat the seventh grade. Latoya questioned how he spent the hours after school when she was at work and often caught him lying about his whereabouts. "Passaic isn't anywhere near as bad as Newark, but you never know," Latoya told me. "I need peace of mind. I don't want to go crazy looking for him." Over dinner one night, she warned Derek that she wouldn't let him play baseball next spring unless his grades improved and he stopped lying. Derek said nothing, just rubbed his face and played with his food. Latoya sighed. Sometimes he seemed no more mature than her daughter, who was less than half his age. But she felt for him. It must have been stressful not knowing where you were going to live one month to the next.

Just before Christmas, Derek's father announced he was checking himself into the drug rehabilitation facility where he'd met Derek's mother, Gail, more than a decade earlier. He wrote a letter endorsing Latoya as Derek's temporary caregiver and got it notarized. He expected to stay in rehab for anywhere between six months and a year; Latoya told him to take his time and do what he had to do to get well.

Derek became further unmoored. His teachers decided that none of their efforts were having any discernible effect. They recommended him for School Based Youth Services, a form of in-school counseling. But it, too, did no apparent good. Derek wouldn't talk about the sessions, and the only thing his counselor revealed to Latoya was that he was afraid to discuss his problems with her. Latoya sat him down one evening and said: "Something's wrong with you. Something's going on with you. Why don't you tell me? I'm here. You don't have to go to a stranger to talk." She began to cry, and he just looked at her, his face revealing nothing.

The only hint of what was troubling Derek came in a letter to his father. For his first few weeks in rehab, Derek Sr. was not allowed to contact anyone, including his family. But once that probationary period ended, he wrote Derek, apologizing and saying that when he got out he wanted to move to Maryland and take Derek with him. Derek wrote back, complaining that no one ever bothered to ask what *he* wanted to do or where *he* wanted to live. If someone *did* ask him, he wasn't sure what he'd answer, because he never wanted to choose one relative over another. But it would have been nice to at least have a voice.

During a break from school in February 2010, I picked Derek up for lunch. Things were getting better, he said. Latoya had managed to get Derek's welfare benefits transferred to her, which she used to buy extra groceries and an air mattress. She set up long-delayed doctor appointments, including a visit to replace his lost pair of glasses; without them, Derek could not recognize Latoya from down the hallway or read the writing on a classroom chalkboard. His work in Saturday school had eliminated two of his Fs, leaving only one, in math. He and Latoya still argued about his grades, but, by and large, they were at peace.

He asked if we could go see Rodney. It had been many months since they'd spoken, and he wanted to say hi. Derek was beginning to think about baseball season, and he hoped that he could somehow return to the Eagles; he thought Rodney might make him a captain. We stopped by Naimah's, and Rodney, surprised by the visit, reached for him. Derek leaned in for a hug. "You got tall, boy," Rodney said, squeezing Derek's arms. "You're going to hit some home runs." Rodney told Derek he wanted him to play catcher for the Eagles next year. When we left, Rodney gave Derek a permission slip for his baseball camp.

In March, Latoya returned home late from work and found the apartment empty. She called her sister, who reported seeing Derek at a high school basketball game. She had told him to go home, and he had refused. When he finally showed up later that night, Latoya pushed him onto the couch and threatened to call DYFS and have him removed from her house. He started clapping sarcastically, saying, "That's what I wanted." He called her a bitch, she slapped him, and he stormed out. He slept at a neighbor's apartment, went to school the next day, then spent the weekend in Newark. Irene told him he needed to show

Latoya more respect because there was no other place to go. "Derek needs a psychologist's help," she told me. "He's hurting. He is really, really hurting. The way he grew up, he always felt his parents never wanted him. When he gets older, who knows what he's going to do? We got to get him help now."

Derek returned to Passaic Monday morning and went straight to school without talking to Latoya. He came home late and fell asleep on the couch. Latoya inflated his air mattress and helped him into bed, and the next morning she asked if he wanted to leave. He looked at the floor and shook his head. That night, she told him: "If something's bothering you, bring it up. It's not like I'll get mad or curse at you or go off on you. Just say it and we'll talk about it. I'd rather talk when I'm not angry." Without looking up, he mumbled, "Okay."

Latoya told me she was running out of patience and didn't know what to do. "He doesn't talk to me so I don't know what's going on. I can't remember him ever opening up to me. I think everything that's going on as far as my dad, his mom, the living situation, he's just taking in a lot. He doesn't know how to express it but to misbehave or just shut down. I don't understand why he doesn't trust me enough, trust anyone."

She called her father. At rehab, along with therapy and 12-step programs, Derek Sr. was taking parenting classes, where clients learned how to improve their relationships with their estranged children. Latoya suspected that her father was afraid of taking care of Derek alone, of being a full-time parent after so many years on the periphery. But now was the time for him to step up. She told him, "I don't know what to do or what to say. I don't know how to help him. *You* need to talk to Derek."

CHAPTER 20

Just before the start of the 2009 school year, Thaiquan Scott moved his family out of their house on Peshine Avenue and into another on the edge of the South Ward, closer to downtown. It was not exactly moving up. In fact, despite all the crime that surrounded them on Peshine, Thaiquan was leery of leaving that neighborhood for another that could be worse. But he didn't feel like he had much of a choice. Shamira, his wife, had started night school to become a respiratory therapist, a sacrifice they hoped would pay off in the long run but for now made their hectic pace of life even more frenzied: Thaiquan worked from eleven at night to seven in the morning, Shamira worked from seven in the morning until three in the afternoon before heading to class, and somehow in between they shuttled five children to and from school, practice, games. "Not much time to sleep," Thaiquan said. "I'm running off of fumes."

Their new place was owned by the Newark Housing Authority, where Thaiquan and Shamira had submitted an application months earlier. The agency offered them a three-story, four-bedroom unit at the end of an L-shaped cluster of town houses on Chadwick Avenue. When Thaiquan saw the address, he thought, *Damn, Chadwick?* Just saying the name made him feel on edge. Anyone who knew the streets knew Chadwick's reputation; it was supposedly controlled by the Bloods. One night he drove by to check out the complex and immediately picked up on the not-so-subtle signs of drug activity: guys posted outside, ducking into back lots, doing furtive business in the street-lights' shadows. On one corner, near Avon Avenue School, menacing-looking young men carefully eyed the traffic that moved past them as they drew on flavored cigars.

The Scotts' town house was set off from the street, accessible by a short driveway that ended in a small parking lot flanked by a scrim of scrawny trees. This courtyard effect made it seem as if they were sepa-rated from what was happening on Chadwick. But maintaining a real-istic sense of detachment required some vigilance. Just before they moved in, Thaiquan politely but firmly approached one of the dealers and told him that his family lived there now and the kids needed a place to play. The dealer backed off, aware that complaining neighbors were bad for business. Every so often, Thaiquan or his father-in-law noticed people slipping through a "cut" in a fence that lined the rear of the property, or idling in cars, and told them to "get that up out of here." The trespassers always went quietly. "As long as they don't come in this courtyard here where my kids play at, I'm good," Thaiquan said during one of my early visits to his new house. "It's for the police to arrest them up there."

The town house complex had been built fairly recently, within the last decade or so, but the cheap construction was already showing signs of serious wear. Thaiquan let his children romp on the spit of mottled grass outside their door, but he forbade them from venturing any farther. Since no one went anywhere on foot, routine trips in the minivan took on the atmosphere of adventure, with kids piling into the seats to accompany Thaiquan to the store, run errands, or to col-lect their siblings. "We come, we go, we keep the kids busy," Thaiquan told me. "Maybe people think we think we're better than them because we don't keep the door open like in the projects, or have people com-ing and going. But we moved here because it was space, and rent wasn't so bad."

Inside, the Scott household operated at various degrees of frenzy. On typical afternoons, girls in braids and cornrows wearing embroi-dered jeans and brightly colored T-shirts bounced around the living room. They snapped folded-paper fortune-tellers, passed around a handheld SpongeBob SquarePants video game, ate from a pot of instant noodles, and gnawed on gobs of Mike and Ikes. Often they were joined by the children of Thaiquan and Shamira's close friends, whom the kids called their cousins; the youngest one, a girl who was just learning to crawl, would get passed from lap to floor to lap and fed whatever the other kids were eating. Nasir and Kaneisha, the two oldest, disappeared into their bedrooms upstairs, emerging to fix a snack or complete their weekly chores, which included scrubbing the stove, sink, dishes, and kitchen counters. Shamira's amiable father sat on the couch, watching talk shows and reruns and taking smoke breaks out the back door, grinding butts into an empty tuna fish can.

Thaiquan left for work with the house teeming and returned as it was waking. He shuttled the kids to school, crashed for a few hours, and rose just before he had to pick them up. All five children attended different schools, none of which met with his and Shamira's approval. That autumn, in what had become an annual ritual, they submitted applications for the kids to be included in the lotteries of several of the city's most popular charter schools. They estimated that they'd put in about twenty applications in all, and they were starting to wonder if the paperwork ended up in the trash. But Thaiquan and Shamira persisted. They had friends and colleagues who talked about how much more attention and discipline their kids were getting in charters: long days, intensive reading instruction, uniforms, lots of homework. The charters were controversial, drawing fire from critics who claimed they drained resources from traditional public schools and skimmed the best students, but Thaiquan and Shamira thought they deserved the chance to be included in the education reform movement sweeping Newark. "It's the structure. The organization. Something about it gives you a sense of pride," Thaiquan said. "They're taking these kids back."

At Beth Israel Medical Center, where Thaiquan worked the emergency room intake desk, doctors completing their residencies nominated him for employee of the year. He won. They invited him to their graduation and gave him their numbers in case he ever needed a hand.

"Anything you want to be you can still be," one of them told him. "We're all behind you. But we need you to take the next step." Thaiquan had yet to decide what that move was because it sapped most of his strength to make it through each day. Working in the ER night after night, he saw firsthand how tenuous life could be, how quickly your future could be snatched from you. That was what propelled him, although the stress and sleep deficit sometimes snuck up and overcame him. For reasons he could not quite understand, these moments most often occurred on Monday mornings, after the last child had been dropped at school and he began his short ride home in the empty minivan. The abrupt silence felt suffocating, and to fill the void his mind drifted to friends and family he'd lost in recent years: his father, his grandmother, countless cousins and "comrades" shot in the streets or off in prison. He thought about whatever crisis was facing any number of his children at the moment and how desperately he wanted to make everything turn out okay; there always seemed to be another obstacle in the way, another potential calamity that required evasive action. He drew so much motivation from his wife and kids, and wanted to protect them so badly, that the burden of his love sometimes seemed too much to bear. By the time he steered into the town house parking lot, he was heaving over the steering wheel, cheeks wet with tears.

Thaiquan worried most about Nasir. He was a good kid—decent student, talented athlete, considerate brother—but he was thirteen now, and he was starting to change. He'd just brought home his first Fs and had received a warning that he was in danger of being held back. He snapped at teachers. He got suspended for throwing an orange in the hallway, breaking a light fixture. Instead of punishing Nasir, Thaiquan tried talking to him. He told Nasir he had a chance to graduate from high school, go to college, and pull himself and his sisters "out of the ghetto." But he had to believe in himself. Thaiquan recounted the story of an old friend of his in Atlanta who blew his chance at a Division I football scholarship because he let his GPA slip. "I want you to go to school and *be* somebody, even if you don't become a baseball, football, basketball player," Thaiquan urged. "Be *better* than me. Raise the bar *up*."

But Nasir seemed deaf to Thaiquan's words. Thaiquan blamed Nasir's mother. He still believed that she abetted his devil-may-care attitude. Adding insult, she'd just filed a request to obtain full custody of Nasir. Thaiquan didn't seriously believe she would prevail; she had tried before and failed, and Thaiquan and Shamira still had the more stable home and jobs. But it required Thaiquan to hire a lawyer, costing money he did not have, and that infuriated him. Sometimes he fantasized about moving to Georgia, where he had family, just to keep Nasir away from her.

Thaiquan was so wrapped up in his fight for Nasir that he barely had time to concentrate on Kaneisha, who was struggling through her first year at Malcolm X. Shabazz High School. A quiet homebody, Kaneisha tended to thrive in intimate settings, whether in class or in the Eagles dugout, where she'd mothered her Eagles teammates. Thrown into mainstream classes at Shabazz, Kaneisha had held her own for a while, bringing home As from her video production class and Cs in the others. But in late autumn, she fell behind. Shamira took away the cell phone her biological father had bought her during one of his weekend visits. When she examined her daughter's text message log, she came across some notes from her father that were sexually explicit.

Shamira was the tech-savvy one—Thaiquan hardly checked his voice mails and didn't have an e-mail account. She, on the other hand, was always connected, punching out texts and updating her Facebook account and returning e-mails as soon as she got them. She confronted Kaneisha, who said that her father had tried to force himself on her, but she fought him off. When Shamira asked why she hadn't said anything earlier, Kaneisha answered that she was afraid no one would believe her.

Thaiquan felt awful for not seeing any warning signs. He wondered if by focusing on making things right with Nasir, he'd failed to protect her. How did he let this kind of evil come down on his family?

They went to the police and filed a complaint, and a state-hired therapist was brought in to counsel Kaneisha. In those sessions, Kaneisha seemed to blame herself for what had happened and expressed concern that she would not be allowed to see her siblings on her father's side. She also was afraid of running into her father, who had been showing up after school, trying to talk to her about the allegations. Thaiquan and Shamira got a judge to sign a restraining order against him, but the case proceeded excruciatingly slowly. Shamira kept calling for updates and heard nothing. It seemed to Thaiquan that the city, especially the police, didn't care. "If this happened in South Orange or Old Bridge"—the suburbs—"they would have been on it, but since this is the Bricks, they're dragging their feet," he told me. Fed up, he picked up a childhood friend, Al-Samad, and they went looking for Kaneisha's father. "If he's out there," Thaiquan announced, "I'm going to whoop his ass." They pulled up to the father's house and saw him standing outside. Thaiquan crept from the car, came through the front gate, and chased him up the steps. The father slammed the door, and Thaiquan would have kicked it off its hinge if Al-Samad hadn't stopped him.

At home, Shamira pleaded with Thaiquan to be patient, to remember what could happen if he got arrested. *Think about how far we've come*, she told him, *and where we are now, and how far we still have to go*. Thaiquan thanked God for Shamira, always there to talk him down from his rages. She was his counterweight, calm and even-tempered, with a remarkable ability to see a problem, even the most personal, with just the right amount of perspective. She had a reasoned way of speaking to him that softened his jangled nerves. Problem was, his anger always boiled back.

"It's turmoil, man," Thaiquan told me one December day at his kitchen table, shaking his head and kneading a pillow on his lap. Recounting Kaneisha's ordeal, he broke down in tears, and it took a minute or two for him to compose himself. "I'm an emotional guy. I wear my pride on my sleeve. My kids mean everything to me. I live for them, and for something like that to happen under our noses . . ." His moist eyes fixed on the ceiling. "We got to change the shit that goes on here. We got to do better." Then he looked straight at me, his hands still jammed in his lap. "Motherfuckers like that, they need to put all them motherfuckers up in front of a *firing squad*. That's my *stepdaughter*. Maybe it could have been worse if my wife wasn't really looking. It was probably God making her look at that cell phone, seeing what was in there. Everything was on the up-and-up, and then this shit come. You never seen him at no game. He never did *nothing* for her. The first bike she ever had, *I* bought for her. I'm not tooting my own horn, but that's *my* child there."

Kaneisha didn't like trouble. She preferred watching the Disney Channel with her little sisters rather than going out with friends. She wanted to grow up to be someone who took care of people. She'd impressed her parents with her maturity and determination. Now Thaiquan worried about the lasting consequences of not only the alleged molestation but of Kaneisha's knowing that her father was still out there. "She's a physical kid. She ain't no pushover," Thaiquan said, working the pillow like a stress ball. "But who's to say what type of mental effect it will have?"

Thaiquan and Shamira tried to maintain a shield around their children. They made sure they knew where the kids were at all times. They drove them wherever they needed to go. They ate dinner together and did not go out at night. But as Nasir and Kaneisha got older, and graduated from Little League and the age of innocence, that shield didn't seem as potent as they once thought. Thaiquan imagined danger, in some disembodied form, lurking in the shadows beyond his doorstep. But despite his angry musings about moving to Georgia, he didn't seem to seriously consider leaving Newark. "At one point I did tell my wife we're going to have to move," he said. "But why do I have to let the violence or what's going on out there run me away from *my* city? This is personal. I'm born and raised my whole life here. This is *my* city. Why do *we* gotta just get up and bail?"

CHAPTER 21

Since he could remember, DeWan had considered two men his fathers. Each of them floated in and out of his world with little predictability, and even after Joicki explained to him, when he was eight, the difference between them—"You came from his sperm," she said of his birth father. "And Kareem is my husband"—DeWan continued calling both of them Daddy. He attached no qualifiers or prefixes, like "biological" or "step," that would diminish their standing; in DeWan's heart, each was equally equipped to be his father, even if neither had proven himself. In the absence of true parenting, potential was enough to fuel his faith.

Hearing DeWan describe Kareem as his "daddy" irritated DeWan's biological dad but, not surprisingly, it had the opposite effect on Kareem, especially in the months leading up to his release from prison in late 2008. DeWan had every reason to resent Kareem for what he'd done to his family, but in that single word DeWan said, in effect, that he still needed Kareem, still believed in him, and still thought he could become the man they wanted him to be. Kareem drew inspiration from that. "He loves me like I'm his father," Kareem boasted in the fall of 2009, "and I love him like my son."

Then Kareem faltered. He got high and descended into an addict's gyre of destruction. He fought with Joicki, stayed out for days, then called from jail, crying to come back. That was when, for the first time I could tell, DeWan started addressing Kareem by his first name.

DeWan wasn't being vindictive; I doubted if he'd even thought it through. It was more a reflex, a spontaneous gesture that signaled his disaffection. Kareem understood that, and, once his head cleared, he vowed to earn back DeWan's trust. When he came home sober and full of promises again, DeWan rewarded him with "daddy" status.

This became a recurring cycle in which Kareem repeatedly relapsed and recovered and DeWan switched titles accordingly. The ups and downs became so frequent that I could barely keep track. One day, Joicki would be packing their things, saying they were leaving Kareem behind because he'd been "sniffing bags of dope" paid for by a loan shark who was now chasing him around the neighborhood. On another, she'd excuse him as "a lost black man trying to find his way" and she'd assure me they were going to make it. Later she'd report that she'd gotten a restraining order against him. "It's finally over. I hate him," she'd announce, adding that she wished she'd married somebody else, someone who gave a shit about having kids. But then I'd hear that they'd gone shopping together at Babies "R" Us and were talking about the advent of the next child as if it were some kind of marital baptism. On Christmas Day they got into a brutal fight outside their building and, a few days after, recalled it to me while nestled on the sofa, as if they were retelling another entertaining chapter in their topsy-turvy—and sometimes joyful—marriage. DeWan acted cool and nonchalant through it all, toggling between "Daddy" and "Kareem" with apparent equanimity. But I wondered if his reserve of forgiveness was dwindling.

On the last day of 2009, I stopped by the apartment, and DeWan answered my knock in a T-shirt and gray baseball pants. Joicki was running errands, Kareem was out somewhere, and little Kareem lay sprawled in front of the television, eyes fluttering at half-mast as he watched the film *AI*. The apartment had been reorganized again. I looked around and saw tokens of a new determination. Tacked to one wall was Kareem's "certificate of achievement" from the drug treatment program he'd completed before coming home. Next to it was a framed Scripture from the book of Joshua: "As for me and my house, we will serve the Lord." A hand-colored chart of the boys' household chores—read Bible, clean room, do homework, take bath, sweep floor—hung outside their bedroom. DeWan's trophies were arranged in a neat row on a shelf near a Wii video game system Joicki had given them for Christmas, along with books of all sorts: children's stories, religious tomes, literature from Joicki's college days, classics she'd grown up reading as an escape to the world outside Elizabeth Avenue. Alongside *Falling Up* by Shel Silverstein and *Great Expectations* by Charles Dickens was a study of Newark's education failures called *Ghetto Schooling* and a marriage guide called *I Don't Want Delilah, I Need You: What a Woman Needs to Know, What a Man Needs to Understand*.

DeWan called his mother to make sure she was on her way home, then excused himself to change. He emerged in a pair of skinny-fit blue jeans and spread a pink Ralph Lauren button-down across an ironing board. As he pressed it, his dreadlocks, which had been no more than nubs when we'd first met, swept across his eyes. After a few passes over the impossibly wrinkled shirt, he gave up and pulled it on, then slipped into a pair of canvas high-top Vans adorned with Popsicles and clouds. This was the skateboarder look he'd adopted after seeing a photo of Tony Hawk in *Sports Illustrated*. When he'd first asked Joicki for a pair of skinny jeans, she'd refused, because she didn't want him emulating the new narrow-assed version of the sagging-pants style that currently predominated on the street. He insistently padded around the house with rubber bands wrapped around the calves of his loose-fitting jeans until she relented. DeWan wore those skinny jeans every day until Christmas, when Joicki added an assortment of pairs in different colors, including red and yellow. "Can I get some skinny khakis, too?" he asked, jeans being forbidden at school. "Boy," she answered, "they don't sell *skinny khakis*!"

DeWan topped his outfit with a stylish, heavy flannel coat with epaulets, another Christmas gift. "Does this look like a girl's jacket?" he asked. I assured him it didn't. He checked his reflection in a mirror and flipped his dreads back, a habit that his social worker at TEAM Academy, Phaedra Ruddock, said made him look like he was in a shampoo commercial. DeWan announced that he was ready, and as we headed out, he hollered to his brother, "Don't answer the door for anyone until Mommy gets home." I noticed for the first time that his voice had dropped and deepened. At the elevator, I saw him slip a cell phone in his pocket. "Kareem's," he explained. I knew by his choice of words that something had gone wrong again. But when I asked what happened, DeWan looked uneasy. "He got in trouble and hasn't been home," he said. Then he asked if we could please not talk about it.

We drove up Custer Avenue and onto Bergen Street, the neighborhood's main commercial thoroughfare, and passed several young men bunched on a corner. "Those are the bay-bays," DeWan said. That was his shorthand for the "bad boys" who set upon many of his classmates as they walked to and from TEAM Academy. The principal and his staff stood vigil outside the building in an attempt to prevent attacks, but once the students disappeared from sight, the veil of protection evaporated. Lately, the TEAM kids were being tormented by a particularly malicious boy from Peshine Avenue School, but he didn't mess with DeWan. A few months ago, DeWan told me, he, William, and some other Eagles were walking from the park when they saw the bully and his crew coming toward them. William panicked and called his mother, while DeWan headed straight for them and offered an outstretched palm. The bully grinned and shook DeWan's hand, and the crew went on their way. "I probably was stupid for doing it, but I did it," DeWan said. "I think I wanted to prove that I wasn't scared. He probably thought I was trying to be funny. I could have been seriously injured."

I told DeWan I was impressed by his ability to diffuse the situation through friendly confrontation. The gesture was very DeWan, a reflection of his poised, mature side—the part of him that his mother and teachers wished he'd exhibit more often. They said he was "a deep thinker," "intelligent," possessing an acute sense of right and wrong and a sensitivity to injustice, but that made his academic underachievement and classroom mischief all the more aggravating: they knew he was capable of so much more.

DeWan worried he was failing them, the same way Kareem was failing him. His grades had sunk from a 3.0 last trimester to something under 2.0. His teachers warned that he was in danger of being held back, and his mother said he had to bring his grades up by spring or she wouldn't let him play baseball, which would be terrible, because Coach Rock was depending on him to lead the Eagles through the 2010 season. "Somehow I just started coasting, thinking I could do it easily, and I stopped doing the work," he said, frowning. "It's embarrassing." He was also ashamed about the way he'd been losing his composure lately. He and a classmate were playing the dozens the other day when the boy said something about DeWan's pregnant mother. "Yeah? So, your mom works at McDonald's," DeWan snapped. It wasn't a good joke. The boy's mother had actually taken DeWan's order there not long ago, which made it not only unfunny but mean. It was the kind of immature behavior DeWan criticized in Kareem and his classmates, but he often could be as bad as they were.

DeWan stared out the window as we left his neighborhood and headed north over Interstate 78 and into the Central Ward. The drive took us past a patchwork landscape that epitomized Newark's fitful evolution: a block of dilapidated wood-frame homes here, rows of newly built town houses there, a cluster of low-rise projects, a rundown but busy retail strip, the construction site of a gleaming new police headquarters, a movie theater whose opening seventeen years ago had been hailed as a symbol of Newark's resurgence, but had recently needed a financial bailout from the city. "Two more years, and I'm going to be in high school," DeWan pondered. Life was moving too fast. He didn't want to abandon boyhood just yet. He was still dwelling on that thought as we slid into a booth at IHOP and stared into oversize menus. He called a waiter over. "Can I get a children's menu?" he asked. "I'm not ready for this stuff."

The next time I saw DeWan, in early February, he was sitting at a small wooden desk facing the wall of the TEAM Academy principal's office, a bright yellow pinny pulled tight over his polo. I'd arrived planning to shadow him through his school day, but he'd gotten into another shouting match with a boy who'd made fun of his mother. A teacher overheard DeWan call the kid a pussy, which earned him a stint in "in-school detention." He was also on "the bench" for giving the finger to someone in class, which meant he wasn't allowed to talk to any other students. DeWan sat at that desk all day, doing homework, nodding off, trying to meet the eyes of passing girls, and wondering how his temper had gotten so difficult to control. When things got particularly rough at home, DeWan said, he retreated to his bedroom, where, "to get rid of the pain," he punched and screamed into his pillows, splashed cold water on his face, and turned to his sketch pad, drawing pictures of wide-eyed boys with flaming hair. "I get mad easily," he said. "My mother thinks I need counseling with Miss Ruddock about that."

Ruddock saw a connection between the turbulence at home and DeWan's troubles in school, but she told him (as the Passaic math teacher had told Derek) that it was no excuse. Many other students at TEAM Academy were dealing with similar scenarios, or worse; DeWan still had to get his homework done and come to school every day ready to learn. She'd signed him up for an after-school modern dance class, hoping it would have the same emboldening effect as last year's *West Side Story.* "He's one of those kids who are easily disappointed because he puts a lot of hope in people, and [Kareem] really let him down," Ruddock told me. "[DeWan] is run a lot by his emotions. I'm sad for him. It's like he's heartbroken."

DeWan had always been willing to grant Kareem another chance to earn back the title of "Daddy," but it was getting more difficult. Kareem had recently kicked in the apartment's front door in a late-night rage, bending it at a corner and rendering it impossible to lock. His mother filed a police complaint, and a judge ordered Kareem to seek counseling. DeWan told her he thought Kareem was a bum and that she was too lovey-dovey with him.

"Mom," DeWan said, "why are you living with him? Why can't you just leave?"

"Because I'm married and it's not that easy," she replied. "You don't just leave when you've made a commitment like that."

DeWan thought that was bull.

"He says he'll change and he never does," DeWan said from his detention desk. He looked at me with a frail grin, then pressed his hands together as if he was praying. "I hope we leave him," he said. "I *hope* so."

As much as DeWan pleaded, and as demoralized as she was herself, Joicki just couldn't let Kareem go. She wondered if it had to do with the fact that she'd grown up without a father in the house. She prayed for Kareem. She begged him to get help, told him she would need him when the baby came. She vowed not to dredge up their past because she knew how it hurt his confidence. But Kareem was sapping so much of her energy that DeWan worried she was losing focus on him and little Kareem. Joicki apologized to DeWan almost daily. "This is an experience we're all going through, and it's going to make us stronger," she assured him.

Joicki hoped the experience wouldn't discourage DeWan from getting married and starting a family of his own one day. Instead of letting DeWan explore and discover himself, Joicki felt the urge to cocoon him. "I just feel bad for him," Joicki told me in mid-February. "I don't want him to be hurt. My concern in life is that my children grow up healthy, mentally. I don't want him to grow up and be like, 'Oh, I did this because my father wasn't there,' or, 'I did this because my mother didn't tell me.' I don't want him to use no excuses. I just want him to be successful. More than I was."

Just after three a.m. on February 23, Kareem came home drunk and high and started banging on the door, apparently forgetting he'd already broken it. He woke everyone up, and Joicki refused to let him in.

"We feel unsafe," she told him. "You gotta go."

"Man, I just want to go to sleep."

"If you come in and go to sleep, I'm going to call the cops."

"You ain't gonna call the cops." And then he crumpled to the floor and passed out.

The police arrived and tried to remove Kareem from the apartment. Joicki didn't like the way they were handling him and told them so. Finding her "belligerent and pushy," they tried to restrain her and, because she was in the late stages of pregnancy, called for backup. As more officers crowded into the apartment, she and the boys grew more upset, and she threatened to call Internal Affairs. The officers pulled Kareem out, searched his pockets, and found two glass vials with cocaine residue. They took him to the local precinct, where they found an open warrant under his name for failing to show up for a prior court date. He was booked and sent to the Essex County Jail on the industrial outskirts of the East Ward.

Later that day, when I talked to DeWan on the phone, he sounded resigned, as if he wasn't surprised by anything anymore. "I'm fine," he insisted coldly. "I don't care. He deserved it after what he's done."

A week later, Joicki told me she'd attended a hearing to update a restraining order she'd taken against Kareem. Against her better judgment, she said she didn't want to pursue the matter any longer because Kareem had promised that when he was released he would go to counseling and live with his sister.

"Don't have the baby without me," he pleaded as she left the courtroom.

"Tell the baby," she said.

When she got home, she felt the first pangs of labor contractions. She told me she was done with Kareem holding her and the boys down. "I don't want him back," she said. "Everyone's at peace now, happy, talking. It's time to move on."

CHAPTER 22

Steering his wheezy scooter through the automatic sliding glass doors of the
Kessler Institute for Rehabilitation's entrance bay, Rodney felt the creep
of ghostly memories. Some details of the place remained vaguely
familiar—the placid-faced nurses, the lost stares of patients sunning
themselves under a window, the tangy olfactory cocktail of antisep-
tics and sanitizer. But most vivid was something he could not see or
hear or smell: the sense of emotional desolation. He had to stop a
moment in the lobby to regain his equilibrium. Perhaps this was why
he'd been avoiding this place for so long.

Rodney could handle most of the indignities that came with his
injury, but the one thing he could not abide was an unreliable wheelchair. Without a good chair, he couldn't go where he wanted or had to
rely on others to get there, which was humiliating. For months he'd
been getting by with a scooter too weak to handle hills and a manual
chair that seemed ready to come apart at any moment. He'd spent
most of winter indoors, at his place or Naimah's, depending on how
they were getting along. But his baseball camp was scheduled for
March, and the 2010 Little League season would begin soon after that.
He was desperate for new wheels.

Rodney made his appointment at Kessler weeks ahead of time, but
his medical-transport company still had him in its records as being
able to walk and would not allow him a Medicaid-subsidized pickup.
So I gave him a ride, and he let me join him in his consultation room,

where his doctor, Barbara Benevento, a woman with acerbic wit and long, thick brown hair, walked in and exclaimed in mock exasperation: "I haven't seen you in years, and *now* you want to see me? With a *reporter?*" She narrowed her eyes and scrunched her forehead, sizing up the scooter. It resembled one of those contraptions advertised on television as a way for the frail and elderly to get around the house—not designed for a six-foot, three-inch, 220-pound man. She perched on a swivel chair and examined Rodney's chart. She'd been seeing him on and off since the day he first showed up at Kessler, shoulders slumped and mumbling short, gruff answers to her questions. He looked the same, doleful and apologetic, only now with a beard. She noted the date of his last checkup and was surprised to see that it had been four years.

She began asking Rodney basic questions about his health, and he replied hesitatingly, almost in a whisper, listing his myriad problems: the festering, year-old skin lesion; a suspected urinary tract infection; the failure of his local medical supply store to keep him stocked with urine-disposal kits; the van mix-up. She shot him a look like a mother scolding a child. She appreciated his self-sufficiency, but he had gone so long without care and his problems had piled so deep that it would take a small team to dig him out. "You're out of the loop, and we need to get you in," she said.

Benevento called a nurse, and together they checked Rodney's sore, gave him meds, and comped him boxes of condoms and urine bags. She told Rodney to come back in a few weeks and urged him to quit the scooter because it was probably making his sore worse. Then she gave him what he'd come for: a prescription for a new manual wheelchair, the first step of a winding, bureaucratic process that would require stacks of paperwork and many return visits. Rodney asked how long it would take, and Benevento said a few months at best. She and everyone else at Kessler knew how difficult it was to get a new wheelchair approved by Medicaid. Even though it was the most essential piece of equipment for people with spinal-cord injuries, patients were only allowed to get a replacement every few years. When their chairs broke, many went to the secondhand market, borrowed from others, or appealed to someone's goodwill; Rodney had gotten his scooter from the family of a dead neighbor.

Before heading home, Rodney stopped by the rehabilitation gym to say hello to his former physical therapist, Denise Delorenzo. She hugged him tightly and told him how she still bragged to her patients about what he'd been able to do in the gym nearly fifteen years earlier. She told him she was pregnant with a boy and was thinking about naming him Rodney. "I wish I could bring you back to motivate the younger guys now," she said. She hung an arm over his shoulder, and Rodney looked down. For a moment he seemed just like the frightened but determined young man who'd wheeled away from her after their last session together in 1996, heading out into an uncertain future.

A couple of weeks later, a latch on Rodney's jury-rigged manual wheel-chair snapped, and he crashed to the floor of Naimah's apartment, his right shoulder absorbing the blow. Naimah tried to pull him up, but Rodney shook her off and sat there for a moment, pissed and humiliated, his bare butt showing above the slipped waistband of his sweatpants. He pulled himself onto her sofa and sat there for a moment, saying nothing. She begged him to pester Kessler for a new chair. He said it wouldn't make any difference; he'd wait until his next appointment. He spent most of the next few days inside, trying to figure out how he was going to make it to spring.

There was so much to do. He needed to find an indoor practice facility for his camp, along with instructors, coaches, food, and transportation. Respect Challenges, the philanthropic group that had agreed to fund the camp, would not give Rodney the money until he created his own tax-exempt nonprofit organization. And Reggie, the father of Versace and Rodney's most dependable assistant coach the last two seasons, had just announced that he was forming his own team, made up of children from Carmel Towers, including several Eagles. Rodney would now have to go on a last-minute recruiting spree to replace the kids Reggie signed up.

When he finally got to Kessler for his appointment, the doctors found that his blood pressure had skyrocketed and his bladder had begun to spasm, putting him at risk of a serious infection. They gave him medicine for both, replaced the wheels on his chair (the order for his new chair was still tangled in red tape somewhere), and warned him to take better care of himself. When he got home, he changed into a T-shirt, long underwear bottoms, gym shorts, and green wool socks. He lit up a Black and Mild cigar, wallowing in a plume of thick, sweet-smelling smoke.

He turned to a pile of clean laundry and began folding XXL-sized white T-shirts into thirds and stacking them on the sofa. His ceiling fan was spinning off balance, clacking in its fixture. On the street, Rodney said, people always told him, "You're the strongest person I know." They said it because they could not imagine living as he did. They pitied him, and Rodney couldn't blame them, because for years he had pitied himself. The Eagles had helped him escape that mind-set by showing him he could make a positive difference in people's lives. But now he wondered if it was worth the physical and emotional toll. Maybe he'd been kidding himself. Maybe he needed to accept that a paraplegic had no place on the ball field. He told me he was thinking about quitting.

That, I said, was a terrible idea. I challenged him to consider where he would have ended up if he'd never been injured. Would he have stopped dealing? Would he have decided to coach?

"There's no telling," he replied. "I *think* I would have. If I'd seen that field over there, even if I was walking, by me loving the game like I did, wanting to save kids' lives, I probably would have coached. So I'd say yeah." He blamed the devil for making him question himself and "keeping me from doing the things I want to do." But he said he also believed that God gave everyone choices, and it was up to him to make the correct ones. "You gotta do what's right, and in my heart, I know what I'm doing is right. There's nothing wrong with what I'm doing. So why should I stop? I'm doing a beautiful thing with these kids. The other thing that drives me? My mother." He frowned and fell silent.

Clara was ill again—with what he didn't know, because she didn't tell him anything. But he assumed it was serious; she'd stopped going outside and wasn't eating much. She'd been admitted to Beth Israel on three separate occasions in the past year, and each time Rodney didn't find out until a day or two later. Rodney tolerated her secretiveness because he was the same way; he never told her about his multitude of ailments because he did not want to make her worry. She was his biggest supporter and was more proud of him now than she'd ever been. What would she think of him if he quit? He didn't want to know.

Rodney's relationship with his mother baffled me. They still lived a few floors apart, spoke every day, and worried obsessively about each other. And yet they concealed so much. Each claimed to want to spare the other pain. But it wasn't healthy, this secrecy. What bothered me most was Rodney's refusal to ask Clara about his father. Rodney had not spoken of it since his early twenties, when he'd expressed his doubts to a family friend, who in turn confronted his mother and got her so upset. Rodney still ran into the people who claimed to be his half siblings, but he wouldn't betray his mother by even thinking they were right. He told himself he'd ask her one day, but he could never find the right time.

I decided to try to ask her myself. I knew I was meddling, but this was too important a detail, too open a question to let lie. Clara was a proud woman. She didn't like to show weakness. I'd heard that she hadn't let anyone see her cry when Rodney got shot or when her older son, Stephen, died from complications related to alcoholism in 1993. But still, someone had to ask. The truth could help Rodney get a better sense of himself, put his life into better perspective.

"I'm seventy-four now, and when you're my age you don't remember things anymore," Clara warned me as I entered her apartment on the twenty-fifth floor of Zion Towers one late winter afternoon. "So don't ask me to remember stuff." She was jabbing at her television remote, trying to find a soap opera that had been taken off the air for a college basketball game. Her wiry gray hair was pulled into a ponytail, and her skeletal frame was folded into her sofa, above which, on her living-room wall, hung rows of photographs of her parents, children, and grandchildren. There was a black-and-white portrait of her with her daughter Barbara on the day they graduated from Essex County College together in 1999, and a diploma from Rutgers-Newark, where she completed a bachelor's degree four years later. Two six-foot bookshelves were stacked with paperbacks, mostly thrillers and romances, titles she did not read but could not part with; they had belonged to Barbara, who died of cancer in 2006. On another shelf sat a trophy, given to Rodney after the 2008 season, with an inscription that said INSPIRATIONAL COACH OF THE YEAR. Behind the television, her window was cracked open, drawing drafts that swirled through the overheated apartment like jolts of cool water.

I asked her how she was feeling and she grimaced. Her ulcer still caused her intestinal distress. She suffered from a slipped disc in her back and was depressed because she hadn't felt strong enough to take assignments as a substitute teacher, the one thing that kept her busy. The antianxiety meds that her doctor prescribed made her throw up. He wanted her to see a therapist, but she refused; therapy was book talk, mumbo jumbo that only benefited the doctors who billed you. "You have to rely on yourself to face your own problems, what's bothering you," she said in her native Virginian drawl. "A therapist can't do that. You have to come to terms with your own problems." The phone rang, and Clara did not move. She let it go to her answering machine. It rang again. Still, Clara sat. "The bill collector has me stressed out," she explained. She'd answered an ad offering to consolidate the swollen balances on her credit cards, then, as she got too sick to work, fell deeper in debt.

"Rodney worries about you," I said.

She shook her head. "If I say I don't feel good, the phone will ring a hundred times. He'll come up here and say, 'What's wrong with you?' I'll say, 'Nothing is wrong with me, I'm all right.' He'll say, 'No, you're not.' He'll get more upset if I tell him. God bless his heart, I'm so glad he cares about me, but I just don't want to tell my kids nothing. If I tell them, they'll make me more upset than I already am."

I told her I found it curious that she and Rodney avoided burdening each other with their personal problems, because the withholding probably caused them even more stress. She smiled coyly, her gaunt cheekbones nudging the coaster-size eyeglasses resting at the end of her nose. "We're trying to protect each other," Clara said. "That's a family trait, being secretive. My father had prostate cancer for umpteen years and he's ninety-five years old. Didn't tell my mother nothing. He was ninety before we knew."

Politely as I could, I asked if she would tell me the story of Rodney's father. "That falls back on personal stuff," she said. "If it's in a book people will read it and hold stuff against you." I persisted, telling her how important it was to her son's story. A corner of her mouth curled disapprovingly and she stood up. "I'm going to have to smoke a cigarette now," she said.

She went to the open window, looked out over the neighborhood's roofs, and lit up. The horizon was lined crimson under the setting sun, and the sky above was darkening from blue to purple. Several long moments passed. She exhaled deeply, the smoke passing through the screen and dissolving into the outdoor air. Finally, she spoke. "I tell my kids their father was the one who passed," she sighed. "James. All of the kids." She did not shift her gaze from the sunset. The lights on the tips of downtown skyscrapers blinked red and white. She took another drag on her cigarette. "This is the thing. Me and my husband, James, separated many, many, many years ago. I was young, and he was out in the street fooling around, and we separated. But he was very abusive. *Very* abusive. He would leave and come back, and every time he came back I got pregnant." She took another slow drag.

"So. There was Barbara and Pam, and my son that passed, Stevie, those were the three. In the meantime, years passed and I did start going out with this other, with this guy. And in the meantime, I was having sex with both of them."

This, apparently, was more than she'd ever told Rodney. She slowed herself down, wondering, perhaps, how far to go. "I never questioned nothing," she said. "And he"—James—"accepted them as his own." The phone rang again, and Clara talked over the trill.

She told a story about an acquaintance who approached her in a hair salon not long ago and said she'd met one of Rodney's sisters. Clara asked which one. The woman said a name, but it was not Pam, or Barbara, or Darlene, none of her girls. It dawned on Clara that the woman was talking about one of her ex-boyfriend's kids. That got Clara very upset, and she told the woman that the "sister" was not Rodney's kin.

"Everyone has dark secrets," the woman pressed.

"Yes, but that's a lie," Clara snapped.

That was the last time she'd discussed the topic with anyone. She'd hoped to bury the matter on the day she laid James to rest and became a widowed mother of five. She did not see the good of bringing it back up. Wasn't it enough that she had raised and cared for her kids, alone, as best she could? What mattered was what she believed, and she believed that James was her children's only father. She raised her right palm to me. "So help me God, that other man was not Rodney's father." And that was all she was going to say on the subject.

I left assuring myself that I'd tried, and although I didn't quite get the answer I was looking for, I did have more information that might help Rodney find the truth. I just had to figure out how to tell him.

For two nights before the first Saturday of March, Rodney could not sleep. He'd plastered street poles and lobby walls with flyers announcing the "First Annual Rodney Mason Mentor Baseball Camp" and pestered any parent with a Little League–age child, but very few had signed up. Instead, just like anything anyone tried to organize in the neighborhood, commitment was put off until the last minute. He went around telling kids that they could just take a ride and see if they liked it. But there was no way to tell how many would show up for the weekend camp, and as the start date approached, all he could do was wait and worry. Lying awake in bed, he imagined an empty bus and the shame of having to explain how he had wasted the grant money.

It was a wonder, actually, that he made it this far. Though he hated begging, Rodney had reached out to anyone he thought might be able to help, and a small group of friends and acquaintances, including some members of the Jackie Robinson South Ward Little League committee, had rallied behind him. Soon he had an agreement with a batting cage complex in a nearby suburb, a bus company to shuttle the kids back and forth, and an arrangement from Respect Challenges to pay the bills directly. Naimah offered to prepare brown-bag lunches, and one of the men who'd approached Rodney at the autumn fund-raiser kicked in $400 for T-shirts.

On Saturday, March 6, Rodney rolled up to the camp's meeting spot at the edge of the park, where a yellow school bus waited. On the field, Reggie was hitting grounders to his new team, the Monarchs. When Rodney first heard about Reggie's plans to field his own team, he wanted to throttle him. But he set his ego aside and told Reggie he hoped their teams could practice together in the spirit of neighborhood unity. But the Monarchs were clearly on their own trajectory. They'd been running drills for weeks, while Rodney scratched around for fresh bodies to fill out his roster. He had a small number of Eagles returning this year, led by Jalil, the diminutive boy who used to suck his fingers, at second base, and DeWan, who would be one of the top pitchers in the league. Another boy, Naseer, a trash-talking holdover from the 2009 season, would play shortstop. Thaiquan's kids, Kaneisha and Nasir, were now too old to play Little League. But if Rodney could somehow get Derek to come back as his catcher, he'd have a solid core around which he could build a team. He couldn't depend on Derek, though. His grandmother Irene had already warned Rodney that Derek wasn't spending much time in Newark anymore and was having a lot of trouble at home. "I don't know if it's a good idea for you to get his hopes up about playing on your team," she'd said.

Gradually, Rodney's face relaxed, as a small crowd of campers formed on the sidewalk. Just before departure time, Rodney counted heads. Twenty-seven. He chuckled. Somehow he'd pulled it off. I admitted that I was surprised, given how bleak things had looked a few weeks ago, when I'd questioned his resolve. He smiled at me. "Once a hustler, always a hustler," he said. "*Never* count me out."

CHAPTER 23

From deep inside a dream, DeWan heard his mother calling for him. He could tell it was urgent but couldn't tell why. He lifted his head. His heart pounded. It was still dark outside but wouldn't be for long. His mother cried out again. She was in her bedroom, watching the clock, timing her contractions, the pain approaching unbearable. "Puda!" she cried. "I'm having the baby! Call 911."

DeWan gasped. "Ooh, yeah!" He found the phone, made the call, then sat a second. He told himself to stay calm. His mother needed him. She'd always said he'd make a great husband and father one day, and, with Kareem still in jail, now was his chance to prove himself, to show that he could be the man of the house. The dependable one.

The medics weren't very friendly: no chitchat, no smiles, no sharing in DeWan's awe at what was about to happen. They hustled Joicki into the ambulance and took off so fast that he barely got a chance to say good-bye. Joicki wasn't much for talking anyway, as focused as she was on getting the baby out. She'd already decided that she didn't want anyone accompanying her to the hospital or sitting at her side. She wanted this moment to herself, to be alone and in control of it to the extent that that was possible. The baby came quickly, in less than an hour, and with her last push she squeezed the hand of a nurse she'd never met. At 7:33 a.m., on March 10, 2010, Sir Elisha Welch—whose name Joicki and Kareem had chosen together, after the miracle-performing prophet from the second book of Kings—presented himself to the world, healthy and wailing like a gale.

Kareem showed up a week later, straight from the county lockup, knocking at Joicki's door after the boys had left for school. In his two weeks behind bars for criminal mischief, he'd been beaten by prisoners who suspected him of being in a rival gang, shared a tier with murderers, endured a twenty-three-and-a-half-hour-a-day lockdown, turned thirty-eight years old, and missed the birth of his son. He looked drawn and desperate. "I'm so sorry," he sobbed. "I'm so tired of this. I'm never going to do it again." Joicki wanted to believe him, as she had so many times before, because she still loved him and still thought her sons needed him. But she didn't want to risk putting the family through another cycle of hope and upheaval. She handed Kareem the baby but didn't let him stay long. She sent him to see her sister, who worked at the city welfare office and could get him placed in a shelter. "You've got to get yourself together," she said.

Later that day, when Joicki told me about Kareem's visit, I asked if she thought he'd been sincere. "Hell, no," she answered. She was wearing a pink sweat suit, her hair in a bandanna, her face flush with the weary bliss of new motherhood. "Well, I'm not going to judge. I can't judge. I don't know what's in his heart. But *been there, done that*, you know? I love Kareem, but I love my children, too, and I need them to have a better start in life than I did. Having Kareem in this home turned everything upside down. I gave him a hundred chances. I don't resent him and I don't regret anything, though. I'm just stronger and wiser."

She got up to use the bathroom, and while she was gone, DeWan burst into the apartment. The baby, a wrinkled, moist morsel of caramel skin and frizzy hair, woke with a squall. DeWan saw the ribbon of light under the bathroom door and dropped his book bag. He draped a burp rag across the shoulder of his white Aeropostale hoodie, leaned into the crib, and scooped the boy up. He rested Sir Elisha's belly against his collarbone. The crying stopped, and DeWan smiled contentedly. He'd exhausted enough energy worrying about Kareem and had decided that they could do this without him. DeWan had recently told his mother that he finally realized they weren't missing out on anything because they had each other; Kareem was the one alone. Joicki thought that was pretty profound for a boy his age.

At school, DeWan had a new adviser, the head of a new "boys group" for underperforming students, who liked to say, "It doesn't matter how hard life is. You should still be able to be successful." The adviser told DeWan he was at an age where he'd soon have to decide whether he would fulfill his potential or accept mediocrity—a choice that would have ramifications for the rest of his life. The message resonated with DeWan. He started staying up late studying and writing papers, including one in which he said he wanted to help change the perception of black boys as people who went to jail "for not thinking before their actions." His grades jumped. He took the advice of his social worker Phaedra Ruddock and signed up for a modern dance class, where he bounded across the gym floor looking as joyful and relaxed as she'd ever seen him. On a lark, he tried out for the school soccer team and made the cut. And soon, of course, there would be baseball. DeWan would probably be one of the league's best players this year, and Rodney had promised to make him the Eagles' captain.

DeWan slowly lowered himself into the sofa. He hooked his hands under his baby brother's armpits, held their faces close, and looked into the child's dark, moist eyes. He kissed Sir Elisha's forehead and sucked gently, producing a short, squeaky vibrato. "What's up, stinky butt?" Joicki returned, took the baby, and began to nurse him. Soon he was asleep in her arms. DeWan slid to the floor and began to do his homework at his mother's feet. A warm tranquillity fell over the apartment. If DeWan couldn't have his vision of a two-parent family, then maybe this was good enough.

The Straight and Narrow drug-rehabilitation clinic sat in the dusty shadow of Interstate 80 in Paterson, a hollowed-out former manufacturing hub a few miles north of Newark. It specialized in helping drug offenders avoid jail, which was how Derek's father ended up there more than a decade ago. Now he was there voluntarily, which earned him quizzical looks from the lifelong addicts with whom he bunked.

Straight and Narrow operated somewhat like a minimum security prison, or a halfway house, with strict limits on movement and communication, including a complete blackout—no letters, phone calls, or anything else from the outside—for the first twenty-eight days and a ban on visits for the first two months. But Derek Sr. didn't mind. In fact, he embraced the restrictions. Straight and Narrow had helped him get clean and stay that way until his recent relapse, and he knew he needed to submit to the highly disciplined environment if he was to ever regain control of his life.

The facility had not changed much, but among the additions was a Family Success Center, where fathers took classes aimed at helping them reconnect with their children. Every so often, the center hosted a Family Day, an extended visit with the clients' kids to test how they applied their new skills. The next Family Day, scheduled for a Sunday in the middle of March, came at a critical time for Derek. He was defiant at home, recalcitrant at school, and making no discernible progress in counseling. He refused to talk to anyone about what was bothering him. Latoya, his half sister, was counting the days until their father finished rehab and took Derek off her hands. But that was still months away, and she didn't think she could make it that long.

The visit took place at a day care center that had been painted bright blue and red, a forced bit of cheer in a neighborhood of row houses, auto repair shops, and greasy lunch counters. Latoya and Derek, along with Latoya's daughter and two sisters, arrived early and found Derek Sr. waiting for them. He hugged them and led them to a classroom where other families were sitting in child-size chairs at child-size tables, eating catered food, smearing finger paints on each other's faces, and listening to tinkly children's music. There was so much to catch up on that Derek Sr. failed to notice Latoya's attempts to steer the conversation toward Derek. Only later, when the event was almost over and the others had left the table to wash up, did Derek Sr. get a chance to speak to his son alone. Both wore blotches of green and red on their cheeks.

"Things are going to get better, D.," Derek Sr. said. "We're going to make things work this time." He promised to find an apartment for the two of them, alone, and to listen to Derek more. "I need you in my life and you need me in yours," he said.

Derek looked up at his father and allowed a smile. "I can't wait."

They embraced, and when it came time for good-byes, Derek told his father he loved him. Walking to the car, Latoya asked Derek if he was happy, and he nodded. She noticed that for the rest of the day, his bearing lightened and his face brightened. He made fun of his sisters and laughed at his own dumb jokes. He ate a lot and talked a lot. Latoya had not seen that side of him for a while. She hoped it would last.

It didn't. Not three days later, Derek was caught tussling with a boy in the Lincoln Middle School hallway, earning him a suspension. Latoya was ready to toss him out of her apartment. "I do everything I can by providing him a home when I didn't have to," she vented to me in a text message. "He eats, has clean clothes, he has freedom, the only thing I ask of him is keep his area clean and do good in school, he doesn't appreciate anything."

The next morning, Derek woke before dawn and watched the sun rise from Latoya's living-room window. He sensed that his days there were numbered. He wanted to make peace, but he felt unfairly pushed around. He was always the one being blamed for acting badly, but the adults in his life failed to recognize that they bore some of the responsibility. They, too, made mistakes and failed to live up to their promises.

He thought about his mother. He often tried to think of her when he felt lonely. He pictured her as he best remembered, her face plump and flush and creased by thick dimples, her big dark eyes, her crescent of uncannily bright teeth. He wished they'd been closer. He didn't blame her, though. She was sick. Weak. But Derek believed that she was looking out for him now, like a guardian angel, from somewhere above.

The morning sky turned from purple to scarlet to blue. Derek imagined going someplace warm and quiet, *a vacation from the drama*, where he could forget about everything and just relax. Maybe his father would finally take him on that summer trip he'd been promising. He remembered Derek Sr.'s Family Day vow, and held on to it.

* * *

This was the first spring in which Rodney struggled to find players—much of his 2009 lineup had either aged out or been signed by Reggie for the Monarchs. Rodney had hoped to recruit reinforcements for the Eagles at his camp, but most of the children who participated on four consecutive Saturdays in March had already been claimed by other teams. Rodney went to the league for help, and one of the committee members hooked him up with kids from a local basketball program, none of whom had played baseball before. They weren't any worse than the first batch of rookies he'd coached in 2008. He could make players out of them, too. "God ain't gonna let me fall on my face," Rodney told me.

Opening day arrived in mid-April with the 2010 Eagles in street clothes. It was largely Rodney's fault; he'd let last year's team customize and keep their jerseys, leaving the league to order replacements. The shipment had been delayed, and all but his four veterans showed up at the field in mismatched assemblages of jeans, basketball shorts, sweatpants, and T-shirts. He could hear parents in the bleachers grumbling. In the visitors' dugout, the Philly Stars wore clean, tightly tucked uniforms. He called the Eagles together. He told them he knew how embarrassing it was to take the field looking so ragtag and that he'd understand if they didn't want to go out there. Thankfully, they insisted on playing, and beat the Philly Stars, 13–6.

A few days later, still with no uniforms, they rolled over the Black Yankees, 13–4. Then they squeaked past the Black Crackers, 8–7. "We undefeated and we gonna stay undefeated!" DeWan roared.

DeWan had always showed promise, but this year, his last in Little League, he was coming into his own. An instructor at Rodney's preseason camp had noticed it right away and pulled DeWan aside to tell him he could have a long future in the game if he stuck with it. DeWan took charge at practice, guiding his teammates in warm-ups and reminding them that he expected a championship. "We're gonna be the bomb squad this year," he cried. "We're gonna be the greatest."

DeWan had the tools of a potentially great player: he was an almost unhittable pitcher, a feared batsman, and a fleet base runner. His signature play was turning a single or double into an inside-the-park home run by zipping around the bases and drawing errant throws. His only pitch was a fastball, but he taught himself to change speeds to keep batters off balance. He was also an instinctive leader. He repositioned outfielders and reminded infielders where to play the ball if it was hit to them. When Nashawn, Naimah's son, struck out and began to cry, DeWan, remembering his own rookie struggles at the plate, put a hand on Nashawn's shoulder and said, "It's all right. You took a nice swing. Don't worry about it. Get 'em next time." Most of the new kids hadn't learned any of the popular chants or chatter lines, so DeWan tried to break the uncomfortable lulls that fell over the bench. "You all asleep. C'mon!" he shouted. "Talk it up! You can do this! Swing harder! Act like this is the championship!"

The fantasy of a perfect season ended against Reggie's Monarchs, who played in sharp new black and red uniforms, their banter peppered with Spanish by a group of newly arrived Dominicans. With DeWan on the mound, the Eagles stayed within a run or two, but Reggie was paying close attention and late in the game called time-out to report that DeWan had exceeded the league's maximum pitch count. Rodney, caught unprepared, brought in a reliever who'd never pitched before, and the Monarchs trampled him, 9–1. The loss was a devastating blow to the Eagles' confidence, and their hopes for winning the league championship—quixotic, perhaps, because many of them still didn't know how to run the bases or pick up a ground ball or throw properly. But Rodney wasn't concerned. "You know that I like being the underdog," he told them. "People will think nothing of us, then they'll be surprised when we beat them."

The Eagles dropped two of their next three games, including a rematch against the Monarchs, and fell to the middle of the league's standings. DeWan continued to pitch well but got erratic support from his teammates, including Derek, his battery mate behind the plate. Derek had a dependable glove and threw out a few runners trying to steal second, but because he lived most of the week with his sister in Passaic, he missed a lot of games and was unable to find his timing at bat. He struck out often and returned to the dugout with a sour look on his face. At various points Rodney caught Derek strolling back to the bench, dawdling after an errant ball, or going nose to nose with a teammate who accused him of crying. Rodney talked to Derek's grandmother Irene, who told him that Derek was difficult to deal with at home, too. Irene told Rodney she was considering keeping Derek from playing baseball as punishment. Rodney urged Derek to apologize. "We need you here," he pleaded. "You gotta buckle down."

Derek told Rodney he might feel better if he could pitch, and Rodney obliged, naming him the starter in a game against the lowly Pittsburgh Crawfords. The Eagles spotted Derek a 6–0 lead in the top of the first, and Derek squandered it by walking in several runs in the bottom half of the inning. Rodney pulled Derek with the score tied, and Derek stormed off the field.

"What's wrong with you?" Rodney asked.

"Whatever," Derek mumbled.

Rodney pulled closer. "I don't ever want to see an attitude like that. It isn't that serious."

Mercifully, it started to rain, and the umpire suspended play. As the Eagles packed up, Derek tried to avoid Rodney's glare. "Look at me," Rodney said. "Don't ever let me see that bad sportsmanship. When you go to high school, they won't accept that." Derek finally looked at Rodney and murmured an apology. "I messed up," he admitted. Naimah offered to give him a ride home. Rodney sat in the front seat, listening to Derek pound his glove in frustration.

Eventually, the rest of the league figured out how to neutralize DeWan by counting his pitches and intentionally walking him. That flustered DeWan, and his attitude spread to the rest of the team. There were times when the Eagles played so haphazardly that Rodney found it difficult to control his frustration. He forced himself to remember that his players came to the field with all sorts of issues that made their moods swing from smiling to sour and back again. They didn't mean any harm. Many of them were ashamed of what was happening in their lives off the field. One of the things Rodney liked most about coaching was being able to relate to them, to let them know that he'd been through many of the same things. Baseball, he told them, had been his sanctuary, and ever since he'd quit he'd wondered what his life would have been like if he hadn't. "You just gotta be strong," he said. "And you gotta remember the part where you're supposed to be having fun. Have *fun*."

In mid-April, about a month after visiting their father in rehab, Derek and Latoya quarreled over plans to see him again. Latoya wanted Derek to stay with her for a weekend so they could make the trip together, but Derek wanted to be in Newark with the Eagles. On Saturday, Derek had Mary take him back to Irene's, leaving Latoya furious. That night, I got a text from Latoya. "I dropped his clothes off at his [grandma's] house. I'm done."

Irene was floored. "We don't know what we're going to do," she told me on the phone. "This is senior housing, so he can't stay with me. We may have to get his dad to come out of the program. Or call DYFS." She put Derek on the line. He sounded stunned. I asked him where he wanted to go, and he said his opinion didn't matter. "I have no choice," he said flatly.

They spent the rest of the weekend frantically trying to find a place for Derek to live. His father called Latoya and begged her to keep him until he got out of rehab. She refused. Finally, late on Sunday, a cousin who lived in the same public housing complex as Latoya volunteered to let Derek stay at her place. Derek made it back to Passaic late Monday, tired and unnerved, just in time for the start of his school's annual round of weeklong standardized testing.

Derek slept on his cousin's floor and struggled through his tests, but by the weekend her beneficence had evaporated. She claimed that she'd volunteered to let Derek remain for only a few days, not the two months until his father came home. Derek shuttled back to Irene's, hoping that his cousin would change her mind, but she didn't return his calls all weekend. He missed school Monday while Mary and Irene scrambled for new options. To Derek, his life had reached a new low. "This is bad," he told me.

Finally, Mary decided to move him back into her crowded

apartment, find him a school in Newark to finish the term, and wait until summer to figure out their next move. Derek slept on a pullout couch in her cluttered living room.

I did the math and estimated that in just two years Derek had moved eight times, never sleeping in his own bed. I shared my tally with him and he shrugged. He didn't bother to keep track of such things. "I'm used to it," he said.

Every day in April, Kareem walked across town from his sister's to see the baby and update Joicki on his plans to find a job and go to rehab. She let him stay for fifteen minutes at a time, then gradually let him linger a little longer, and soon he was hanging out while she tidied up the apartment or cooked or ran errands. One night, DeWan went to play the new Wii and discovered it missing. Kareem confessed, saying he'd pawned it for $100 to cover "things I shouldn't be spending on," and promised to buy another as soon as his unemployment check arrived. Joicki considered filing charges, but she knew that a theft conviction would ruin him.

It frustrated DeWan that his mother allowed Kareem another opening to wriggle back into their lives. He reacted by disengaging: when Kareem was home, DeWan tried not to be, and when they did cross paths DeWan didn't acknowledge him unless forced to. "He's not my father," DeWan told me. "He's just someone I know."

DeWan and I were at the ball field one afternoon, listening to songs he'd recorded off Hot 97 with his cell phone, when Kareem turned up, eyes bloodshot, in a floppy knit hat and stained shirt. He looked like he hadn't slept or changed his clothes in days. He asked DeWan to call Joicki and let her know he was there. DeWan took a moment to consider the request, paused his music, and dialed the number. "Kareem wants to see you and the baby," he said. A few minutes later, Joicki showed up, pushing a stroller, and Kareem shuffled alongside her. They continued up the hill, Kareem peeking under a layer of blankets for a look at Sir Elisha. DeWan watched them with a disapproving glare. He wished his mother could see what he saw: a man who would not stop taking advantage of them.

Kareem pressed his case, telling Joicki she was his only friend, and his family his only support. He offered to stay the night and help with the baby. She didn't need the help, but agreed anyway, thinking it might make him feel useful. The next morning, she let Kareem tag along to the supermarket, and he stuck around the rest of the day, ending it in the bleachers for an Eagles game. Later that week, he replaced the Wii and announced that he'd visited one of the city's "one-stop career centers," where he'd come up with a plan to work days and study at night to become a drug counselor. On Sunday, they went to church, and when they returned home Kareem told Joicki, "I'm not leaving. I can't leave. I can't keep going back and forth. I need to be here."

Joicki cursed herself for being "too damn nice" to Kareem. A part of her wished he'd leave her alone. She'd never gotten over her anger at his failing to fulfill his end of the bargain they'd made during her visits to him in prison two years earlier. But she also wondered whether she'd been too quick to dismiss him, too eager to prove that she could raise the boys by herself. Maybe she'd treated him too much like a boyfriend and not enough like the husband with whom she'd vowed to remain, for better and for worse. "I wasn't raised by a man so I never learned how to love a man," she told me. "I was raised by strong women who were like, *Let's keep it going*, even when men weren't around. But Kareem needs my support. My emotional support." The night after church, Joicki gathered the family in the living room and presented a question: Do we want Daddy back in the house? DeWan was the only holdout but acquiesced because he didn't want to disappoint his mother and brother. "Okay, give him a chance," he said. "Because everyone deserves a chance."

In his first few days back home, Kareem seemed clearheaded and well-groomed, a dramatic difference from the day I'd seen him at the ballpark. "I just came to my senses," he told me one morning, his eyes puffy from a long night with a gassy baby. He was barefoot in a clean T-shirt and jeans, flipping television channels while Joicki nursed Sir Elisha in the bedroom. "I told myself, 'Man, it's over. Time to stop playing.'" He knew his family's faith in him was thin. He'd been arrested so many times since his return from prison that the new charges, mostly low-grade misdemeanors relating to his getting high and fighting with Joicki, had become hopelessly tangled, and if he didn't start going to court to sort them out, he'd likely end up behind bars again. At his next scheduled hearing, he was supposed to give the judge an update on his progress with drug and anger counseling. He claimed that he'd finally come to grips with his dark side. "I know that getting high is just a fake solution to my problems. So the first step for me is not getting high and letting that selfishness go. You see, what I learned about myself is that I have some traits that the devil has. The devil is selfish."

Kareem was a remarkably intelligent man, a talented writer and devout Christian who seemed to understand the roots of his illness—childhood abandonment, chronic insecurity, greed. I knew that he often felt jealous of my access to Joicki and the boys, especially when he'd been kicked out or put in jail. But he never showed me that side. I couldn't remember a time when he didn't greet me with a warm, long hug and a mischievous smile. He could be, when sober, charismatic and deeply lovable, and I saw how it was possible for his family to keep letting him back.

He still had a long way to go to earn back DeWan's trust, however. "Puda don't like me. I'll come in, he won't say nothing to me, he won't speak to me. Even that day when I saw you in the park he wasn't feeling me. I can't blame him. I hurt his mother. I hurt his little brother. I hurt him." The only thing he could do, he told me, was to rededicate himself to the basics: working, paying rent, being reliable. "Then he'll see that I'm serious."

Joicki called his name from the bedroom, and Kareem jumped from his groggy perch on the couch. She handed him Sir Elisha, and he returned with the baby. He sat down again, patting the boy's back. "This is the reason I'm here. This is how I got through to her"—he nodded at the bedroom—"to come home. Being here, taking care of him, is cheering me up, bringing us closer." Sir Elisha fell asleep, face-down in Kareem's chest. Kareem's mouth curled into a satisfied grin. "You ever see one of those children, and the mother got the baby and the father come around and the baby won't go to the father, and it's crying *aaahhhh* and he don't know 'em? That's what my fear is. Him not knowing me. I can't allow that. He'll never see me high, he'll never experience anything like that. He helped me change my life. He helped me change my life so I can help him come into his. So I can be there for him."

Kareem impressed everyone that spring by landing a job in the "ring room" at Kearny Steel, removing and cleaning industrial drums for $8 an hour. They celebrated with a weekend at the shore, where Joicki snapped photos of Kareem, happy and heavier, holding Sir Elisha while little Kareem laughed over his shoulder. DeWan, though, would not reveal any suggestion of hope. When I asked him how he thought things were going, he scrunched his face. "Good, I guess," he said. "So far."

On April 15, I had a conversation with a community leader in the neighborhood that inadvertently led me to some disturbing revelations about Rodney. It began innocuously enough, with the community leader telling me how much Rodney's work with the kids had elevated his standing in the neighborhood. But in an offhand comment, she told me that she'd heard talk about Rodney, that he'd been doing "some things" that didn't comport with his reformed image.

"What kinds of things?" I asked.

"Illegal things."

I pressed her for more information, but she declined to go any further. Perhaps she didn't want to be the source of any adverse publicity for Rodney. She dismissed the talk as unsubstantiated rumors. She told me that she admired what he was trying to do, and knew many men in similar predicaments, trying to transition from the streets but "scarlet lettered" by their criminal records.

"I think Rodney is absolutely wonderful," she insisted. "I also think he's living in a world that could pull him back into the fight on any given day. So who am I to say what might motivate him to do what he does? What's not right to me might make sense to Rodney. We don't know the negotiations he has to make. He's surviving by any means necessary and I'm not going to criticize how he gets it done."

I understood her point, but I was more concerned about those rumors. I called Rodney and told him we needed to talk. Over lunch, I asked him if he'd stopped dealing. He told me he had. I asked him when. He looked at me sheepishly and told me he wasn't exactly sure—he'd always been bad at dates—but it must have been sometime after my 2008 article about the Eagles was published.

It took some effort to control my disappointment—in him and myself. He must have noticed because his body tensed and he tried to explain. He insisted that he'd only been "dippin' and dabbin'"—nowhere near the frequency of the old days, just enough to buy things when he ran out of money: food, a bat or glove, extra baseballs, Gatorade, pocket change for a hungry kid. He compared it to playing Russian roulette: he knew the risks, but he still could not resist.

"I don't understand," I stammered. "Did you ever stop and think that you were essentially poisoning the same people you were trying to help?"

Rodney shook his head. "You can't understand it if you haven't lived it," he said. "People who live in this neighborhood, especially those who have done drugs or sold drugs, would understand. It's an addiction. Selling drugs and doing drugs are damn near the same addiction. You keep doing it even when you know it's wrong. It's the only way I know how to get what I need without having to rely on someone for it."

But my article, and the reaction to it, had made it more difficult to justify his duplicity, he said. "That really made me change. I felt like I knew what my purpose was, and I wanted to take full advantage of it."

Over the next few weeks, I kept pressing Rodney for more details about his dealing. Eventually he admitted that he hadn't really quit in 2008; he'd trimmed his business to just one customer, a white suburban woman who commuted into the city every day with a $200-a-day coke habit. How he could still justify that to himself puzzled me. In his mind, apparently, still doing bad, but less of it, was a virtue.

He told me he'd dealt with the cokehead personally at first, then had a friend make the exchanges in her car. But one day in late 2009, she was short on cash, and Rodney's friend refused to give her the coke.

She flipped out and held his friend captive until he handed over the drugs. He returned to Rodney and said, "You gotta stop now. It's too risky." That, Rodney insisted, was his last drug deal.

I hated myself for being so blind. *This* was why reporters weren't supposed to get too close to their subjects. I wasn't naive. I knew that the odds were against Rodney's succeeding. I'd been writing for years about men who tried, and repeatedly failed, to leave the streets. Maybe I'd been distracted by my desire for Rodney to fulfill some fairy-tale story line—a story line that was becoming increasingly difficult to sustain. Rodney didn't want to ruin the ending. Neither, apparently, did anyone else: not one person on Elizabeth Avenue had hinted to me that Rodney might not be the reformed man that I thought he was.

Until this point, I'd visualized Rodney's journey within a fairly clear, defined narrative: an ex-con and survivor who finds redemption in coaching Little League baseball. But now his story was much more morally ambiguous. I thought about all the times he'd told me how hard it was to make ends meet and how badly he wanted a job. I thought about the pep talks he'd given to his players, to the kids around the neighborhood, and the students at the synagogue. I thought about all the people who'd been inspired by his story, including the superintendent of schools, who'd offered to give Rodney a job. I thought about the times Rodney had complained how bad shit still happened to him even when he did good, and about the advice he'd given his murdered friend Yusuf against "playing both sides." Had he been dealing through all of that?

I still believed that in his heart Rodney wanted to change, to become a good man, one who didn't tie himself up in contradictions. I knew that he had come to see coaching as his life's calling and hoped that it would somehow lead him to honest work. He often told me that as long as he kept doing good and thinking positively, an opportunity would eventually come along. That was true, to an extent; since the 2008 season, all kinds of people had offered to help him in some way. But none of them explicitly offered him employment, and Rodney never explicitly asked, and the months and years floated by, with Rodney telling me that he just needed to finish the next baseball season, or get a new wheelchair, or overcome his latest health problem, or get his mind right, and then he'd start his job search. After years of simply surviving, Rodney now had to think further into the future, to consider his potential as a human being and citizen. But he was not used to this, and he never moved past the thinking-about-it stage.

I told him I knew he could do it. I now saw his story as part of a larger journey, of a city struggling to redeem itself. But I'd come to realize that personal transformation, like a city's, didn't come quickly, or even over a couple of years. Change, real change, was the culmination of countless everyday decisions, large and little, that challenged you to do more than just get through each day. Transformation was a series of starts and stops, of small victories and nagging disappointments.

This may have been a revelation to Rodney, but Derek and DeWan were already witnessing this dynamic in their lives. They were crossing into adolescence just as the adults in whom they'd invested so much hope were faltering. The question was whether they could maintain faith in themselves and the world around them.

They quarreled a lot, and Rodney often visited Naimah's hangout when he wanted to make peace. Even if their romance withered, Rodney still wanted to remain in her life. He'd always love her, in some way, even if as a close friend. And he'd grown attached to Naimah's oldest son, Nashawn, who still called Rodney "Daddy" and had asked to play for him this year. Naimah warned Rodney not to take lightly his responsibilities as coach and stand-in father; Nashawn's heart had been broken once already, and a second time would crush him.

But there was no sign of them today.

Rodney lurched up the hill toward Bergen Street. The sidewalk was lumpy and uneven, and he had to pop wheelies to keep from getting stuck in the rutted concrete. He pivoted over the curb and clanged into the street. Dark patches of moisture formed on his shirt. Gradually the slope softened, and after a quarter mile he reached its crest and swiveled right onto Bergen. He glided a few blocks to the First Class Championship Gym.

Inside, men were rolling prayer rugs across the boxing gym's wood-plank floors and securing tapestries over mirrored walls in preparation for *jumu'ah*. Rodney took off his Yankees cap. His smoothly shaved head was beaded with sweat. An imam in a white kufi, his graying beard cinched with an elastic band, shook Rodney's hand: "*Assalamu alaykum*." Rodney continued into a back room and removed his white Nike high-tops. Back on the gym floor, men in stocking feet—some wearing jeans and polos, others in loose-fitting cotton tunics and pants—faced the room's eastern corner. They kneeled and touched their foreheads to the floor, then stood with their palms up, murmuring. Rodney took his place in the back. He bowed his head and lowered it to his lap in silent prayer. A peaceful look fell over his face. The imam stepped to a lectern, led the opening prayers, and began his sermon. Sunday was Mother's Day, and the imam wanted to talk about mothers' place in Islam. "When you have been blessed with a loving, nurturing mom," he said, "you should celebrate her every day. Do not wait for a circle on your calendar. A true mother is a divine gift and should be treated as such year-round."

CHAPTER 24

Rodney leaned into the slope of Elizabeth Avenue, grabbed hold of an iron
that ran along the sidewalk, and tugged himself forward with a g
He rolled a couple of feet and, just before his momentum died, c
another grip. He heaved again. Another couple of feet. Then
and again, rhythmically working his way up the street, the mu
his back and arms knotting under his T-shirt. A stabbing pa
through his shoulder. He sucked air into his chalky mouth. At
ner he caught his breath, worked himself around the bend, and
his one-armed jerk-and-coast up Renner Avenue.

About a hundred feet ahead was Naimah's apartment bu
was a dazzling Friday afternoon in early May, and on days li
often found her sitting in her car, door open, listening to m
her two sons played baseball using a broken broom handle
rubber ball, and imaginary bases. Naimah liked that sp
it was as close as she could get to the front stoops of her y
where she could just sit, watch her boys, and ignore tl
waiting for her upstairs. She still hadn't found a new job
ing handmade jewelry to try to stave off eviction. Rodn
for cable and electric and still had her registered as his
care aide, which was good for a few hundred dollars
Medicaid, but she'd taken in her mother, who was on r
wanted Rodney to contribute more. "Damn, I can on'
he griped. "I ain't no motherfucking baller."

Rodney listened, eyes closed, head down, hands clasped between his knees. He thought about Clara. She was the one who'd loved him, truly and unconditionally, through everything—his dealing, his injury, his depression, his awakening. She was a devout Christian, but she respected his conversion to Islam, and they often discussed his struggle with faith and his desire to mend his broken life. "What we see as horrible, God sees in a different way," she assured him. "God kept you here for a purpose."

Services ended, and Rodney coasted out into the sun. The ride home through Weequahic's side streets was downhill, and Rodney took his time, slowing to examine a row of neat homes with small columned porches and postage-stamp front lawns. He had always wondered what it would be like to live in a house, a real house. When he was a boy, he visited his mother's family in Norfolk, Virginia, and was amazed by how much room everyone had. Their Zion Towers apartment, by comparison, felt like a cage. He didn't want to grow old in that claustrophobic high-rise. He had friends who'd moved away, to other parts of the city, to Atlanta and to Miami, and they all urged him to get out, too. But he could not leave Clara. He never mentioned his thoughts of moving, because he didn't want her to feel guilty, and she never told him about her own desire to retire to a quiet senior citizens home down South because she didn't want him to think she'd abandon him. As a result, neither of them went anywhere.

Rodney rolled on.

Every year, in the first weeks of spring, a striking metamorphosis took place on the streets of Weequahic. The maples, locusts, Callery pears, ginkgoes, white pines, and sycamores erupted into a riot of colors: greens, pinks, reds, yellows. The plumage, bright enough to make Rodney's weary eyes squint, garlanded the darkest, most dilapidated streets, an annual promise of renewal, even in places where nothing much changed. The ballpark, too. At the bottom of the hill, across Elizabeth Avenue, blooming maples, tulips, and cherry trees girdled the Little League field, welcoming children. At first hint of warmth, they trampled onto the turf, its tiny blades of UV-resistant polyethylene shimmering in the late-afternoon light. They brought baseballs and bats, footballs and bicycles. They ran each other down and rolled around, brittle leaves from last autumn clumping to the backs of their shirts. Soon a white box truck decorated with pictures of snow cones and toasted almond bars would pull to the curb, predictable as spring itself. From somewhere inside the idling vehicle came the tinny first bars of "Turkey in the Straw," an organ-grinder jingle that would remain on constant twenty-second loop through summer, serenading every practice, every game, and most of the daylight hours in between. Rodney was never far behind, arriving early to watch for potential recruits. The sight snapped him out of his gloom, rejuvenated him. It still had that effect today, several weeks into the season. *This*, he told himself, *is the only thing that makes me feel human again.*

May 11 was Election Day in Newark. Cory Booker was seeking his second term as mayor and was all but assured a victory over a poorly financed former county prosecutor. Booker had many impressive accomplishments to campaign on: a reduction in crime, including the city's first murder-free month since before the riots; the renovation of city parks and ball fields; the luring of millions of dollars in grants from Bill Gates, Oprah Winfrey, and other wealthy celebrities to fund an array of civic initiatives, including new charter schools. All over town, government buildings were adorned with signs that boasted: BUILDING A STRONGER, SAFER, PROUDER CITY. Booker bragged about his connections to President Obama, for whom he'd fervently campaigned, and how his relationship with the White House could be used to reclaim the engines that once powered the city's economy: the river, the rails, the port. "We were a city who God gave all the assets," he told an audience at Rutgers Business School that spring. "There is gold under our feet." But Booker's ties with rich non-Newarkers—and his ongoing appearances on television talk shows—fed criticism that he was more concerned with his national reputation than with the people back home. Worse, Booker faced a gargantuan budget deficit that would require drastic, painful cost cutting. What exactly that meant for his constituents he did not say; they would have to wait until after they'd elected him to another four years in office.

Though Booker was the odds-on favorite, he wasn't so popular in the South Ward. Of Newark's five wards, the South Ward was where people felt most removed from whatever progress the city had made. It was the most violent part of Newark, and had among the highest concentration of residents losing their homes to foreclosure. Every one of its public elementary schools was ranked as "consistently struggling" or "chronically failing." Although Booker lived in the South Ward, so did most of the city's old-guard political elite, to whom Booker's mere existence in city hall was an affront. They included Booker's archrival, Sharpe James, the former mayor who returned from federal prison two days before the election and was met by hundreds of cheering supporters. If there was one place where cynicism and distrust of Booker most flourished, this was it.

Booker didn't win the South Ward, but he still took 59 percent of the citywide vote, a landslide victory. Safely back in office, he laid out his fiscal plan, which included a huge property tax hike and more than six hundred layoffs, including scores of police officers whose union had endorsed him a few months earlier, after Booker promised them raises. As if on cue, the city exploded in violence, with thirty-five murders over three months, making the summer of 2010 Newark's bloodiest in twenty years. Most of the violence was related in some way to the drug trade, the result of older dealers, like those Rodney had come up with, returning from prison and trying to push younger guys off the corners they once controlled. In most shootings, both the attacker and the victim had some kind of criminal record. Studies on recidivism showed that the average ex-con didn't go more than three years after prison without getting arrested again, a staggering failure rate that produced a relentless churn of poorly educated, jobless, hardened young men who soaked up an inordinate amount of the city's resources and fueled its sense of desperation. More than a thousand of them hit the streets every year, giving Newark the highest concentration of parolees of any American city. Booker knew this, and part of his crime-fighting strategy was to develop programs to help ex-cons find legitimate work and reconnect with their families. But it was difficult to prove it was working.

One afternoon, as the Eagles were wrapping up practice, the sound of gunshots reverberated along Elizabeth Avenue. Everyone dropped, and when the pops stopped, Rodney called Naimah, who drove the kids home. Another night, while Rodney was at Naimah's, Nashawn started yelling that someone had been shot outside their building. Rodney looked out the window and saw throbbing police lights and yellow tape blocking the intersection of Elizabeth and Renner. He began to wonder whether all the hope and hype about Newark's rebirth would hold. "I think Booker's doing the best he can do under the circumstances," Rodney told me. "But Newark is a tough city. Look at it out here. It's like the Wild, Wild West. What the mayor say or do, it don't seem like it really touch us. Shit's the same as it always been for us, way before he got elected. The only thing he's trying to do is try to clean up the mess the best way he can and try to slow that shit down. He's got a load on his hands."

Back in the Newark school district that May, Derek no longer had to worry about the Fs he was going to receive on his year-end report card in Passaic, or about being held back, because there was no system in place to transfer his old grades or the record of his behavioral problems. Days after his abrupt departure from his sister's, he was behind a desk at Avon Avenue School, his slate clean, a stranger to his teachers with a couple months left in the term.

Avon had just been placed on a list of New Jersey's thirty worst-performing schools—along with eight other Newark schools, including Malcolm X. Shabazz High School. At Avon, just 38 percent of eighth graders were proficient in reading and writing, and 14 percent were proficient in math. The state Department of Education, which had run the city's schools since the 1995 takeover, had thrown lots of money at Avon to improve conditions there, but it remained widely regarded as a dumping ground for failing students and disgruntled teachers. Avon had been through four principals in seven years, and enrollment had ballooned to more than six hundred kids, double the number of many other similarly sized schools. Derek's aunt and grandmother knew Avon's reputation but didn't have time to go through the complicated process of requesting a school outside of their neighborhood.

Derek found Avon far more disorderly than Lincoln Middle School or any of the other schools he'd attended. Boys and girls were separated into different classrooms as a way to lessen distractions, but that did not seem to make much of a difference, at least on the boys' side. They were louder and much more hostile, making his old Passaic hijinks seem quaint. Teachers struggled to get lessons started. Some kids acted like they ran the classroom. Derek tried not to attract any attention to himself, lest he become the bullies' prey.

He was sitting alone at lunch the first day when a teacher came up to him and said, "You look like a drummer." A sharply dressed, thickly built jazz bassist from New Orleans, Thaddeus Exposé led a small student band that had lost its drummer on the eve of a gig at a parent-teachers conference. Exposé had noticed Derek in the office that morning and made a mental note to introduce himself. He prided himself on his ability to spot young talent and sensed something about this new kid. Perhaps it was his coiled-up energy or the way he bounced his legs in his chair. Or maybe it was the tapping fingers. Exposé wasn't sure. Anyway, it couldn't hurt to ask.

The question threw Derek because as far as he knew, no one at Avon was aware that he played drums.

"Yeah, I am," Derek said.

"I knew it," Exposé said. "You play jazz?"

"Yeah," Derek lied. He had no idea what jazz was. But he could fake it.

"I want to hear how you sound."

"Okay. When?"

Exposé walked Derek to his next class and asked the teacher if he could borrow Derek for a few minutes. They continued to the music room, where three boys had already assembled: a bassist, a pianist, and a guitarist. Exposé offered him a seat at a small drum kit.

"What do you want me to play?" Derek asked.

"The best thing you know how."

Derek launched into a funky back beat that he often used with the Golden Lights, a gospel band he'd formed with two boys at church. Although Derek clearly didn't know swing from the blues, Exposé was impressed. Not many kids thrown into such a situation would respond with such poise. He got permission from Derek's afternoon teachers to keep him in the band room, and they practiced for the rest of the day, running through "It's Only a Paper Moon," "When the Saints Go Marching In," "Summertime," and "All Blues." Some of the tunes Derek picked up quickly, while others required techniques that he didn't know. But he struggled through them, and by the end of the day Exposé pronounced them ready to perform.

The next morning, Derek dressed in one of his church suits—dark gray checks with a thigh-length double-breasted jacket—and walked to school, where the band piled into Exposé's SUV and headed to the Robert Treat Hotel. They played for a few hundred people in the ballroom, closing with "Saints," during which a woman in the audience opened an umbrella and began dancing in the aisle. They received a rousing ovation.

Derek arrived home exhilarated, without books, sweat coating his forehead. Wanting to know more about the music that had gotten those people so worked up, he hoped to get on the computer and look up some jazz drummers or find the jazz channel on cable. But there was no chance of that. Mary and her daughter Alnisa were arguing over Alnisa's long-delayed move into her own apartment; their stuff remained among the piles of folded clothes, laundry racks, suitcases, crates, chairs, and children's toys spilling across the living room where Derek was supposed to sleep. The jetsam left little room for Derek to unpack his plastic bins, to practice on his snare drum, to concentrate on his homework. But he didn't mind. He was still riding the buzz from the show. Jazz. It wasn't as tough as metal, or as spiritual as gospel, but it was cool. Exposé said Derek had the talent to make a career if he studied and practiced and took himself seriously. No one had ever told him that before.

*　*　*

The Eagles slumped through the season's final weeks. Their record dipped below .500, each defeat sapping their drive. Their uniforms arrived, but caps quickly went missing, stirrup socks disappeared, and umpires admonished them for stepping to the plate in undershirts. Rodney appeared tired and disheartened. I encouraged him to remember why he'd starting coaching in the first place: to give kids a chance to get off the street and play. But it wasn't easy working with children who sometimes didn't seem to care, who considered practice optional or without warning failed to show up for games. His frustration boiled over on a late-season weekend, when the Eagles were scheduled to make up an earlier rainout against the Black Senators. They met at Weequahic Park, but no one else was there. Just before game time, the league president called from the field at St. Peter's Recreation Center asking where they were. She'd changed the venue. Rodney claimed she'd never told him, and she insisted she had. She gave them fifteen minutes to show up.

Rodney told his team they wouldn't make it in time and would have to forfeit. DeWan insisted they try to find rides. Rodney refused, but DeWan persisted and Rodney blurted, "If you don't like it, then you don't have to be part of the team." DeWan, tears welling in his eyes, pulled off his jersey and handed it to Rodney. Then he walked away and called his mother. Joicki immediately dialed Rodney. "You *never* tell a kid that. Don't tell a kid he should quit. *Never*. That's *crushing*."

Rodney felt horrible. He apologized to DeWan, and DeWan apologized in return. Both said they were cool with each other. But after that day, DeWan's attitude changed. He no longer got fired up in the dugout, no longer talked about baseball at home. He wore shorts to one game and skipped warm-ups to chat with a friend. He walked to his position just before the first pitch. "Something is broken between them," Joicki observed. "They've known each other for a long time and they've been through some things. But this hurt."

Joicki knew Rodney better than most people—better, in many ways, than Naimah. That bothered Naimah. She had come to see herself not only as Rodney's fiancée, but also as his protector. She suspected that Rodney and Joicki talked about her behind her back, and she worried that they saw her as an overly jealous woman. What she really felt was disrespect. One afternoon, Naimah came upon Rodney talking to Joicki at the field and exploded.

"What are you doing talking to that bitch?" Naimah said.

Rodney, shocked and embarrassed, turned to leave. "Yeah, go ahead," Naimah yelled. "Roll your cripple ass away."

"Fuck you, you gay whore bitch," Rodney answered.

Naimah vowed that it was finally over between them. Rodney moved back to his apartment, and they didn't speak for days. Eventually, their tempers calmed and they went out for Chinese food to smooth things over. She invited him to go to the beach for Father's Day with Nashawn and Zion. But they weren't the same. Rodney still had feelings for Naimah but didn't want to sacrifice any of his independence. Naimah, meanwhile, had come to believe that Rodney was never going to let himself trust a woman or be happy. "He doesn't talk, he just sits inside there like he's mad at the world," she told me. She started looking for a new place to live, somewhere out of the neighborhood, a place with a backyard for her boys, where they could start over again.

In mid-June, the league president announced that she was running out of money and would have to cut the schedule short and start the play-offs immediately. The Eagles, in fifth place at 8-9, drew their old rivals, the Black Barons, for a best-of-three series. Before the first game, Rodney met his players on the mound. They crowded around him. Some chomped on corn chips, others, fruit pies.

"Look, y'all. Play time is over now. This is for real." Some boys were bickering in the back, and Rodney shushed them. "We lose this, that's it. No more baseball. Ya'll want to keep playing?"

"Yeah."

"We gotta step our game up now, all right?"

"Yeah."

"Serious, this ain't no play, we're trying to win. I know you all want to win, right?"

"Yes."

"Huh?"

"Yes!"

"C'mon we gonna crack they a . . ."

The kids laughed at Rodney's near curse.

"I almost said it, boy. I almost said something . . . All right, so I don't want to see no attitude. We just gonna play, all right? We gonna give it all we got. No arguing. No pouting. Remember, if y'all play the way I say, we gonna beat them. If you don't listen to me we gonna have problems. So when you get up to plate, swing, swing, swing, and when you get on base, run, run, run."

The Eagles lost, 10–8.

They jumped out to a 5–0 lead in game 2 before it started to rain. The umpire suspended play, and the Barons' coach filed a protest, arguing that the Eagles weren't wearing their full uniforms: some didn't have hats, others wore mismatched socks. The league president upheld the protest and awarded the game to the Barons.

Suddenly, just like that, the season was over. Rodney was despondent. He told me he felt like everyone—opposing coaches, the league president, disgruntled parents, Naimah—was trying to bring him down. I agreed that it wasn't fair to cut the season short on a technicality. But I told Rodney that there was no conspiracy, and it didn't do any good to mope about it. Besides, he bore some responsibility for being disorganized and for failing to ensure that they wore their uniforms correctly. Rodney snapped at me, "You only know what people tell you. You don't live with this shit. My people get jealous when they see others doing something good. I *know* I did a good job this year. I did everything right." The next day, he filed a counterprotest, and after consulting national Little League officials, the president reversed herself: the Eagles and Barons would resume the suspended game from where they left off.

Derek's father got out of Straight and Narrow in late June and found in the mail a notice to appear in Essex County Family Court to answer a request by Mary to obtain full custody of his son. The document enraged him, not least because it described him as having been "locked up" for the past several months, which was not true—he'd gone to rehab voluntarily. Although he had no money, job, or permanent home, he vowed to do whatever he could to get Derek back. "She's not getting him," he told me at Latoya's apartment in Passaic, where we'd arranged to meet on the afternoon of his release. "If she wants to fight dirty, I can fight dirty. I know how to fight dirty."

But, deep down, Derek Sr. knew that he was in no position to battle Mary. His history of drinking, drugging, woman-chasing, and long absences would not look good to a judge, and it would take months to piece his life back together. By the morning of the July 9 hearing, he was conciliatory, contrite even. He showed up at the courthouse in downtown Newark in a pressed blue button-down shirt, jeans, and brown workboots, and found Mary and Irene in the hallway. "This is all my fault," he told them. "But I'm trying to make it right." Irene hissed and waved him off. Mary walked inside the courtroom.

The hearing was closed to anyone not directly involved in the case, so Irene and I waited on a bench among a sullen crowd of Family Court clients—overburdened mothers, estranged fathers, grumpy teenagers. Irene told me she wanted Mary to sever ties with Derek Sr. completely. "Derek has been through too much," she said. "Every time his father gets him, he breaks his promises, and that's when Derek gets the attitude. All those promises, they go in one ear and out the other now. Our main goal is stability for Derek. We are not going to do this all over again."

Mary, as it turned out, wasn't as hostile. She said she'd filed the motion not because she wanted to keep Derek from his father, but because she worried she wouldn't be able to obtain health insurance for him unless she was his sole legal guardian. She and Derek's father emerged from the courtroom an hour or so later, speaking amicably. In the courtroom, they said, Derek Sr. had told the judge he was now in a better position to become a dependable father but needed Mary to keep Derek while he got back on his feet. Mary said that would be fine with her, as long as she still had the final say over Derek's care. The judge agreed, reaffirming Mary as the primary guardian, with Derek Sr. eligible for regular visits. "My focus now is getting myself straight so I can take care of Derek," he told Mary. "He's been through a lot. My life was in shambles. It still is. But I'm going to make it work. I'm not perfect. But I'm doing what I have to do to be there."

They lingered in the hallway, waiting for a court officer to deliver a copy of the judge's decision. Derek Sr. asked what his son was up to. Mary said Derek was doing well, playing gigs at church and getting more deeply involved in jazz. His Avon Avenue School band teacher, Thaddeus Exposé, had become a mentor, enrolling Derek in a four-week summer camp at Arts High School and getting him a scholarship to a prestigious clinic in suburban Montclair called Jazz House Kids. "The drums keep him focused and calm," Mary said. "They don't give him time to explode. We're trying to keep him busy so he don't have time to think of nothing else." She invited Derek Sr. to come to see Derek play that Sunday, and Derek Sr. said he would try. They exchanged numbers and drifted to opposite ends of the hallway.

Derek Sr. leaned against a wall and ran a palm over his shaved head. He motioned for me to come over. He told me he wished Mary and Irene and everyone else could look into his heart and know how much he hurt for Derek, how badly he wanted to set things right. "I don't want Derek to think I'm abandoning him. I don't want his grandmother or aunt to think that way. They know who I am and from my actions they know I'm a trying person. I took him out to eat from time to time, I did things to make him feel good. I'm going to do better at this."

A court officer called his name and handed him a copy of the judge's order. He started to walk to the elevator, then stopped and turned back toward Mary and Irene. "Tell Derek I'll see him soon," he called.

Mary and Irene looked at each other knowingly. It had already been more than two weeks since he'd come home from rehab, and he had yet to contact his son.

Kareem announced in early July that he wasn't going to go to rehab or anger management classes; he'd decided that he could handle his problems on his own. "You go away to a program, you come back sober, what's the difference from staying with your family and doing the same thing?" he said. "It's not the program, it's the person's tenacity to want to do something different." He and Joicki fought, and the cycle began turning again. One night he stormed out of the apartment and called hours later from the street, high. Afraid he'd get jumped or killed, she picked him up but wouldn't let him stay at the apartment. Not long afterward, he got stopped for "wandering," police jargon for looking like you're trying to buy drugs, and was held on warrants relating to missed court appearances. When he got out, he huddled in abandoned buildings or crashed with people he knew from the street.

DeWan was annoyed but not altogether unhappy because this time he hadn't allowed himself to get too invested in Kareem. "I prefer it with him not around," he told me when I stopped by the apartment one afternoon, before the resumption of the Eagles' second play-off game against the Black Barons. His words caught in his throat and a faint, involuntary chirp slipped out, a lingering sign of puberty. "It's more peaceful."

He said he'd begun to reconsider his biological father who, for the first time DeWan could remember, had attended one of his baseball games this season. Since then, they'd been spending more time together—not one on one, as DeWan would have preferred, but among extended family. That was enough to see his father in a new light: as someone who was "calm and collected," who didn't smoke crack or break in doors or fight his mother. DeWan figured that if he could forgive Kareem for all he'd done, he could do the same for his birth dad. "He made a mistake. People can make mistakes," DeWan told me. "No one is perfect, after all. I'd still like to carry his name and one day show people that he made a man."

DeWan had also decided that football, not baseball, was going to be his main sport from now on. Although the Eagles' season had not yet ended, he'd lost interest. He insisted it had nothing to do with his argument with Coach Rock; it was just that his Little League career hadn't turned out to be as triumphant as he'd hoped.

*　*　*

The Eagles returned to the field against the Barons looking like they would have rather stayed home. DeWan lost his command on the mound, and Derek, catching, couldn't hold on to his errant pitches. DeWan barked at Derek. Derek glared at DeWan. Rodney called them into a huddle. "Get it together," he pleaded. Someone suggested he switch Derek to a different position. Rodney did, and Derek pouted. "He *still* got a funky attitude," Rodney told me. Then he pointed at DeWan. "Look." His onetime star player was on the mound with his head slumped, lobbing pitches and walking slowly back to the rubber. The Barons took a 9–6 lead.

In the bottom of the fourth, DeWan hit a towering shot into center field that bounced over the fence for an RBI ground-rule double that tied the score. The Barons jumped ahead again in the fifth, and the Eagles failed to score in the bottom half of the inning, leaving them one last chance to save their season. An urgent cheer rose from the bleachers. I scanned the crowd and saw Joicki and Kareem, Derek's aunt Mary, Thaiquan and two of his daughters, and Naimah, all shouting for the home team. In the top of the sixth, DeWan, playing shortstop, killed a Barons rally with an adroit double play, and in the bottom half of the inning smacked a two-run inside-the-park home run, tying the game at 11 each. Derek reached on an infield single, then advanced to third on a passed ball. The Barons pitcher walked the next three batters, bringing Derek home. The Eagles mobbed him, and when he made it back to the dugout he gushed, "I redeemed myself!"

Rodney's skin tingled with pride. He felt more like a coach than he ever had. "Y'all didn't give up," he told them. "You could have lost that game, so I give all praise to y'all. You did not give up. Don't never, never, *never* give up on yourselves."

The Eagles whooped.

"One! Two! Three!" DeWan shouted.

"EAGLES!"

The tiebreaker, played a couple of days later, was as exciting and tense as game 2. The Eagles and Black Barons completed six innings with the score tied, 5–5, and remained deadlocked until the bottom of the eighth, when the Barons won on a close play at home. Several Eagles burst into tears. The Barons gave the Eagles a standing ovation. "They played hard," Rodney told me. "They left it out there on the field. They showed me their determination. They didn't give up. I can't be upset about that, win or lose."

DeWan and Derek disappeared into the dusk, their Little League careers over, their paths likely never to converge again. Rodney remembered what had happened to him after his last year in Little League. He wished there was a way to keep looking after them, to keep teaching and coaching them. He always told them to have faith, that things were going to get better. If only he could be sure about that.

CHAPTER 25

Among the three dozen people killed in Newark in the summer of 2010 was a man named Al-Samad Davis, a reedy, dreadlocked thirty-three-year-old father of five who was sitting on the porch of a house in the West Ward one night in early July when a gunman opened fire on him from a passing SUV. His death got little media attention, just a cursory mention in the newspaper, and police, slogging through one of the bloodiest seasons in the city's history, never publicly identified a suspect or discussed a motive. The uptick in crime, they said, was largely attributable to drug and gang rivalries, part of the regular "ebb and flow" of violence in Newark, and an anomaly given the sustained drop in gunplay since Mayor Booker took office four years prior. With no witnesses talking and nothing particularly newsworthy to keep Al-Samad's death in the public consciousness, the search for his killer went cold, and the case joined the list of dozens of murders that went unsolved each year.

Thaiquan had known Al-Samad since they were eight. They grew up together, called each other cousin, and babysat each other's kids. They'd also made trouble together; each had spent time in prison for dealing drugs. And, just like Thaiquan, Al-Samad had renounced that life and was trying to build a new one; he'd recently gotten married and embraced his wife's children as his own. Thaiquan was sure that Al-Samad's murder was a mistake, that the gunman had meant to shoot someone else. Even in the unlikely case that Al-Samad had made such an enemy, he wouldn't have put himself at such risk; he was a child of the streets, but he wasn't reckless or stupid. Al-Samad was the one who'd persuaded Thaiquan not to kick in the door to get at Kaneisha's father. Not long before his death, Al-Samad had expressed concern about the uptick in shootings that summer, reminding Thaiquan to stay safe. Thaiquan advised Al-Samad to do the same.

The sudden loss of his best friend, the senselessness of it, seized Thaiquan with a sadness so complete that he suffered a panic attack when he returned from his vigil at the hospital. He stepped from the car and felt like he was on the deck of listing ship. He collapsed at the gate to his yard, and his wife and kids helped him inside, where he tottered around like a specter, moaning, "They killed him, they killed him . . ." Shamira and the kids were heartbroken for him, but as his despondency continued into the next day, they felt a growing sense of dread.

Al-Samad's wife asked Thaiquan to come to the funeral home for the ritual Islamic washing of the body. "He looks like he's at peace," she told him. But when Thaiquan saw Al-Samad on the gurney, he knew she was wrong. Thaiquan looked at the gaping wound in his friend's chest, and then his face, his eyes. The expression Thaiquan saw was not peace but shock. The listing feeling returned, and Thaiquan suddenly felt a rush of heat. He threw up, staggered outside, and threw up again. Somehow, he made it home and dressed for the funeral, but at the cemetery he broke down and was unable to join the other men at the grave site. Everything was moving too fast. Islam required that the body be put in the ground as quickly as possible, but he wasn't ready to say good-bye.

Thaiquan felt like everyone he was close to—his father, his aunt, his grandmother, a young cousin who'd recently succumbed to leukemia, and now his best friend—was being taken from him. As the days passed, he retreated into himself, unable to sleep and unwilling to eat. He was out of work on temporary disability with a painful but treatable cyst in his wrist, so there was no routine to fall back on, and he slipped deeper into despair. He looked at himself in the mirror and told himself to get it together, that the bills had to be paid, the kids had to be fed. There were brief moments when the depression lifted, but the space was quickly filled with anger—for the killer, for the cops, for Newark.

To live and survive in this city, you needed to absorb its toughness, make its resilience your own, find purpose in the briefest flashes of light. You had to believe that if you kept yourself and your family out of trouble, trouble wouldn't find you. But if someone could sneak up and take Al-Samad's life and get away with it so easily, then who was to say that it couldn't happen to him? Or Shamira? Or one of their kids? He hoped it was true that everything happened for a reason and that one day he'd be able to make sense of Al-Samad's death. But he couldn't see how.

For a while, after the election of Mayor Booker and their two seasons with Coach Rock and the Eagles, Thaiquan felt like good things were happening in Newark. He'd twice voted for Booker, but it had now become clear that there was a limit to what the mayor could do. Money troubles had forced Booker to lay off hundreds of city workers, including dozens of cops, and people were saying that things were going to get worse before they got better. In his second inaugural speech on July 1, Booker had urged the city to draw strength from the city's struggle.

Newark today is more hopeful, has more promise, possibilities and potential because this is a city where its people did not give up on their American dreams when others abandoned their faith in them; stood their ground when others cut and ran.

This is Newark, a place where faith is stubborn, hope is intractable, and the will to fight and win towers over cynical surrender, resignation and retreat.

The American spirit needs the Newark spirit. The values that have helped our city survive and thrive, endure and overcome are the solid bedrock that is needed during these shifting, uncertain times.

Those words, so inspiring just a few days ago, now seemed like a blindly optimistic fantasy. "Newark ain't my city anymore," Thaiquan said when I stopped by the house a week after Al-Samad's killing. He was wilted against a wall, head in his arms, while Shamira and their children, dressed for a day at the city pool, eyed him uneasily from across the room. "It ain't my city anymore . . . It hurts . . . It hurts so bad."

It wasn't just Al-Samad's death that made Thaiquan feel this way. It was the steady, grinding stress that burned a pit in his gut when he sent Nasir to stay with his mother, or when he contemplated what Kaneisha's father had allegedly done to her, or while they waited to hear if their kids had been accepted into a charter school. Each decision they faced, small and large, seemed to have potentially dire consequences—life-and-death consequences, if Thaiquan obsessed over them long enough.

This had been Thaiquan's toughest year with Nasir. He'd barely passed the seventh grade at Peshine Avenue School and was placed in summer school. Nasir's mother had filed court papers seeking to take full custody of him, forcing Thaiquan to hire a lawyer and submit to home inspections. One night, a sixteen-year-old girl Nasir knew from hanging out with his mother's family was gunned down in a park. Nasir came home shaken. Thaiquan wished his son would realize how real the risks were. "These are the times when he has to make the right choices," Thaiquan said. "It's the fourth quarter for him."

Kaneisha had transitioned from special education into mostly mainstream classes at Malcolm X. Shabazz High School and earned steady Bs and Cs. That was doubly impressive given the distraction of the pending charges against her father, who still had not been arrested. Kaneisha and Shamira testified to a grand jury, which indicted him. After that experience, something in Kaneisha seemed to break. She fell in with a group of girls who cut school, lied about where she'd been, and toyed with running away. Her grades plummeted. She acted as if she didn't care for any of the things—family, home, sports—that had previously kept her centered. Maybe it was typical teenage rebellion, but Thaiquan saw something more sinister, rooted in the charges against her father. "I think it crushed her," Thaiquan told me. "She genuinely thought he wanted to give her that fatherly love." Thaiquan told Kaneisha he'd never let anything happen to her again. But if the case went to trial, she'd have no choice but to relive the trauma on the witness stand. Thaiquan couldn't protect her from that.

Thaiquan was only thirty-three, but he felt ancient and exhausted. His weight dropped by more than twenty-five pounds. He conjured plots of street justice: finding Al-Samad's killer and Kaneisha's father and closing the cases himself. Shamira, calm and reasonable as always, told him he needed counseling and urged him to think of his family. "You've come such a long way from the streets and the violence and the way you used to be," she said. "You have too much to lose. If you do something irrational, we'll be going through the same thing you're going through now."

She was right. Thaiquan had always told his children that things weren't as bleak as they seemed. They still had so much growing up to do, so many big decisions still to make, so much to accomplish. But he couldn't pretend: there were times, like now, when all the working and striving and hoping really did seem futile.

Whenever I made plans to meet Derek, he goaded me into taking him to Guitar Center, a cavernous music store on Route 22 with a back room dedicated to the drums. He and the clerk greeted each other by first name, and then he headed to the most exotic drum set—an electronic one that retailed for several thousand dollars—and launched into a medley of jazz tunes and covers of Metallica and Slipknot until someone asked him to turn down the volume. Then he'd look at me, sweat dripping into his face, and ask if I had any requests. When his grandmother bought him a cell phone as an early birthday gift, he used the voice-memo function to record those sessions at Guitar Center, and as we drove back to Newark he replayed them, over and over and over, gloating about his "freaking awesome" chops and exclaiming, in mock awe, "I can't believe I did that!"

For the first time in his life, Derek was focused on a single goal: becoming the best drummer he could be. At the Arts High School summer music program, he was learning basic music theory, and at

Jazz House Kids in Montclair, he was becoming a student of the blues, swing, bebop, and Latin jazz and was immersed in the work of Max Roach, Philly Joe Jones, Herbie Hancock, and Art Blakey. This was his talent, his calling, his future, and he knew it. On the drums, Derek carried himself with a self-assurance that his teachers said could not be taught. But the downside of his rampant enthusiasm was that he played too aggressively, especially for a genre that emphasized subtlety and an unselfish exchange of solos. His instructors told him that he didn't have to play loud to prove that he was good and chided him for drowning out his fellow musicians. "You can get *fired* for that," his mentor, Thaddeus Exposé, told him. "You do that when you're working and you'll *lose your job*. You gotta lay in the cut, Derek. Let it *breathe*." One day, the renowned drummer Billy Hart sat in as a guest lecturer at Jazz House Kids and asked to hear Derek play. Hart told him he was impressed with his skill, "but all you've done is show off. Jazz isn't just playing a bunch of loud notes." He advised Derek to use brushes instead of sticks to learn to play "small and smooth."

When he got home, Derek went right to work on his old snare drum. His cousin Alnisa and her two-year-old daughter had moved into their own place nearby, allowing Mary to clear a tiny bedroom for him. He'd crammed in his air mattress and filled the remaining space with a small television, his PlayStation, his plastic bin of clothing, a pair of electric fans, and Alnisa's daughter's leftover menagerie of stuffed animals. That left little place to practice, so Derek cleared a spot in the living room, amid Mary's racks of drying laundry, and pulled up a chair so his snare sat between his legs. He opened his composition book to an exercise called "paradiddle around the kit" and balanced it on a knee. He began to sweep his brushes against the head of the snare, slowly at first, then a little faster, settling into a steady drum roll. His lips curled around his teeth in concentration. His hands quickened. His body loosened. His head lolled back. His mouth slackened. Beads of perspiration formed on his forehead and streaked his temples. "Small and smooth," he murmured. "Small and smooth . . ."

Derek started composing his own riffs and scratching the notes onto paper. He borrowed Mary's laptop and punched up YouTube videos of the jazz masters, and came across a clip of Blakey. Derek grew fascinated with the way Blakey closed his eyes and beamed beatifically as he played. Derek believed he understood that ecstasy, the sense of release that came with losing yourself in a tune. "It just feels so . . . good," Derek told me when I asked him to put the feeling in words. His voice betrayed a tiny but distinct pubescent quiver. "You can't do anything but smile."

Derek still dreamed of starting a rock band, or at least joining one, but there weren't many kids in Newark who liked to play metal, and the bands he found online weren't interested in a kid who couldn't guarantee a ride to practice. His consolation was the Golden Lights, the gospel group he'd formed with a pair of young brothers at church. Every other weekend, they dressed in matching yellow suits and played for their small congregation on Clinton Avenue, earning $60 a performance. Relatives joked that he was going to eclipse his older cousin Ozias, Mary's son and a respected drummer in Newark's gospel community, who'd never had a formal music lesson. Ozias smirked at the suggestion. Derek grinned.

Derek was frequently examining the kids around him for signs that they were better than he was. Some had more natural ability and experience, but Exposé told him he could surpass them if he worked hard enough. Exposé lectured Derek about the "Ten-Thousand-Hour Rule," which stated that mastering a specific task—like playing an instrument—required not just talent but obsessive practicing; that's what he had done growing up in New Orleans. The earlier a boy like him set his sights on a career, the better, Exposé said, because Derek would have to develop his talent in a harsh and unforgiving environment, without the advantage of private lessons. It was a lot to expect of a twelve-year-old boy, but Exposé believed Derek could make all-city band as a freshman and promised to help Derek get into Arts High School. "A lot of black kids in America, they usually don't have a mentor to take them under their wing to help them," Exposé told me. "Instead they have older kids telling them things they can do to ruin their lives. We don't get the opportunities that most white males get. So it's in my heart to do it."

I mentioned Derek to Rodney's music producer friend, Jeff, who invited him to jam at his downtown studio in August. When the time came, Derek took a seat at Jeff's drum kit with a sense of entitlement, like he'd done this a hundred times, and crashed through a five-minute improvisational solo that combined elements of rock, jazz, and gospel. Jeff, leaning back in a swivel chair, eyes hidden behind wraparound sunglasses, nodded along. He told me afterward that Derek had the potential to make a living onstage. Derek was still too young to be considered for a scholarship program Jeff had developed with the Berklee City Music in Boston, but in a year or two he'd be a promising candidate. Jeff urged Derek to stay in touch—and out of trouble.

Derek's summer culminated at Dizzy's Club Coca-Cola, a performance space in the sleek black-and-blue glass Time Warner Center in midtown Manhattan on a stage that featured a panoramic view of Central Park. Jazz House Kids, which was run by the bassist Christian McBride and his wife, had booked an early evening showcase there. Derek played drums and congas with a Latin jazz ensemble, his head tilted skyward, eyes clenched, not unlike the rapturous Blakey. They finished the set with a rousing cover of "Tin Tin Deo" that drew a standing ovation. I squeezed backstage to congratulate him, and I found him resting against a wall, in black slacks, white dress shirt, and a white tie, noodling on a bandmate's bass. He nodded at me and shook my hand coolly, as if he did this every night, and with a look that said: *This is where I belong.*

At not one of Derek's music performances—or any baseball game, for that matter—did I see his father. Weeks had passed after his release from rehab without word from him, and all the talk he'd fed Derek during his time in rehab made his continued absence all the more conspicuous. Derek, as usual, told me he was fine, that he was happy to have a place to sleep, to be with people who cared about him, and to be focusing on his music. Still, what boy didn't want his dad to see him doing something he was really good at?

I contacted Derek's father for an interview. He was, understandably, skeptical of me and my motives for wanting to spend so much time with his son. For months, he'd resisted meeting me and had agreed to see me on the June afternoon of his release from Straight and Narrow only after Latoya and Derek argued on my behalf. We'd spoken once since then, briefly, at Family Court, so most of what I knew of him had come from others: cynical assessments from Irene and Mary, and charitable but vague descriptions from Derek. This time Derek Sr. agreed to meet me at a diner near Latoya's, where he was crashing.

He started with the story of how he'd met Derek's mother, Gail, at Straight and Narrow, and took me through the time he got the call that she'd given birth. He recalled rushing to the hospital, thinking, *I finally got my son*, and finding baby Derek twitching from drug withdrawal. "I felt horrible. Horrible," Derek Sr. told me. "Hurt. I wanted to cry. I'm surprised I didn't relapse right then." By that point he hadn't seen Gail for months, and in that moment he vowed that it was over between them. "But Derek—that was my pride and joy right there," he said. "He was an angel sent from heaven. I loved Derek. I *still do* love Derek." Because of his drug record, Derek Sr. had to fight for permission to see his son for more than a few hours at a time. It was a battle he'd repeat often over the next few years, as he went to prison, struggled to rebuild his life, and succumbed again to addiction.

Derek Sr. acknowledged that he was probably to blame, at least in part, for his son's emotional volatility. His own parents had been drug addicts and alcoholics, and he couldn't remember ever living with his father. He now realized that he'd put Derek in the same predicament. "I tell him, 'What happened is not your fault. It's *my* fault,'" Derek Sr. said. "The buck stops here. I'm not getting any younger, and Derek doesn't deserve to be put in these situations. I'm going to be a good parent. Derek was and is the most important thing in my life."

But he was still broke, still unemployed, still sleeping on his daughter's sofa, and he couldn't let Derek see him like that. "Not for one instant is Derek not on my mind," he insisted. "I am so afraid of him hurting. I miss him so much. I don't want him to think I'm abandoning him."

Not long after our conversation, Derek Sr. called his son. Derek sounded blasé, as if he'd grown weary of waiting, and his interest in reuniting had waned. "He's up in the air, I guess," Derek Sr. told me. "I tell him I'm working on getting my own place and he doesn't respond. Other times he says he wants to come back to me. I guess he misses me. I really miss him. I really need him to be with me. But I need to get on my feet."

Derek told me he'd decided that he still accepted his dad's word but wasn't going to put his life—his music—on hold while his father figured himself out.

Rodney returned to Kessler several times to be fitted for the new wheelchair he'd needed for so long. In August, a tire on his old one sprung a leak, and I drove him to Kessler for help. He went to see the wheelchair technician who'd been working on his application and found out that she'd quit. Her replacement examined Rodney's chart and told him that recently rewritten Medicaid rules would no longer cover the new chair he wanted. She would have to start the process over again, and he'd probably only be eligible for a "nursing chair," the heavy, standard-issue, nonportable model common in hospitals.

Rodney looked confused. "But I've had these other chairs for fifteen years now," he said.

"It's not fair," the new technician agreed. "But it's what's happening." She advised Rodney to make an appointment with his doctor to see if he had any "preexisting conditions," like a shoulder or back injury, that would make him a candidate for a better model.

Rodney pointed out his flat tire. She told him to call the chair company or go to a bike shop. Rodney said that the last time this happened to him, someone at Kessler fixed it.

"Well, someone did you a favor," the technician said brusquely.

Rodney rolled away, trying to contain his anger. "Did you hear that backward-assed shit?" he said.

We went to see his regular doctor, Barbara Benevento. She looked at his chair and grimaced. It was likely the cause of his shoulder pain and could be cited in his renewed request for a better, lightweight chair. But there was no guarantee. "We can fill out a sixteen-page report on why you should have a new chair and not a nursing chair, but they could deny it," she said. "The problem is the insurance." She prescribed three weekly sessions of physical therapy for his shoulder and sent him on his way, the rubber of his flat tire squeaking across the waxed tile floor.

Often, when he ran into such roadblocks, Rodney would tell me, by way of explanation, "Welcome to Niggertown." This, he said, was how life was for his people. "It's hard for us to get simple shit done," he said, "and you don't see that in other places." I told him that maybe he just had to learn to be more of a nag. But Rodney said people listened to me because I was white, and a reporter, and there could be repercussions if I wasn't treated with respect. He believed people generally treated him better when I was at his side—today's experience notwithstanding. I didn't want to admit it, but he was probably right.

We got into my car and traversed Essex County in search of a bike shop or medical supply store that could replace his tire. After getting turned away at a half-dozen places, Rodney told me to take him home; he'd find a ride to the chair company's warehouse another time. "Sometimes you just gotta say *fuck it* and start over tomorrow," he said. "Get out of this mood I'm in, forget about this messed-up day."

All summer, Newark pulsed with talk about ways to save its schools, which, fifteen years into a state takeover, spent an average of $24,000 per pupil and graduated only half of them. Governor Chris Christie, a former prosecutor who'd won office on a promise to cut government waste, called it "an absolutely disgraceful public education system, one that should embarrass our entire state." He cut financial aid to the district, which forced Superintendent Clifford Janey to lay off hundreds of teachers, and prompted students to march in protest. Under pressure to speed up the pace of reform, Janey outlined a series of ambitious proposals to turn around Newark's worst schools. But just before the start of the term, Christie fired Janey, saying change had come too slowly. The governor formed an alliance with Booker to leverage private philanthropic money to underwrite more vigorous reforms, including the expansion of charter schools. The founder of Facebook, Mark Zuckerberg, offered in September to donate $100 million to improve Newark schools, mainly by closing the underperforming ones and replacing them with charters. He went on *The Oprah Winfrey Show* with Booker and Christie to announce it, and the governor told a story about a mother who entered her son in a lottery for a spot in one of the city's top charters. "When I was waiting in that room, I knew that whether his number got picked out was the difference between him going to college or going to jail," Christie quoted the mother as telling him. Oprah and the audience gasped. Christie told Oprah: "No mother in America should have to sit there and by chance have to decide that."

Thaiquan watched the announcement on TV. He empathized with the mother. His seven-year-old daughter, Tanasia, had just become the family's first child to get accepted into a charter, and Thaiquan already noticed a dramatic improvement: she stayed in class longer, brought home more homework than any of her siblings, and was excited each morning to go back. Every child deserved to go to a school like hers, and the $100 million should help make it happen. But already the politicians, activists, and labor unions were squabbling over how the money should be spent. Some were debating whether the donation represented a sinister plot for outsiders to influence how Newark taught its kids. Thaiquan couldn't understand why anyone wouldn't want more options. "It's the education that our youth have been deprived of," he said. "It's something new, a change. Why not?"

He just hoped the bickering would end in time for the innovations to reach all of his kids. The younger ones he didn't worry so much about; nine-year-old Surrayyah and four-year-old Amirah were already guaranteed spots at Tanasia's school, and they still had a shot at other more prestigious charters. But time was running out for Nasir and Kaneisha. Kaniesha's high school, Shabazz, was among the state's worst and had proven resistant to previous reform efforts; she frequently came home with stories about how her day had been disrupted by false fire alarms and fights and general classroom chaos. And now Nasir wanted to follow her there, because that's where most of his friends from Peshine Avenue School were going. The thought of his two oldest children stuck at a "chronically failing" school where only 40 percent of juniors tested proficient in reading and writing and only 22 percent were proficient in math compounded Thaiquan's malaise.

Derek returned to Avon Avenue School as an eighth grader and found that it had been revamped and renamed. It was now BRICK Avon Academy and had become the site of a reform experiment in which a small group of teachers, instead of principals or bureaucrats, was given the power to decide how the school was run. Derek came home on the first day and declared the new look "nothing big," just a bunch of new rules, onerous but well meaning, nothing that would affect him much. All he really cared about was remaining under the wing of Exposé, who freed him from the classroom and the alpha boys who harassed him. These kids were bigger, more hostile, and more ruthless than anything he'd seen in Passaic. They made fun of any perceived weakness, smacked you on the back of your head, and bumped your shoulder in the hallway, daring you to fight back. Some boys obliged, but not Derek. His instinct was to absorb the abuse and wait for their attention to move to the next victim. But that didn't always work.

Derek's teachers worried that he was too passive, too willing to let the other boys take advantage of him in order to be liked, or at least let alone. Soon after the start of classes, Derek said he'd lost his new cell phone. Irene called the school, and his English teacher, Janet Bone, investigated. She found out that Derek had loaned the phone to another boy, who claimed to have left it somewhere and refused to try to get it back. Derek thought that if he snitched he'd get beat up, so Irene and Mary asked the school not to pursue the matter. "We don't want any trouble, we don't want any retaliation," they said. Bone told them they were making a mistake; Derek needed to stick up for himself or things could get worse. "Don't let them push you around," she said.

Derek's teachers described him as respectful, friendly, and relatively intelligent, with a quirky sense of humor. His math and English skills were of a typical sixth grader, which was above average for Avon, where it wasn't unusual for boys his age to be stuck at a second- or third-grade level. But Derek was easily distracted, a daydreamer, a lousy note taker who incessantly drummed his pens, pencils, and fingers on his desk. "Shut *up*, Derek," his classmates complained. "Cut it *out*." When his teachers called home to report that he was blowing off his homework assignments, Mary threatened to take away his music and told him that he'd need better marks if he wanted to go to Arts High School next year. But Derek didn't take the warnings seriously. He seemed to think that he could get by on chops alone.

Many of Derek's teachers disapproved of Exposé taking him out of class to play with the jazz band. Exposé, on the other hand, argued that music gave Derek a better sense of himself and could even help him in some academic subjects, like math. The real problem, Exposé said, was that while Avon's curriculum and rules had changed, the students had not; they were still rowdy and insubordinate. Perhaps as a way to survive, by mid-fall Derek began to act out, too, not only in the school band room but at Jazz House Kids and at a second after-school program Exposé had gotten him into at the New Jersey Performing Arts Center. Derek snickered and made jokes during rehearsals, and defied Exposé by continuing to play too loud or using the wrong type of beat for a particular song. When Exposé admonished Derek, Derek snapped back at him. He began showing up for practice without his sticks, and Exposé discovered that he was letting the bullies take them. He'd offered to write Derek a recommendation for Arts High School, but when he asked about the application Derek looked at him blankly. Exposé warned Derek that he was losing respect for the music, his equipment, his bandmates, and himself.

Derek struggled to express why this was happening to him. His outbursts seemed to come at the end of tough days, when he'd been picked on, or when the boys in class were so wild that the teachers couldn't get their lessons done. Even if he did really care about school-work, it was just about impossible to concentrate. The place was out of control. It made *him* feel out of control.

Just before Thanksgiving, Derek brought home his first report card: three Fs, a C–, and a C+. Mary went ballistic. "That is a disgrace to society," she boomed, standing over him as he slumped into the sofa. "That is a disgrace to the *universe*." Derek smirked, and Mary looked at him hard. She gave him until the end of the next marking period to bring his grades up, or she would take away his drumsticks. "You got from now till February if you want to play drums anymore. The choice is yours."

The smirk faded. "You can't do that," Derek moaned. "I can't get into Arts without music."

Mary tapped the report card with a fingernail. "You can't get into Arts with those grades."

She handed him his blank application to Arts and sent him into his bedroom. Derek pulled the door closed and put on a jazz CD. A half hour later, he emerged and said he was finished and was going to relax with his PlayStation. Mary cocked the back of her right wrist against her hip and shook her head. She didn't have the time to watch over Derek as much as she wanted to. She was still working two jobs, still had two of her grown kids at home, and was also babysitting her granddaughter several afternoons a week. Her house remained chock-ablock with stuff, leaving Derek no place to study in peace. It seemed like Mary's only conversations with Derek lately involved her punishing him or threatening to punish him, and each confrontation made Derek more disobedient. "He'll say, 'I'm calling my father, I don't want to be here, I'm leaving,'" Mary told me. "I point to the door and say, 'There you go.' But he never leaves."

She knew that Derek knew he was better off with her. His father was still saying how much he missed him, still promising to find a place for them to live, and still making the same excuses why that hadn't happened. "I tell Derek, 'I'm not going to keep you from your father,'" Mary said. "I really do think he needs more time with his father. But for the life of me, I don't understand what's going on."

Derek didn't want to hurt his father's feelings, but he had decided that he wanted to stay in Newark. He wasn't ready to return to an unstable environment, where he and his father would have to make amends and salve each other's wounds. Besides, he didn't want to risk upsetting his music plans; he managed to submit his application to

Arts just under the deadline and hoped his acceptance would ignite his career. "I worked so hard to get where I'm at, so I don't want to change my living situation," he told me. "Changing would really mess me up."

Inexplicably, Derek continued to misbehave. In January he nearly got into a fight with a bandmate at Jazz House Kids, and Exposé confronted Irene and Mary when they came to pick him up. Derek angrily interrupted him, and Exposé walked away, hands up, as if in surrender. Irene grew furious. She told Derek he needed to apologize; if he kept it up, he'd lose the support of the people who wanted to help him the most. "You have to realize," she said, "that we're all you got."

Exposé told me he was going to report the incident to the management of Jazz House Kids, which could lead to his expulsion. "Derek is in a downfall," Exposé told me. "I don't know what's happened with him. I'm so disappointed. I want him to continue with the program, but it seems like he takes this for granted. He's fortunate to be in this situation. His environment plays such a crucial role in his behavior, but he's got to start taking advantage of these opportunities. The problem will get worse if he doesn't change."

Just before Christmas 2010, five teenagers were shot in a drive-by on a late afternoon a few blocks away from Thaiquan's home. Two died. Thaiquan compared their ages to Nasir and Kaneisha's: they were all just a year or two apart. Friends who didn't live in Newark told him he had to get his family out of there as soon as he could. But Thaiquan refused to be run off. He didn't want to move to South Jersey or Pennsylvania. He wanted to stay where his struggle began and see it through. "We live in the ghetto, man," he told me one morning. He'd recently returned to work on the overnight shift at the hospital. He settled into a black faux-leather sofa in his living room and tried to relax. A six-foot fir tree adorned with candy canes and silver balls sat in one corner; seven red stockings, each embroidered with a family member's name, hung from the stairway. On the stoop outside, an inflatable Santa Claus waved a droopy arm, and the front door was covered in gift wrapping that said "No Peeking!" His three youngest

daughters scampered about, their giggling and chattering filling the house in defiance of Thaiquan's somber mood. "The other day I asked my kids, 'Tell me, what is the ghetto?' None of them could give me any straightforward answers. I said, 'We *live* in the ghetto, but there's no reason why you have to *be* ghetto.' It's really tough coming up here, but I'm going to be on their back every step of the way."

But what was the endpoint? How would he know if he'd succeeded, if the sacrifice had been worth it? Every day was a fight; sometimes he felt like he'd turned a corner, and other times, like now, it seemed like the journey would never be over. But maybe that wasn't the point. Maybe what mattered most was that he, all of them, kept trying, kept striving. The same could be said about anyone in this town. Even the mayor. And Newark itself. The important thing was not to admit defeat. To hold on to your pride and instill it in your kids. If you managed to do that, well, that was a victory right there.

Every now and then, Thaiquan ran into one of his old "comrades," the guys he used to deal drugs with. Thaiquan had been the firs among them to leave the street and stay away. Most of the othe remained in the game; some had joined gangs. "I respect what y did," they told him, to which Thaiquan shrugged. "I did it for my s he replied. "I'd do anything for him."

Nasir. He was not only Thaiquan's first and only son, but als touchstone, the one who'd inspired him to change and in whor invested so much hope. Thaiquan still believed—he had to be that Nasir would come out on the right side in the end. "In my hearts, I believe my son has taken the things I've gone throu going to make the best of it," Thaiquan told me. "There's still chance for him. He has a chance to be somebody. But we him. That's my only son, and I'm never going to give up o

And then there was Kaneisha. She seemed to be doir was interested in school again, and was better able to even though her father had not yet been arrested. (His happen until the following September, and he would r nearly a year, until August 2012, when he would plea gle third-degree charge of endangering the welfare

sexually explicit text messages, and be released.) Perhaps she was tougher than even Thaiquan had expected.

"But what about you?" I asked. Like his family, I'd grown worried about Thaiquan. It seemed like we were all waiting for him to have a breakdown. Shamira asked Thaiquan how their children were supposed to have any faith in the future with their father walking around depressed. "They're looking at you, watching you," she told him. "It's starting to affect them." She suggested therapy, but he didn't want to admit needing it.

Thaiquan didn't want his kids to see him this way; he knew they missed his laughter and his playfulness, even his lectures. If he kept letting himself drift, what message would it send them? He'd be just like the men who came before him, and he'd doom his own son and daughters to a similar fate. He tried to convince himself that Al-Samad would have wanted him to keep living his life, fighting for his kids. His father, too. He wished his dad was still around, just to see how far he'd come, to see that he was not bound to a life of failed expectations. "I wish we could have had a bit more time together," Thaiquan said. "He was just starting to believe in me. That meant something, for him to believe that I was going to do the right thing."

CHAPTER 26

In late September 2010, Kareem called Joicki from the Essex County jail. He'd been arrested outside Penn Station for allegedly trying to rob two people by pretending an empty water bottle under his shirt was a gun. The evidence appeared damning: the first victim had flagged down a police officer, who canvassed the neighborhood and came upon Kareem holding up a second victim. Kareem could not make bail and, if he was convicted, he could end up in prison for a long time. He wept in Joicki's ear and said what he always said when he was locked up—how sorry he was and how he was going to change. Joicki tried not to listen. But when she hung up, she couldn't stop thinking about him.

After two decades with Kareem, after everything he'd done to himself and to her and their family, Joicki knew that she would always save a place in her heart for him. Was it love? Yes, at first, it had been. But that had been teenage love, intense and infatuating but not sturdy enough by itself to sustain them through the rough spots. It was true that Kareem had messed things up, but she bore some responsibility, too; there was a part of her that still felt guilty for having her first child with someone else, though having DeWan was a blessing that could never be eclipsed by any regret about her choice in men. It was also true that Joicki could be stubborn and play on Kareem's insecurities. But despite all that, she remained loyal, if not to Kareem himself, then to his potential as a husband and father. Joicki never relinquished her vision of a tightly bound family with lots of kids and Kareem at the center. She knew Kareem had it in him. He just had to stop anesthetizing himself against life's downturns, learn to deal with the emotional wounds from his childhood, and realize that she and the boys were his salvation. But she couldn't stand passively by, waiting for a miracle. She'd have to show him that there was something worth coming home for.

Joicki attended his court hearings, just to see his face and let him see hers. Months passed without progress because the Essex County Prosecutor's Office was having trouble persuading witnesses to testify to a grand jury. Joicki talked to Kareem on the jailhouse phone just about every day, urging him to get well.

"I tell him, 'You need to deal with your past, because you're not getting high just because you like it. You gotta stop lying to yourself,'" Joicki told me. We were sitting together at a TEAM Academy basketball game in December. DeWan, who'd finally earned good enough grades to join the school team, was bringing the ball up court. Sneakers squeaked on the hardwood.

Joicki had recently returned to work from an extended maternity leave and found out that she'd been transferred from Malcolm X. Shabazz High School as part of a sweeping reorganization to comply with a federal reform grant. She was now teaching at Barringer High School in the North Ward—another deeply troubled place but, in her assessment, nowhere near as chaotic as Shabazz. The Barringer students paid better attention and showed her more respect, and her supervisor said she might one day be a candidate to chair the English Department. She aspired to start her own day care center, but that was impossible with three young boys to support by herself. She needed her husband at home making money, not shuttling in and out of jail. "Kareem's so smart—smarter than me," Joicki said. "Just imagine if he had none of these drug charges. How different things would be." Sir Elisha tried to wriggle out of her lap, and she set him on the floor beside us so he could crawl. Just then, DeWan stole the ball from the boy he was guarding and made a cautious drive to the basket but was hacked. He stepped to the foul line, bounced the ball, and flexed his knees. "C'mon, Pudaaaa!" Joicki cried. Her voice reverberated around the gym. DeWan's first shot clanged off the rim.

DeWan wasn't much of an offensive player, which was why he'd started the season on the bench. But he was a hustler, and a fierce defender, using his speed and body control to smother opponents. He'd become adept at taking charges—falling to his back dramatically after getting bumped, a talent that was just as attributable to his quick feet as it was to his acting abilities. He was also unfailingly sportsmanlike: he smiled as he elbowed opponents for position, made cordial small talk with them after the whistle blew, and pulled them up off the floor when they fell. At school, his teachers remarked how mature and "comfortable in his own skin" he'd become. He was winning special privileges for good behavior and planned to attend Newark Collegiate Academy, the high school run by KIPP, the charter-school company that ran TEAM.

DeWan sank his second foul shot and backpedaled down the court, accepting high fives from his teammates. "He's becoming a real leader," Joicki observed. "I'm proud of him." She had no doubt that DeWan would go to college, but she worried that staying in Newark would stifle him. "I know it isn't enough just to leave for college," she said. "Because you come back to the same place with the same people and no one to learn from or bring you up." At the same time, though, Joicki couldn't fathom moving out of the city. Newark was in her DNA—the defiance, the sturdiness, the sense of collective struggle— and she felt like she'd be giving up on it if they left. She resolved to wait until Kareem returned home before making any decision.

This was the longest Kareem had been away since his last prison bid, and during that time DeWan seemed to develop a better understanding, an empathy, for his stepfather's frailties. Much of it had to do with DeWan's new confidence in his ability to grow up without a father. He didn't *need* Kareem anymore, so he didn't have to worry so much about what would happen if Kareem failed. That revelation freed DeWan to accept Kareem for who he was and to maintain a relationship without so much disappointment or regret. Whenever DeWan talked to Kareem on the phone, Kareem recited the same worn claims: how badly he missed his family, how tired he was of "doing bad," and how he really was going to make it right when he got out. DeWan rarely gave much thought to those promises anymore, but lately he'd noticed something different—not in the words, but in the tone of Kareem's voice. He sounded old. Tired. Sad. Really sad. DeWan felt bad for him. He told me he didn't want to hate Kareem because grudges had a way of manifesting themselves in other parts of your life. It was better, he'd decided, just to let them go. "I forgive him," DeWan told me after the game. "You can't just keep all that pain inside. You have to forgive in order to move on."

When Joicki heard DeWan say such things, she marveled at his sensitivity and wisdom. Lately, she was having trouble getting Sir Elisha to sleep, causing many long, stressful nights, and DeWan had been taking him off her hands so she could rest. "He's a lot more mature than a lot of men around here, young men in their twenties and thirties," she said. "He knows as much about responsibility as they do. Even though he still sometimes does things like a fourteen-year-old."

The most troubling example occurred in early spring, when DeWan came home in a panic and told Joicki that some boys in the neighborhood were going to jump him. She asked him why, and he told her that he and a few friends from school had aligned themselves with a group that called itself the "EA Posse." DeWan hadn't thought much of it, just that it would be cool to have bigger guys to hang out with and holler the group's name. But when one of them got into a fight, and DeWan didn't show up to defend him, DeWan realized it was more serious than he'd anticipated. One of his friends told him he was facing retribution for his supposed betrayal.

Joicki sprung into action. She called the Newark Police Department's gang unit, who told her that the "EA Posse" was not a legitimate gang in the sense that members "put in work" or committed serious crime, but that didn't mean they weren't potentially dangerous. She called DeWan's principal, Sha Reagans, who had some contacts in the streets, and helped smooth things over. She knocked on DeWan's friends' doors, telling their parents that DeWan wasn't fighting anybody. Then she went to DeWan, who was still at home. "You're an attention seeker, but you get enough attention on your own, with your own talents," she said. "This group isn't even close to you. But now you know that this is what you get if you join a gang: fear, violence, even death."

When DeWan returned to school, Sha told him he'd just learned an important lesson in how a seemingly small decision at such a young age had the potential to cause real damage. "Every choice you make has a set of responsibilities you have to adhere to," Sha said. "If you want to be a street kid, you have to be prepared to be a street kid. Even if the way you're doing it is unofficial. It's all the way out or all the way in. How do *you* want to live your life? What path do *you* choose?"

DeWan said he was sorry, and nothing more came of it. Everyone knew he wasn't really at risk of joining a gang. "He's not a daredevil. He doesn't have that kind of heart," Sha told me. "He's just figuring out who he is."

In June 2011, DeWan received his TEAM Academy graduation certificate at a ceremony that featured a slide show looking back at the class's past four years. When photos of DeWan flashed on the screen—one of him in long dreadlocks, another as a sixth grader in a tie and short-sleeve dress shirt, another on a camping retreat in a wool cap and flannel—the girls squealed. With each picture was a word chosen by his peers to describe his personality: Athletic. Confident. Animated. After the ceremony, DeWan lingered with his friends, mugging for cameras in a gray silk three-piece suit that Joicki bought him for his fourteenth birthday. He'd also worn it to the George Washington Carver School's eighth-grade prom as the date of a girl who'd asked him out on Facebook ("I guess she wanted to go with a smart young man," he'd told me). I waited outside the auditorium with Joicki, her mother, little Kareem, and Sir Elisha. They had plans to go out to dinner to celebrate, but Joicki didn't try to pull DeWan away. He was milking the moment, as if he sensed that his boyhood days were numbered. Finally, he stepped outside and slipped on a pair of mirrored aviator-style sunglasses, eyes hidden from the world spinning out ahead of him.

That summer, I paid DeWan a brief visit. He greeted me with a handshake and the same amiable, gap-toothed smile that had drawn me to him more than three years before. It was the kind of look that made it seem like he was trying to stifle a laugh or keep an amusing secret. Seeing him smile that way always made me smile, too.

DeWan had resisted growing up, but there was no longer any avoiding it. His face was leaner, his cheekbones more defined, his body longer and more sinewy. His dreadlocks, those cute nubby things that he'd started growing as an Eagles rookie, now brushed his shoulders and were dyed golden brown at the tips. He invited me to have a seat, and he walked into the galley kitchen to fix himself lunch.

Since Kareem's arrest, DeWan had expressed a desire to have a closer relationship with his biological father. They'd seen each other a few times since then, but his father didn't seem to be too interested. He probably would never be the father DeWan wanted. But DeWan decided he was alright with that. "Now I'm starting to understand that even with them not around, I can still make it through," he told me.

Kareem's case finally reached a grand jury. Nine months after his arrest, he was indicted for one of the two robberies (the other victim wouldn't testify). Prosecutors offered him a plea deal that would put him in prison for five years, but he had yet to decide whether to accept it or go to trial. A few weeks earlier, after he'd gotten off the phone with Kareem in jail, DeWan had told me that he really did think this time that Kareem was going to do better. "Him staying away from the family hurt him more than it hurt us, because as a father you want to be around the people who look up to you," DeWan said. "He realizes that, and I hope he does well when he comes back."

When he comes back. Not if. *When.*

I'd asked him why, after all this time, he still thought it was possible, and he shrugged. "You know how you have a feeling that something's going to change?" he said. "I just have that feeling."

In April 2012, a jury would acquit Kareem of the one remaining robbery charge.

I worried that DeWan was headed toward more heartbreak. But then I reminded myself that he was still a boy in many respects. He still saw the years ahead of him as mysterious and thrilling and dripping with possibility. He'd yet to become cynical, and that was a gift.

CHAPTER 27

Derek returned to school after the 2010 holidays and learned that his music teacher and mentor, Thaddeus Exposé, had left. The district's budget cuts had trickled down to BRICK Avon Academy's music program, and Exposé was asked to teach more general music classes, so he requested a transfer to a school where he could focus on a smaller group of committed musicians. Exposé had been the one who'd nurtured Derek's love of music. He'd driven Derek to rehearsals, taken him out to dinner, let him hang out at his home studio, given him lessons in jazz history. Exposé had broadened Derek's world, but he'd also taught Derek restraint: control your emotions, follow directions, never get too full of yourself, and always "lay in the cut" when someone else has the mic. Not long ago, at a gig in the suburbs, Exposé had cracked a joke while introducing a tune, and Derek had hit a rim shot. Exposé paused mid-sentence, glanced back in disapproval, and turned the awkward moment on its head. "I tell my drummer, 'You can't do that, because you'll get fired.'" The audience laughed—Fire a kid!—but Derek got the message and didn't repeat the mistake. Exposé could be demanding and tough, but he was a rare male voice telling him how to make his way in the world, and he expected a lot of Derek. Now Derek would be on his own again. He apologized to Exposé for misbehaving.

Drumming was all that really mattered to Derek, more than baseball now. "It gives me a *reason*," Derek once told me. "Like I have something bright ahead of me." But with Exposé gone, and with his aunt on his case to pull his grades up, he would no longer attend Jazz House Kids or any other after-school music program. On his last report card, he'd received two Fs, three Cs, and one A, in writing. That might not have even been good enough to graduate from the eighth grade, let alone get him into Arts, one of Newark's most competitive public high schools, without Exposé to help him through the process.

The Avon Avenue School jazz band's final show took place in the basement conference room of a hotel in central New Jersey, where Exposé was scheduled to give a seminar on teaching music to urban schoolchildren. He brought the band to help illustrate his point that inner-city kids had at least as much talent as their suburban counterparts but often lacked the resources to develop it. Exposé started by telling the teachers in the audience about their ride to the hotel that morning, during which he and the kids had discussed why it was so difficult to envision themselves becoming successful. The answers fell into three categories: lack of attention at home, scant exposure at school, bad influences everywhere else. "Kids in urban areas don't have much, so it's harder to get them to learn," Exposé said. "They don't have the money for private lessons or to get to practices and gigs. But when you have nothing, you have to make something. That's why the city is where the music comes from."

Derek, in a mohawk, black suit, and black polo, sat at his drum kit, bouncing his legs, itching to play. He savored his moments onstage, and with his time in the band waning, he didn't want to waste it on talk. But Exposé went on. Jazz was "America's music," he said, and Newark, the birthplace of Sarah Vaughan, Willie Smith, and Wayne Shorter, had long been a cradle of the genre. But that tradition was disappearing. Exposé pointed at the band. "Even if they don't become professional musicians, they will have a connection to the music. It will enrich their lives. They'll feel connected to their roots." Then he counted off, Derek hit a quick *ba-dum*, and the band launched into "Milestones." That was followed by "Cantaloupe Island," and for the finale, Exposé joined in on bass for a rendition of "Cissy Strut" by the Meters. They sounded like pros: tight, sharp, and well-rehearsed, and

Derek played just as Exposé had taught him: authoritative but not overwhelming; attacking his solos, then receding into the background. When they finished, Exposé boasted, "You are not going to hear many elementary-age kids performing at this level."

Derek began packing up his kit, disassembling this phase of his life with the same resignation that he'd handled so many other downturns. I drove him back to Newark, and we ate lunch at a diner on Clinton Avenue, around the corner from his aunt Mary's house. He didn't say much, which I took for gloom. I urged him not to let the loss of Exposé get him down; he'd already proven that he was able to handle much more than what any kid his age should have to deal with, and he'd find a way to persevere this time, too. But Derek looked at me like I had it all wrong. "I'm not sad," he said.

"You're not?"

"I've seen so much that I don't get sad anymore."

Derek coasted through the rest of the school year. Avon's principal, Charity Haygood, who was leading the school's reform effort, was aware of him, but he was one of more than six hundred students in her charge, and because he wasn't a troublemaker and nowhere near one of the worst students, she didn't really know him or what he needed. She was constantly distracted by one crisis or another: a looming grant deadline, complaints from the teachers union, wrinkles in her plan to recruit parents into a tutoring program, the search for the culprit who'd stomped on the hood of her car. Haygood was a tenaciously determined woman, but she sometimes had overly ambitious expectations of how quickly she could change things. She'd once accompanied me to Derek's classroom and found the teacher playing the kids a reality TV show about conjoined twins; Derek had sat near the back, running an Afro pick through his hair, appearing to pay little attention. Back in her office, Haygood momentarily let her frustration show. "That class you sat in on? That sucked," she told me. "Derek should have a rigorous schedule every day, throughout the day. He has been failed. I want him to have the same opportunity I'd want my own child to have, but at this point we're not offering that." That was the cruel side of education reform: it was often too late for many older kids to reap the benefits.

Derek's English teacher, Janet Bone, worried that Derek was at risk of losing his way. "He's so meek and mild, he wants everyone to like him," she told me. He still got picked on, and Bone pressed him to stick up for himself. One day he did. The bullies were roughhousing in the hall when one of them wrongly accused Derek of hitting him. The boy got in Derek's face, and Derek barked, "Let's do it." He didn't know what possessed him to say that, but the boy must have seen something in Derek's eyes because he immediately backed down. Bone congratulated Derek and told Mary about it. But Mary didn't see it as good news; she worried Derek would face retaliation. Bone disagreed; in a place like Avon, she said, you had to show your strength if you didn't want to be a victim. "You know where you live, this is what it's like here," Bone recalled telling Mary. "You have to realize that this is a tough area. Derek knows it now. He's starting to show some aggression. He's just trying to find himself." A few weeks later, four boys jumped Derek after school, knocking him to the ground and laughing at him. Derek picked himself up, palms dotted with blood, and walked home, wondering why kids like that always singled out the peaceful ones.

Derek withdrew to his bedroom, thrashing his snare and playing video games. On weekends, he slept late. The 2011 baseball season came and went without Derek bothering to sign up for senior league, the next step for kids who had graduated from Little League.

He sometimes went days without talking to Mary or Irene. If they asked him if he was going to graduate, he said he had no idea. They were flummoxed. "I don't know what's wrong," Irene told me. "He's got too much going for him to blow it now." She helped Derek make arrangements to see his father, who agreed to pick him up on a Friday night but didn't show up. Derek played it off like he didn't care. Irene asked if he was okay, and he shrugged. He understood that his dad was still trying to get his life in order, but he wasn't going to call to reschedule. "What's the use?" Derek said. "He's only going to come up with an excuse."

Not long after that, Derek got a rejection letter from Arts High School. He knew it was coming, but seeing it in black and white made it final. His heart had been set on Arts, and nothing else. *Forget it*, he told himself.

But there was good news, too: Derek was informed that he was indeed going to graduate, even with the two Fs. Derek's guidance counselor told him if they didn't act quickly, he'd end up at Shabazz. She suggested a new school, called Newark Hybrid, that was opening up with just one freshman class in the coming fall. When Derek told me he'd agreed to enroll there, I asked him what he knew about it. "Nothing," he said. "I guess we'll find out at orientation." I looked the place up. Hybrid was an experiment, a collaboration between Newark Public Schools and a private company aimed at blending traditional classroom work with online learning. According to its literature, Hybrid was "designed to help students who may not be on track toward graduating or who might benefit from the following program features: learning through projects, starting with curiosity rather than a curriculum topic, credit for demonstrated mastery, flexible time schedule, a significant amount of adult attention and coaching." I wasn't sure what that meant. It seemed to me that Derek was getting shuttled off to a school for kids who couldn't learn in typical classrooms. Little thought seemed to have been put into the decision; the main redeeming quality of Derek's new school was that it wasn't Shabazz. Hybrid didn't even have its own music program. I wondered if Derek was becoming one of the countless Newark children who were pushed toward high school graduation without being properly prepared for what lay beyond.

Derek's eighth-grade "promotion exercises" took place on the Avon Avenue School playground, under a tent that blocked the pounding June sun but not the heat that radiated from the asphalt. Derek wore a white guayabera, white cotton slacks, and black square-toed dress shoes. His hair was cut into a fresh mohawk/fade hybrid, with lightning bolts shaved from his temples to his neckline. Puberty had been good to him so far: he was slimmer, his chin and cheekbones squared, with a trace of hair darkening his upper lip. He sat at a drum kit and accompanied his classmates as they sang a song called "I Believe," then returned to the tent to receive his certificate. Afterward, he posed for photos with Irene, with Mary and her fiancé, and with Haygood, who hugged Derek and wished him luck.

The playground began to empty out. Irene told me she worried that he would spend the summer sitting around with little to do. A week ago, a thirteen-year-old boy had been shot to death a few blocks from her apartment in what police described as a "targeted attack" by another teenager. Although Derek was not the type to be out on a corner at midnight, Irene fretted all the same. "We need to keep him off the streets," she told me. Derek's new music teacher overheard and offered to get him into some kind of summer music program. Irene urged Derek not to waste the opportunity. "I won't, Grandma," he promised.

In September 2011, Derek started at Newark Hybrid. He resumed playing with the Golden Lights at church and saved up enough money to buy himself a new snare. He joined the marching band of a high school in the North Ward and performed at Friday night football games. He developed a new obsession for drum lines, the percussion section of marching bands that often performed as a separate unit. He studied them on YouTube, just like he'd studied jazz and gospel and heavy metal. He told me he wanted to go on to college and study every kind of musical genre possible, because the more versatile he became, the better chance he would make a living at it. "I just need to keep practicing and not let my ego get too big," he said. "And, God willing, someone will pick me up, and I'll keep getting myself noticed and hopefully I'll become a famous artist."

Derek told me that he felt he was better able to deal with all the things that for a long time had made him so angry—his mother's death, failing classes, getting sent to a new home every few months, his father's unfulfilled vows. He realized that part of what made him lose his temper was the fear of being ignored, overlooked. Now he saw things more clearly. Getting upset only threatened to throw him off his goal. So he tried to let it go. "I've learned to accept the fact that sometimes life doesn't go your way," he said.

He saw his father from time to time, but usually not for more than a day or two, and the permanent reunion never materialized. But he tried to be more understanding about his father's own struggles. "He's a good person," Derek told me. "I can't really blame him for anything, because I know it could have been worse. Because at least he still cares enough to say hello, good morning, that stuff. Many kids like me don't even have that. What I have now a lot of people don't have. A lot of kids don't even have families to go to. I appreciate that there's people there for me."

CHAPTER 28

Never in his life had he seen a sky so clear and blue and bright. Never had he been able to see so far, from such a height. It was godlike, this view. This was what it must have felt like to be rich and powerful and have the world, literally, at your feet, looking down from a black-glass skyscraper over midtown Manhattan. He scanned the western horizon over New Jersey and made out Giants Stadium miles away, across the Meadowlands. He traced the squiggly brown path of the Passaic River until he came upon Newark, a jagged line of silhouetted high-rises. Another world.

The last time Rodney was in New York, it was to buy drugs in Washington Heights fifteen years ago. Now he was nearly five hundred feet in the sky, in a glass-walled conference room outfitted with a huge flat-screen TV, a glossy wooden table, a bar stocked with soft drinks, and an antique brass telescope. It was December 2011, and Rodney had an appointment with a young woman who worked at Pershing Square Capital Management, a hedge fund whose owner, William Ackman, was a major financial supporter of Mayor Booker. Through the firm's philanthropic foundation, Ackman had pledged $25 million for Newark schools to help Booker match the $100 million donation announced earlier in the year by Facebook's Mark Zuckerberg. The woman, named Helena, worked at the foundation. She was from California and a graduate of AmeriCorps, and was looking for ways, outside of her duties with the foundation, to continue her volunteer work. While researching Newark, she came across my 2008 story about the

Eagles, tracked down Rodney, and asked if he needed help. He told her he did, and she took a bus to meet him. They discussed how he could put together another preseason baseball clinic and create a year-round mentoring program. She seemed earnest and sincere, but Rodney wanted to meet her at her office, to make sure she was who she said she was. He asked me to come along, to see what I thought.

We stood waiting in the forty-second-floor meeting room, gazing out the windows. This was one of those moments when I felt less like a reporter than Rodney's traveling companion, a buddy along for the ride. We spoke nearly every day, often just to check in on each other, and as far as I knew, he'd stopped dealing for real and was back to living on his disability checks. I was disappointed that he still hadn't made better use of the opportunities that had already presented themselves. I repeatedly told him that finding a job, even one that had nothing to do with helping kids, would bring him more financial security and confidence. Instead, he drifted. He spent his off-season days watching TV, hanging out with friends, maybe taking a bus downtown for a haircut or to shop, or pestering Kessler for the new wheelchair that he still hadn't received. Sometimes he met up with Naimah, but they were just friends now, nothing romantic, although Nashawn still called him Daddy. There were many days when Rodney woke up drained of resolve. "I don't have the fire anymore," he'd tell me. In the background there was always the television, tuned to Sports Center or a twenty-four-hour news channel, the noise that distracted him. I reminded him how far he'd come and that he didn't want to look back with any more regret. Sometimes it worked, and other times he remained in his mood for days or weeks.

Rodney told me that he still couldn't understand why people like Helena found his story so compelling, why they wanted to help him so badly. "But I know it's all good. This shit still might open up doors for me. Make my life a little better than it is."

Helena walked into the conference room, her hair pulled into a loose bun, a mug of tea in one hand and, in the other, a calendar and a document labeled "Rodney Mason Baseball Camp." The foundation she worked for didn't make donations to individuals, but she had a bunch of ideas to help Rodney raise money on his own: a raffle, a bake sale, a candy sale, a holiday craft sale, a refreshment stand. She envisioned him raising enough to become a full-service charity, arranging outings to restaurants, ball games, ice rinks, New York City. She recommended, just as the Respect Challenges philanthropic organization had suggested when it awarded him a grant, that he create his own tax-exempt nonprofit group, which would make it easier to seek money from charities. Rodney hadn't expected Helena to have such ambitious goals, and he wasn't prepared to answer her questions. He promised to have a clearer plan the next time they met, after the holidays.

We drove back to Newark. The towers of Elizabeth Avenue became visible from the New Jersey Turnpike. It was late afternoon, and the city was darkening under a shroud of gunmetal clouds. Rodney considered the towers for a moment. "That's no-man's-land right there," he mused. Most people in New York probably didn't even know where Newark was, Rodney said, and the few who did probably wanted nothing to do with it, because it seemed so fucked up. "I can't blame them," Rodney said. "But that's why I like to work with kids. They're innocent."

His current and former players still stopped by his apartment to say hi and ask about his plans for the coming spring. The visits usually snapped him out of his funk. "I got my own personal issues to deal with, and sometimes I blank everything else out," he told me. "But then I see those kids, their faces."

A few days before Christmas, the people at Respect Challenges invited Rodney and the Eagles to a party at a shelter for battered women that the group supported. Rodney brought his mother, Clara, and Nashawn. Two friends also came along: Jeff Billingsley, who'd helped Rodney apply for the grant that had funded his baseball camp, and Jeff's music production partner, Marcel, who'd just gotten out of the hospital after getting shot in the gut during a robbery of his hot dog cart. Marcel walked with a cane and was glassy eyed from painkillers, but he was grateful to be alive; he told Rodney he had a whole new level of respect for him. Joicki brought DeWan, who looked handsome in a black leather jacket, gray dress shirt, dark jeans, white Nike high-tops, and one of those Elmer Fudd–style caps that had become fashionable that winter. Joicki told me she'd just spoken to Kareem on the phone from jail. I asked how he was doing. "He always sounds good when he's on 'vacation,'" Joicki sniffed. "When he gets home, that's when he changes."

Several men hoisted Rodney up the brick front steps and into a cramped dining room, where everyone gathered around a TV to watch the Giants play the Eagles while grazing from platters of pasta, chicken, potatoes, bread, cheesecake, and tiramisu. Then the festivities moved into an adjacent living room. Wrapped gifts were stacked beneath a tree. A woman from Respect Challenges led everyone in a round of Christmas carols. Someone screwed a Santa's hat onto Rodney's head and asked him to hand out the presents: baseballs and Modell's gift cards for the boys, sweaters for the women. They posed for group pictures, with some of the boys in green Santa's-elves caps. Rodney smiled self-consciously, his arm curled around Nashawn. Someone brought out a Wiffle ball and bat, and the boys scrambled into an alleyway for a game. The ball skidded across the shelter's windows, followed by a welter of shouts and jostling feet.

There were moments, now being one of them, when Rodney couldn't believe how much his life had changed. Before his injury, he'd been the kind of guy who might have put one of his girlfriends in a battered women's shelter; if he'd shown up at the door, the residents would have called the cops. Rodney hardly recognized that old self. That old self would never have been comfortable singing "Jingle Bells" while handing out Christmas gifts in a floppy red cap. His injury had altered his perspective on many important things, not least of which was an understanding of what it was like to be the victim of a violent crime. His injury had also led him to Islam, and without Islam, without starting a conversation with God, Rodney doubted whether he would have been able to move past the hate and anger and shame that had consumed him in the years immediately after the attack. He also never would have been able to forgive Hawk, the man who'd shot him—forgiveness was the only way to move on with his life. Moving on also meant leaving the drug business behind. It wasn't easy to resist going back to that well of quick money. He'd slipped too many times to count, and there still were moments when he was tempted. Surrounded by the kids and the toys and the caroling, playing Santa Claus, Rodney could think of no other place he'd rather be. *"Damn,"* he marveled. "Ain't it strange where life takes you?"

Even with Helena's help, Rodney didn't get his plans together in time to hold another preseason baseball camp; he settled on a single afternoon visit to an indoor batting cage. All of his original Eagles had aged out of Little League, with the exception of Jalil, the finger-sucking infielder, so it would be another rebuilding year. At first, Rodney cringed at the thought of teaching the game to another batch of undisciplined kids, enduring the blowout losses, keeping them from crying, and talking them out of quitting. One of his new recruits was a sickly asthmatic boy who had never been on any kind of team before and could not go anywhere without his inhaler. He was a terrible player, but just before the start of the season, the boy's mother thanked Rodney for giving her son the opportunity—it meant the world to him just to be able to play, to be part of something. That helped Rodney remember why he was doing this.

Just after the 2011 season got under way, on the day Rodney turned forty-four, his mother checked herself into the hospital with chest pains. As usual, she played it off, telling him it was only some discomfort. But Rodney knew better. Clara had always been gaunt, but now she looked like a wraith, pale and weak and hardly able to eat. Too frightened to wait and wonder, as he had so many times before, Rodney cornered Clara's doctor, who revealed that she had late-stage lung cancer.

Rodney wasn't necessarily surprised, but hearing the news devastated him. He found a place to be alone, and when the panic subsided, he returned to Clara's room. She was asleep. He spent the night there, watching her chest rise and fall, and when she woke up she was calm, like she'd known the diagnosis for a while. She was too old for surgery and too weak for chemotherapy, and had decided to accept whatever fate God chose for her. She held out her hand, and Rodney put his in it. It felt fragile and weightless, like a bird's wing.

"You got to stop coming in here looking so down," she told him. "Don't be sad. Stay strong."

Rodney nodded. "Okay, Mom," he said. But he wasn't sure if he could.

He called me later that day and broke down in sobs. It was the first time I'd heard him cry. "This is the hardest thing I've been through yet," he said.

I drove into town to see Clara myself, and afterward I took Rodney to lunch. I had yet to tell him about my meeting with Clara last winter, when she'd acknowledged having a boyfriend before Rodney and Darlene were born. I'd put it off because I didn't want to drive a wedge between Rodney and his mother, even as I planned to write about it. The time never felt right, but now I had no choice.

When I finished, I told Rodney that if there was ever a time to ask his mother about his father, this was it. He shook his head wearily. He'd been telling himself for years that he would confront Clara before something happened to her, but now it was too late. He didn't want her spending her final days worried about decisions she'd made decades earlier. He said he'd rather carry the burden of never knowing. "I guess it's something I gotta live with," he said. "I'm still curious about the truth, and I don't know if she's wrong or right, but I'm with her. I'm always with her. I can't go against my mom."

One morning, he arrived at the hospital and found Clara in a morphine-induced sleep. The woman who shared her room said Clara had been moaning his name all night. When Clara woke, she saw him and croaked, "Help me, Rodney. Make it stop." He asked where it hurt. "All over," she said. He found a nurse to administer more painkiller. Clara drifted off.

As Clara weakened, she could do little more than ask Rodney to summon the nurse, or bring a cup of water to her lips, or hold her hand. He and one of his sisters were at her side when she drew her last breath. Her funeral was held at Greater Mt. Moriah Baptist Church, where, when he was a teenager, Rodney had gone in a panic after bingeing on crack-laced joints. Rodney said in his eulogy that he finally accepted "that it was her time and that she fulfilled her requirement here on Earth. But I miss her and just want her to know again that I'm thankful for all her sacrifices, her teaching, and her love."

The next day, Derek called.

"I heard about your mother," he said. "I know what you're going through. I've been through the same thing. My prayers go out to you."

"Thanks, Derek."

"All right, Coach Rock. See you later."

After he hung up, Rodney thought it curious that in his darkest hour, one of his players had called him to make him feel better. Wasn't it supposed to be the other way around?

Clara once told me she believed that God had kept Rodney around for a reason: so he could teach people. I asked her what his lesson was. "No matter what a person did in life, they can change," she replied. "Drugs is a big deal, but it isn't the worst thing. People have done worse things than Rodney. The story is that if you want to, when you've been to jail, prison, or whatever, you can make it. You can change. But you have to want to change. That's the key. You have to want to change."

Clara had been right. All this time, I'd been waiting for Rodney's journey to come to some kind of climax, a final turnaround at which point he could declare that he was saved, redeemed, a new man. But that was not going to happen, not the way I hoped. My mind turned to the speech by Dr. Martin Luther King Jr. that Rodney's doctor had referenced during his visit to an after-school program just before the 2009 season, the one about unfulfilled dreams. "Salvation isn't reaching the destination of absolute morality," King preached, "but it's being in the process and on the right road." Whether Rodney reached his goal or not, what mattered was that it was in his heart to get there.

It wasn't just Rodney who'd shown me that. I'd learned it from DeWan and Joicki and Kareem; from Derek and his father and Irene and Mary; from Thaiquan. Even Mayor Booker. They were all trying to do their best in the way they knew how. It was difficult—a step forward followed by a half-step back, messing up and starting over—and after all this time, I still had no idea whether any of them would fulfill their dreams. But I still felt good about their chances. Because if there was a single abiding truth about the people of Newark, it was this: they did not give up.

NOTE ON SOURCES

This is a work of nonfiction. The bulk of it, particularly the chapters that occur after I first met Rodney in early 2005, are the result of first-person reporting—interviews, hanging out, watching, and listening. Most of the scenes and dialogue I witnessed, but there are many I reconstructed based on the recollections of people involved. In some cases I was able to corroborate their accounts through public documents or other records. But there were instances in which I had to draw from the memories of one person, and their retellings reflect their perspective of what happened. Some quotes have been edited for clarity.

The scenes and dialogue that comprise the earlier chapters are based on historical records and participants' memories, particularly Rodney's. Whenever possible, I checked these accounts with others, and with whatever documents were available, publicly or otherwise.

Much of my secondary research relied on the work of my former colleagues at the *Star-Ledger*. Their insightful and thoughtful coverage of crime, politics, education, development, and sports in Newark—and the career of Cory Booker—allowed me to put this story in broader context and to describe scenes where I was not present. I depended to a lesser extent on work by journalists at other newspapers, magazines, television stations, and websites. That included the *New York Times*, the *Wall Street Journal*, Bloomberg, *The New Yorker*, *GQ*, *Esquire*, *Education Week*, *Time*, *Sports Illustrated*, PBS, *City Journal*, and NJ Spotlight.

For insight into Newark's history, I mainly consulted two volumes: *Newark* by John Cunningham and *How Newark Became Newark* by Brad R. Tuttle. I also drew from *Crabgrass Frontier* by Kenneth Jackson and *The Tenement Landlord* by George Sternlieb. The writings of the late historian Charles Cummings proved immensely helpful. I spent many hours with the enthusiastic and unsung staff of the Newark Public Library's New Jersey Information Center. They helped me navigate decades-old archives of the *Star-Ledger* and the *Newark Evening News*. They also granted me access to a collection of documents from the Newark HUD Tenants Coalition, which contributed to my understanding of the development of the Elizabeth Avenue high-rises.

Historians at Rutgers-Newark, particularly Dr. Clement Price and Tom McCabe, were gracious enough to share their knowledge.

I also watched the documentary films *The Lottery* and *Street Fight*, and the first season of the television series *Brick City*.

My research of Newark's school system included *Black Mayors and School Politics* by Wilbur C. Rich and *Ghetto Schooling* by Jean Anyon. To better understand the evolution of the Weequahic neighborhood, I read *The Enduring Community: The Jews of Newark and MetroWest* by William B. Helmreich; *New Jersey Dreaming: Capital, Culture, and the Class of '58* by Sherry B. Ortner; and *Jews of Weequahic* by Linda B. Forgosh. I found these volumes, and many other helpful texts, at the John Cotton Dana Library at Rutgers-Newark, with guidance from Natalie Borisovets.

I consulted the work of journalists at *Sports Illustrated*, ESPN, and many small newspapers across the country who have documented the state of baseball in urban neighborhoods. *Baseball in Newark* by Robert L. Cvornyek and *Shades of Glory: The Negro Leagues and the Story of African-American Baseball* by Lawrence D. Hogan and Jules Tygiel also came in handy.

My reporting on the narcotics epidemic in Newark in the 1980s and 1990s included the RAND study, *Substance Abuse Problems and Programs in Newark*.

I also relied on research by social service organizations and think tanks. They included the Brookings Institution's analysis of U.S. Census data; the Association for Children of New Jersey's annual *Kids Count* survey; the New Jersey Institute for Social Justice's reports on prisoner reentry; and Living Cities, a project of the National Community Development Initiative.

ACKNOWLEDGMENTS

Behind this book is a community of people who helped me through four years of reporting, researching, writing, and rewriting. I am indebted to all of them.

First, none of this would have been possible without the generosity, patience, and candor of Rodney Mason, Derek Fykes, DeWan Johnson, Thaiquan Scott, the rest of the Elizabeth Avenue Eagles, and all of their families. They agreed to let me into their lives without really understanding what it would entail, and allowed me to stay much longer than they—or I—anticipated. They endured hours-long interviews, invasive questions, unexpected visits, and late-night calls and text messages, but they never wavered. They not only put up with me, they welcomed me and my family into their homes. Their grace and poise in the most difficult of circumstances inspired me. There is no greater gift than the story of one's life, and I am honored to have been entrusted with theirs.

Rodney in particular. When we first met, he was angry and distrustful, but he gave me a shot at telling his story, and for that I am blessed. Not once did he refuse to answer any of my questions, no matter how dark the subject. I hope this meets his standard that a book about his life be "raw and uncut."

This project began as a vague and mildly impractical story idea for the *Star-Ledger*. As a crime reporter, I had no business writing about a Little League team, but my direct supervisor, city editor Bruno

Tedeschi, immediately saw the idea's potential and encouraged me to develop it. When the time came to formally pitch the story, Bruno's boss, Steve Liebman, gave me the green light. Bruno and Steve arranged for me to work with photographer Jennifer Brown, who not only took beautiful pictures, but combined them with audio recordings for a multimedia package that expertly evoked the Eagles' spirit (and helped me add context to my later reporting). David Tucker guided me through early versions of the story. When scenes were cut, Bruno found new life for them as online sidebars. All told, I spent nearly three months on that original story. In many newsrooms, that is an impossibility. But I was fortunate enough to work at a paper run by Jim Willse, who encouraged reporters to pursue long-form narratives. Thank you, all.

When the story was published, and I returned to my beat, investigative reporter Ted Sherman looked across his desk at me and said I should write a book. I laughed. But he was serious. "If you don't do it, someone else will," he said. Thank you, Ted.

I thought about it, and called my friend, author David Kinney, who put me in touch with his agent. Thank you, Dave.

That agent, Larry Weissman, and his wife, Sascha Alper, not only saw the story's broader potential, but treated it as if it were their own. They became its champion. They urged me to think big. They wanted the proposal to be perfect, and they was relentless. It took me nearly a year to get it right. There were times when I was ready to give up. But they kept pushing me, and just when I thought there was no hope, they guided my proposal into the hands of someone who understood it best. Thank you, Larry and Sascha.

Immediately upon meeting Gillian Blake at Holt, I knew I wanted her to publish this book. Where other editors were unsettled by the lack of a clear ending, Gillian embraced it. She provided sharp advice early on, and helped me work through several versions of the manuscript. Thank you, Gillian.

My father-in-law, Dick Hughes, whose heart practically pumps newspaper ink, read early versions of the manuscript and provided incisive and much-needed suggestions. My former colleague Mark Dilonno did, too. I thank you both.

During the long process of producing this book, I received timely and generous support from the J. Anthony Lukas Prize Project. I owe a debt of gratitude to Linda Healey, Leslie Garis, Robin Marantz Henig, Craig Unge, the Nieman Foundation for Journalism at Harvard University, Columbia Journalism School, and the rest of the project's committee.

I received similar support from Leela de Kretser, who repeatedly gave me work when I needed it, and granted me leave when the book's demands pulled me away.

In Newark and beyond, dozens of people helped me obtain documents and provided insights to complete my research. Most of their names do not appear in the preceding pages, but their contributions were crucial. They include Anthony Ambrose and Harry Moskowitz at the Essex County Prosecutor's Office; Neil Minovich, John Chrystal, Anthony Perillo, and Lydell James at the Newark Police Department; Gail Solomon, Steven Kirschblum, Denise DeLorenzo, Susan Sauer, Barbara Benevento, Gabriella Stiefbold, Joyce Fichtenbaum, Eric Kolodin, and Todd Linsenmeyer at the Kessler Institute for Rehabilitation; Valerie Merritt, Vincent Mays, and Patrick Council at Newark Public Schools; L. Shawadeim Reagans, Phaedra Ruddock, Ryan Baylock, Zonya Melendez, Ben Cope, and the teaching staff at TEAM Academy; John Scozzaro, Glenny LaPaix, and Naomi Glugeth at Lincoln Middle School; Charity Haygood at BRICK Avon Academy; Clement Price, Tom McCabe, Marc Krasovic, and John Johnson Jr. at Rutgers-Newark; Kelley Spear, Donna Judd, Reggie Graham, and Herbert Calloway of the Jackie Robinson South Ward Little League; Joseph and Vincent Divincentis, Mike Alban, and Luther Robeson of the Newark Little League Committee; David James at Major League Baseball; Cheryl Coxson, Sherry Bradshaw, and Joyce Lanier-Daniel at the Newark city clerk's office; and the staff of the Newark tax assessor's office.

In addition, Anton Wheeler, Kevin Jenkins, Johnny Jones, Ron Christian, and Obalaji Baraka shared their recollections of the evolution of Elizabeth Avenue. George Hawley and Natalie Borisovets helped me negotiate the stacks at the Newark Public Library's New Jersey Information Center and the John Cotton Dana Library at

Rutgers-Newark, respectively. David Livingston and Mitchell Reiter took time to explain the treatment of spinal cord injuries, particularly those caused by gunshot wounds, at University Hospital. Aqeel Mateen provided lessons on Islam in Newark and welcomed me into his place of worship. David Mactas, Father Lou Bihr, and Brian Amorello patiently answered my questions about the drug-rehab work at Straight and Narrow. Prudence LaFortune and Sam Malone overcame deep reservations to speak with me about their relationships with Rodney. Dennis Beury gave me a crash course in urban landscaping. My former colleague John Mooney helped me translate Newark education data. Gus Miniotis shared his experiences working for the NYPD in Washington Heights.

I don't know how I would have made it this far without my family: my parents, David and Barbara Schuppe, who nurtured my love of reading and journalism and encouraged me to believe in myself; my sisters, Susan and Elizabeth, and my brother-in-law, Alex Weinstein, who helped keep me grounded; and my in-laws, Sid and Kathleen Boren and Dick and Kathy Hughes, who provided loads of unconditional support.

Finally, and most importantly, I am forever grateful to my wife, Amy, a woman of boundless love and unwavering faith. It is because of her that I've reached the point of writing these final words. This book is as much hers as it is mine.

ABOUT THE AUTHOR

JONATHAN SCHUPPE is an award-winning journalist who has shared a Pulitzer Prize for coverage of New Jersey governor Jim McGreevey's resignation. He won the coveted J. Anthony Lukas Work-in-Progress Prize for this project. He lives with his wife and daughter in New Jersey.